"This album is dedicated to all the teachers who told me I'd never amount to nothin.'"

—Notorious B.I.G.

PUBLISHER'S ACKNOWLEDGMENTS

Some of the people who helped bring this book to market include the following:

Editorial and Production
VP Consumer and Technology Publishing Director: Michelle Leete
Associate Director–Book Content Management: Martin Tribe
Associate Publisher: Chris Webb
Assistant Editor: Ellie Scott
Development Editor: Sydney Argenta
Copy Editor: Maryann Steinhart
Technical Editor: Steven Hoober
Editorial Manager: Jodi Jensen
Senior Project Editor: Sara Shlaer
Editorial Assistant: Leslie Saxman

Marketing
Associate Marketing Director: Louise Breinholt
Marketing Executive: Kate Parrett

Composition Services
Compositor: Indianapolis Composition Services
Proofreader: Susan Hobbs
Indexer: Potomac Indexing, LLC

About the Author

Jon Raasch is a freelance web developer specializing in frontend engineering with HTML5, CSS3 and JavaScript. A regular contributor to *Smashing Magazine*, he also writes on his personal blog at `http://jonraasch.com/`.

Jon Raasch built his first website when he was 14. It was hosted on GeoCities and was particularly terrible. Now he builds cutting-edge websites and web-based applications using modern technologies. He is passionate about web standards, frontend performance and user-experience design.

Formerly based in Portland, OR, Jon now travels the world working remotely (with a particular fondness for Berlin, Germany).

Follow him on Twitter: `http://twitter.com/jonraasch`.

Acknowledgments

I'd like to thank Paul Irish for his suggestions for the performance chapter, and Estelle Weyl for her CSS-only iOS interface.

Otherwise, thanks to all the people who write tutorials, give talks on frontend development and release open-source software: Jonathan Snook, Stoyan Stefanov, Remy Sharp, Nicholas Zakas, David DeSandro, Nicole Sullivan, Peter-Paul Koch, Luke Wroblewski, Chris Coyier, Zoe Gillenwater, Christian Heilmann, Kyle Simpson, Steve Souders, Stephanie Rewis, Jacob Gube, Mathias Bynens, Bruce Lawson, Ethan Marcotte, Jan Lehnardt, Jed Schmidt, Nicolas Gallagher, Robert Nyman, Jake Archibald, Lea Verou, Ben Alman, David Kaneda and all the others I'm forgetting.

I'd also like to thank the Smashing Magazine team and Vitaly Friedman, as well as the editors at Wiley, especially Sydney Argenta and Steven Hoober. Finally, I'd like to thank Kate Knappett for looking over Chapters 3 and 4.

Contents

CONTENTS

XVII

Introduction

When my editor approached me about writing a book on WebKit, I initially thought the topic was a bit strange. While I certainly love developing with the advanced features available in WebKit, websites are rarely confined to a single environment, and I've never worked on a project that is geared towards only WebKit browsers.

But the more I thought about it, the more I realized how useful a book on WebKit could be. That's because learning about this engine does not mean supporting *only* WebKit-based browsers. Rather, learning WebKit is about learning standards.

Several years ago, CSS3 features such as rounded corners and gradients were only available in the WebKit-based Safari. At that time, building a site with these features might have been a fun exercise, but certainly was not feasible for production websites.

Fast-forward to today, where most of those capabilities are now supported across all major browsers. CSS3 has gone from a fringe hobby for Safari nerds, to a mainstream approach used in major websites. That's because the features that once originated in WebKit proved so useful that they became standards across all web development.

Today, WebKit continues to push rendering to the next level, innovating new features and sculpting the future of web development. Many of the CSS3 and HTML5 capabilities in WebKit have already been adopted by other browsers, and you can expect more to be adopted in the months and years to come.

Thus learning WebKit provides a window into the future of web development. In this rapidly evolving field, it is crucial for developers to keep on top of modern trends and practices. Focusing on WebKit allows you to go one step further, learning not only the technologies that are used today, but also those that will be used tomorrow.

So should you build websites only for WebKit? Definitely not.

While *Smashing WebKit* focuses on the capabilities of WebKit-based browsers, this engine is not studied in isolation. Whenever possible, cross-browser solutions are discussed, whether they are native support of universal web standards, or alternative workarounds that can be employed as graceful degradation.

This book is divided into five parts:

PART I: INTRODUCING WEBKIT

Part I starts with a brief history of WebKit, where you learn how the engine evolved as well as which platforms and devices use WebKit. You then learn how to set up your local environment for WebKit development: installing a variety of browsers and mobile device emulators. Within each of these environments you learn how to use tools to track down and solve JavaScript bugs, test styling options on the fly and profile the performance of your site. Finally, you learn how to set up testing environments for non-WebKit browsers such as IE and Firefox.

PART II: CSS3 SUPPORT IN WEBKIT

In Part II, you discover how to use a variety of CSS3 properties to expand your styling capabilities and reduce your dependency on external images. WebKit innovated many of the CSS3 properties available in modern browsers and continues to push the envelope with other more experimental styling options.

You then learn how to use advanced CSS3 selectors better select elements and reduce the need for classes and ids in your markup. Finally, you learn about cross-browser support for CSS3 properties and selectors, including how to use native support where it's available, as well as fallback solutions for older browsers.

PART III: HTML5 SUPPORT IN WEBKIT

Part III covers a wide variety of HTML5 functionality. First, you learn how to use video and audio tags to embed media directly in the browser. You also learn how to use HTML5 form elements to create richer web forms that are more interactive and easier to use.

Finally, you dig into drawing complex shapes using HTML5 canvas and SVG. These unique elements allow you to render 2D and 3D scenes, creating stunning applications that rival those built with Flash.

PART IV: MOBILE WEBKIT

Part IV teaches you about the mobile arm of WebKit, discussing a variety of techniques for developing web apps for iPhone, iPad, and various Android phones and tablets. You learn how to take advantage of the unique capabilities of these devices, such as the accelerometer, touch screen, and geolocation.

You then learn how to mirror the look and feel of native iOS and Android apps. You explore JavaScript libraries such as Sencha Touch, and learn how to take web apps offline so they can be accessed regardless of internet connectivity. Finally, you learn how to create fully fledged native apps using the PhoneGap framework and the HTML, CSS and JavaScript skills you already have.

PART V: ADVANCED WEBKIT

Last but not least, Part V covers performance tuning. You start by reviewing best practices for optimization as well as generalized approaches for improving performance in all browsers. Then you learn WebKit-specific optimization techniques that take advantage of the way WebKit renders pages.

Finally you learn where WebKit is headed in the future, as well as how to contribute to the WebKit project, by submitting both bug reports and patches to the WebKit core.

COMPANION WEBSITE

Smashing WebKit has a companion site at `http://wiley.com/go/smashingwebkit`.

The site includes code samples and demos from the examples in this book, as well as links to various resources such as the canvas examples in Chapter 7 and the performance tests in Chapter 12. It also contains links to some resources not found in the book.

START BUILDING BETTER WEBSITES

This book discusses how to build websites and apps that run in WebKit-based browsers, as opposed to native apps that leverage the WebKit core itself.

Smashing WebKit is geared towards frontend developers, but anyone with a grasp of HTML, CSS and JavaScript can benefit from this book. Since *Smashing WebKit* focuses on the cutting-edge WebKit engine, it will be more interesting if you already have a firm grounding in the basics. However, each section starts at a level that is accessible to anyone with some knowledge of frontend development.

So get ready to dive in and start building more modern websites.

3

INTRODUCING WEBKIT

1

WHAT IS WEBKIT?

WEBKIT IS AN open-source rendering engine designed to display web pages. It powers Google Chrome and Safari as well as a variety of mobile devices such as iPhone, iPad, and Android phones and tablets. It also controls rendering in a variety of desktop applications such as Apple Mail and those created with Adobe AIR.

WebKit basically consists of two components: WebCore and JavaScriptCore. WebCore controls all layout and rendering tasks, creating HTML visualizations based on DOM markup and Cascading Style Sheets (CSS). JavaScriptCore compliments this layout engine with a high-performance interaction engine that provides feature-rich JavaScript functionality.

This chapter provides a short history of WebKit and a discussion of which browsers, devices, and applications use the engine. You learn the various components that WebKit supports, as well as how these differ across various implementations.

QUICK HISTORY

The code that would later become WebKit began in 1998 as part of KDE's web browser, Konqueror (designed primarily for Linux).

As part of an effort to build their own web browser, Apple forked the HTML and JavaScript engine from KDE in 2002, naming the ported engine *WebKit*. Initially Apple and KDE cross-developed the engines, exchanging code patches and enhancements. Then Apple made a number of unilateral decisions, including converting a portion of the codebase from C++ to Objective C, and dramatically altering other coding approaches. This along with Apple's source control and poor documentation led to a split between the KDE project and WebKit in 2005, which some KDE developers characterized as a "bitter failure."

In June 2005, Apple announced that it was open-sourcing the entirety of WebKit (previously only WebCore and JavaScriptCore were open-source). This was reportedly part of an effort to work "more closely with KDE and the rest of the open-source community," according to Safari developer Maciej Stachowiak.

As part of the Safari web browser, WebKit gained notoriety in the web community by being the first browser to support a number of CSS3 attributes. While other browsers offered more limited rendering tools, Safari provided a variety of innovative styling controls such as rounded corners and gradients that could generate richer graphics in CSS.

Even as other browsers began supporting these attributes, WebKit-based browsers stayed ahead of the curve by implementing new features, such as CSS animations and 2D and 3D transformations. These impressive features provided a robust rendering toolkit, allowing developers to smoothly animate, rotate, and skew HTML elements using CSS alone. These WebKit innovations proved so useful that they eventually informed the W3C CSS3 recommendations, and became standards used across all modern browsers today.

WHERE IS WEBKIT USED?

WebKit's speed, power, and versatility make it an ideal rendering solution for many situations. The engine is used in a wide variety of implementations, from desktop browsers to mobile devices and web-enabled applications.

WEB BROWSERS

An incredibly feature-rich and fast rendering engine, WebKit is ideal for desktop web browsers. It has been adopted by Google Chrome and Safari as well as a variety of niche browsers.

At its inception, WebKit represented a very small portion of the browser market share because it was powering only the relatively underused Safari and Konqueror. Although Safari usage is increasing, it still comprises a modest 7% of the market, and Konqueror's share is still negligible.

WebKit's share of the browser market climbed considerably when it was adopted by the Google Chrome project. Between Chrome and Safari, WebKit comprises 28% of the desktop browser market (at the time of this writing).

MOBILE DEVICES

Recently Mobile WebKit, a special build of WebKit, has become the emerging standard for mobile device browsers. Lightweight yet surprisingly powerful, Mobile WebKit is an ideal engine for creating rich applications and web experiences on underpowered mobile devices.

The vast majority of smartphones built in recent years use the WebKit framework. Apple iOS devices such as iPhone, iPad and iTouch are all built upon WebKit. Additionally, WebKit is used by most Android devices, which include a wide variety of phones and tablets. Newer Blackberry devices, such as the Blackberry Torch, as well as Symbian-based devices use WebKit. Also, WebOS, which powers the Palm Pre and a number of tablets, is also based on WebKit, however at the time of this writing WebOS' future is uncertain since it has been abandoned by HP.

RIAS

In addition to web browsers and mobile devices, WebKit is also used in a number of desktop applications. Due to its roots as a web browser, the vast majority of these apps are rich Internet applications (RIAs).

WebKit powers apps built with Adobe AIR, a cross-platform framework that allows developers to simultaneously program applications for Windows, Mac, and Linux.

WebKit also is used in Mac OS X dashboard widgets, as well as a number of miscellaneous Mac and Windows apps, such as Apple's Mail and Microsoft's Entourage.

MISCELLANEOUS DEVICES

The same features that make WebKit ideal for mobile devices also make it an attractive option for other underpowered devices such as eReaders and video game consoles.

A variety of reading tablets such as the Kindle and Nook use WebKit to offer a stripped-down web browser on their devices. The Nintendo 3DS, a portable video game console, offers a WebKit-based browser as well.

As more devices become web enabled, you will likely see them adopting WebKit as a powerful open-source solution to integrate a web layer.

WHAT DOES WEBKIT SUPPORT?

The WebKit engine is known for supporting a wide variety of advanced functionality. WebKit leads the pack when it comes to browser support for innovative new features in CSS3, HTML5, and JavaScript.

9

CSS3

WebKit is perhaps best known as the first major engine to support a variety of CSS3 attributes. These features provide developers with an advanced toolkit for rendering complex web pages without relying on images. WebKit supports rounded corners, gradients, drop shadows, custom fonts, and alpha transparency, to name a few. Additionally, it supports CSS animations both through transitions as well as keyframes. Furthermore, WebKit is constantly innovating new experimental attributes and pushing CSS standards into the future.

WebKit also supports a variety of advanced CSS3 selectors, allowing you to choose elements based on their HTML attributes and location in the DOM. You can select direct descendants and siblings, or even the fifth paragraph in a `div`. You can leverage the `:before` and `:after` pseudo-elements to inject content directly into the page, and apply special styling based on the state of elements.

You can even take advantage of CSS media queries to tailor styling to different screen dimensions. That means you can create flexible layouts, which change in response to smaller and larger screen sizes.

HTML5 AND SVG

WebKit also supports a number of advanced features in HTML5. For instance, media tags allow you to embed audio and video directly in the browser, as you learn in Chapter 6. Furthermore, a variety of new form elements can be used to provide a richer user interface without relying on JavaScript. Additionally, these elements can be coupled with HTML5 form validation to ensure the user fills required fields, enters the correct information, and sees appropriate error messages.

WebKit supports canvas as well as SVG, enabling you to draw complex vectored shapes directly in the browser. Combining these drawings with JavaScript interaction, you can build rich applications that rival those built in Flash. With the introduction of WebGL, you can use these elements to create stunning 3D applications.

NOT ALL WEBKITS ARE CREATED EQUAL

One common misconception about WebKit is that the engine is identical across all implementations. Applications not only use different versions of WebKit, but there are additionally a number of modified versions of the core.

USING DIFFERENT VERSIONS OF WEBKIT

You probably expect certain changes across different versions of a single browser, or between browsers that use completely different renderers. But even the latest versions of different WebKit browsers do not necessarily use the same version of the engine.

10

Although browsers typically use a recent build of WebKit, different browser release schedules lead to disparities at any given time. For instance Apple took more than a year between releasing Safari versions 5 and 5.1. Throughout this time, the WebKit engine in Safari slowly became outdated compared to that of Chrome, which had more frequent releases.

Furthermore, browsers often make decisions about which parts of WebKit to support. For example, the default configuration of Chrome enables WebGL, which is also enabled in recent versions of Safari if the user has Mac OS X version 10.6 or higher. Thus the user's operating system can affect how much WebKit functionality is supported in his browser.

MODIFYING THE CORE

As mentioned earlier, the WebKit engine is open source, which has led to a variety of modified versions. For instance, Mobile WebKit differs substantially from the standard core, which means that web apps can behave differently between Desktop and iOS Safari.

Mobile implementations of WebKit even differ from device to device. For instance, Nokia ported the WebKit core to create its Symbian operating system, and Palm used WebKit to create an interface for WebOS, both of which differ from Mobile WebKit.

This means that you will notice incongruities between different implementations of WebKit, which can prove much more complicated than disparities between different versions of a single browser.

11

SUMMARY

WebKit began with open-source, standards-driven principles at its core, and these values continue to shape its development today. From improving its already lightweight and powerful core, to innovating new standards in web development, you can count on WebKit remaining a dominant force amongst web browsers.

Constant refinement of the library ensures that future platforms will continue to view WebKit as the ideal option for web rendering. Furthermore, creating new standards in CSS, JavaScript and HTML shapes the future of not only WebKit-based browsers, but all other browsers on the market.

2

GETTING STARTED WITH WEBKIT DEVELOPMENT

BEFORE YOU CAN dive in and start building WebKit applications, it is important to set up your development environment. To streamline your coding, you need a number of tools, from those that provide accurate testing environments to informative debugging utilities.

Although the specific tools may differ across platforms, you will use the same techniques regardless of whether you are developing for desktop browsers or mobile devices.

In this chapter you learn how to set up your computer to test WebKit apps in the desktop browsers Chrome and Safari. You also learn how to use emulators to test the default browsers in the mobile platforms iOS and Android. These emulators allow you to test a wide range of phones and tablets without having to actually purchase any physical devices.

In addition to basic testing, you learn how to debug apps in each platform, track down JavaScript and styling errors, test styling options on the fly, and even graph download times of external resources.

Finally, you learn how to set up testing environments for non-WebKit browsers. You learn how to run multiple versions of IE, Firefox and Opera on a single machine, as well as how to install alternative mobile browsers for iOS and Android.

SETTING UP TESTING ENVIRONMENTS

Prior to sending an app into production, it is important to test everything in the platforms and browsers you support. It is not enough to simply test your code on a single WebKit browser on a single platform because WebKit implementations differ considerably.

If you are building a web app that needs to support desktop and mobile browsers, you have to test a variety of environments: Desktop Safari and Chrome as well as iOS Safari and Android browser. Although this should be sufficient for most apps, you also may want to test older versions of Safari and Chrome. Additionally, to be safe you may want to test iOS Safari and Android browser on a variety of different devices. Even mobile devices with the same OS version can have bugs and variations, as well as different screen sizes.

TESTING APPROACHES

There are a variety of approaches to cross-browser and cross-platform testing, from quick and easy screenshot services to virtual machines and emulators.

Testing Desktop Browsers

First, there are a number of services such as `http://browsershots.org/` and `http://litmus.com/` that provide screenshots of your site across a variety of browser versions and platforms. While these remote services are unparalleled in the number of browser versions and platforms they support, screenshots can only provide feedback about static styling. Although this offers a useful first look, you usually still need to test dynamic functionality and styling changes.

You might consider using a one-size-fits-all solution such as Adobe CS5 Browser Labs, but these types of solutions are often buggy and do not accurately reflect the experience users have in their native browsers.

Ultimately, the only foolproof way to test across desktop browsers is to install all the browsers and versions you want to test, and then manually perform the tests.

Testing Mobile Devices

Testing mobile devices can be more difficult, due to the large number of devices in the marketplace. While it is best to test your app on any physical device you want to support, it is usually unfeasible to purchase an array of mobile devices for testing.

Fortunately, a variety of mobile device emulators fill in these gaps; however, keep in mind that these emulators are not entirely accurate.

Alternatively, there are paid services such as `www.deviceanywhere.com`, which allow you to test your site across a wide variety of mobile devices. Although costly, this service provides an impressive amount of device testing opportunities.

There are also a couple of free services that are similar to DeviceAnywhere that are released by individual device manufacturers. Although they offer testing only on their proprietary devices, you can still test a number of devices from these companies for free.

Nokia Remote Device Access allows you to test on Nokia devices for 8 hours per day absolutely free (after signing up for Forum Nokia). This includes access to all Symbian-based devices, among other Nokia devices: `www.developer.nokia.com/Devices/Remote_device_access/`.

Samsung Lab.Dev is a similar service offered by Samsung. Here you can test Samsung Android devices for free after signing up for developer program: `http://innovator.samsungmobile.com/bbs/lab/view.do?platformId=1`.

MAC VS. PC

When it comes to testing WebKit, Mac users are in a much better position than Windows users. Because WebKit was originally designed for Mac, the tools and community for WebKit development are still fairly Mac-focused.

Windows users will encounter a number of issues—for instance, you can test Chrome on any platform, but accurately testing Safari is difficult on Windows. Furthermore, the official iOS simulator is not available for Windows.

To make matters worse, it is much easier to run a virtual machine to test Windows on a Mac than vice versa.

However, don't be discouraged if you're a Windows user. Although WebKit testing is certainly more challenging on Windows, there is still a variety of tools that provide decent testing capabilities.

CHROME AND SAFARI ENVIRONMENTS

For Mac users, testing Chrome and Safari is as simple as installing both browsers on your computer.

Windows users can easily test Chrome because it is almost identical across Mac and Windows. There are some minor differences across the platforms, which are mostly related to third-party plugins. Thus to be extra careful, Windows users should double-check Chrome on Mac, and vice versa.

Unfortunately, Windows users will run into major problems testing Safari, which are related to issues with Safari for Windows. Although the Windows version can provide some insight into Safari implementations, it differs so greatly from the Mac version that it is practically useless for cross-platform testing.

To test Safari, Windows users need to test it natively on OS X, either by running a virtual machine, or checking on another computer.

Mac users should not concern themselves with testing Safari for Windows because it has a very small market share (mostly developers testing for Mac).

TESTING OLDER BROWSERS

While testing the latest version of browsers is a good start, it will not always give you a complete representation of the browser spectrum used by your user base. Users often take a while to upgrade browsers, and some may be facing roadblocks such as corporate IT departments, lack of admin privileges, or even hardware/OS issues that prevent them from upgrading. Thus, a thorough testing effort usually includes older browsers.

The best way to determine which older browser versions to support is by looking at your site's analytics data.

Installing Older Versions of Chrome

Testing multiple versions of Chrome is as simple as using multiple user profiles.

Chrome installations are user-specific, so you can test older versions of Chrome by logging out and then logging back in as another user. With this alternative user profile, you can install any version of Chrome you want, a trick that works on both Mac and Windows.

Installing Older Versions of Safari

Installing multiple versions of Safari is a little more complicated. Safari installs at the system level, so you cannot rely on the same user profile trick you used for Chrome.

Although you can keep multiple versions of Safari in your Applications folder, the older versions use the latest WebKit found on your computer. Thus, although you may be seeing an older Safari UI, it will not accurately reflect the experience of a native user.

Fortunately, there is a project called Multi-Safari, which allows you to run multiple versions of Safari on the same machine (similar to MultipleIEs). This project bundles the correct WebKit version into the various instances of Safari, thereby providing a more accurate testing environment.

For more information, go here: `http://michelf.com/projects/multi-safari/`.

DEBUGGING CHROME AND SAFARI ISSUES

Debugging issues in Chrome and Safari is easy using the developer panel that is built into WebKit. In Chrome the developer options are enabled by default, but in Safari you will need to enable them using Preferences → Advanced → Show Develop Menu in Menu Bar as shown in Figure 2-1.

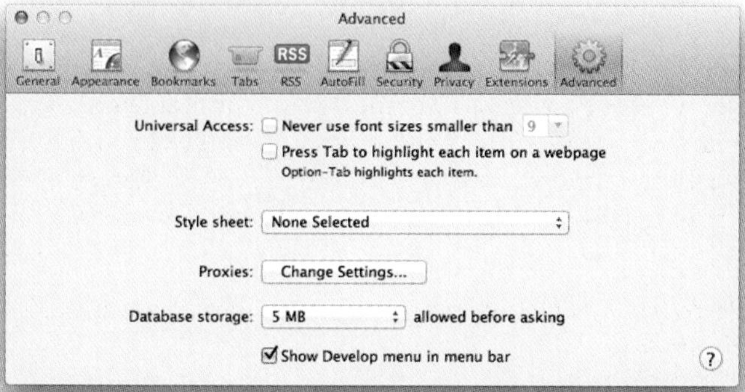

Figure 2-1: You have to enable the developer tools manually in Safari.

Once they are enabled, you can use the developer tools for a variety of debugging tasks, from solving styling and JavaScript problems to network resource tracking.

DOM Inspector

Perhaps the most useful tool in the developer menu is the DOM inspector. To access the inspector, right-click any element in your web page and select Inspect Element. This calls up a panel that shows the element's position in the DOM source and any styles that have been applied, as shown in Figure 2-2.

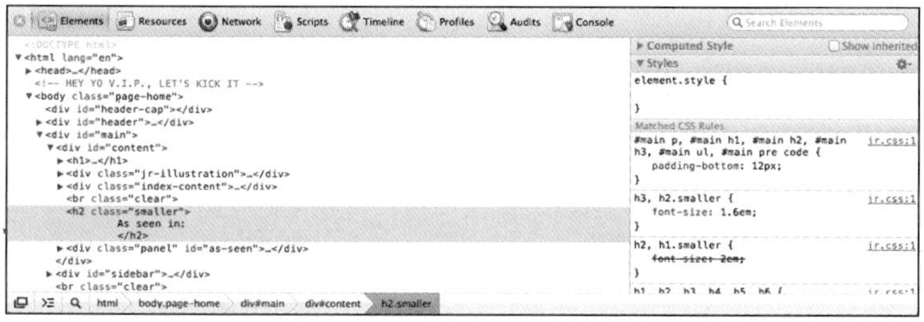

Figure 2-2: The DOM inspector provides a lot of useful styling information.

With the DOM inspector, you can see which styles are being applied from which style rules, as well as any styles that are being overwritten. You can also view the element's overall styling by expanding the Computed Style tab. You can even set your own styling rules on the fly by editing any of the rules you see in the inspector.

17

JavaScript Console

Another extremely useful tool is the JavaScript console. It allows you to track down JavaScript errors by providing a message describing the error as well as the line number and file at which it occurred, as seen in Figure 2-3.

Figure 2-3: A syntax error reported by the JavaScript console.

In addition, the console allows you to output text and objects from JavaScript using `console.log()`.

The JavaScript console even enables you to execute JavaScript on the fly by typing into the console.

Network Graph

The developer menu provides the network graph, a tool you can use to track the download, lookup, and instantiation time of various network resources, as shown in Figure 2-4:

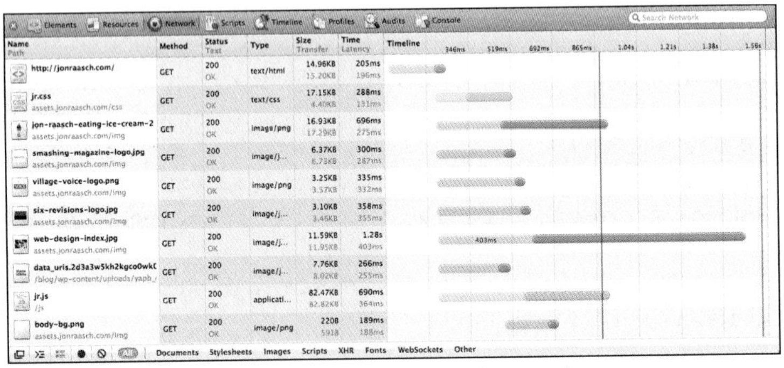

Figure 2-4: The network graph gives useful information about the external resources on your page.

Using the network graph, you can get a good idea of how quickly various resources are being downloaded, and gain insight into how well your server's backend is relaying files to the browser.

iOS AND ANDROID ENVIRONMENTS

When testing WebKit on mobile devices, nothing beats testing natively on all the devices you support. However, actually purchasing all of these devices is rarely cost effective. For instance, just to test a reasonable market share of iOS devices, you would need to buy an iPhone 4, iPhone 3GS, iPad 2, iPad, and iTouch. This is not to mention that there are literally hundreds of Android devices on the market.

Although it might be nice to convince your employer to buy you hundreds of mobile devices, in all likelihood you will need to rely on device emulators for the majority of your testing.

Additionally, device emulators can sometimes be easier to use than the actual device, since you can type on your computer keyboard and freely take screenshots.

> *You should still test on any mobile devices that you already own, however don't be shortsighted and only develop for your particular device.*

SELECTING AN EMULATOR

Device emulators rarely mimic the native experience perfectly, and often contain minor differences from the actual device. These issues can be more pronounced in certain emulators, so it is important to choose the best one. If you choose a buggy emulator, you will spend hours tracking down and solving bugs that do not occur in the native device, or even worse, not see bugs that do exist.

When it comes to device emulation, there are basically two options. The first is simulators, which approximate the native device experience. Although these may be superficially similar to the device, there are certain key technical differences from the actual device.

The other alternative is emulators, which attempt to mimic the native experience exactly by running native code in a virtual machine. Ideally, the only difference between emulators and native devices is that the emulator runs a simulation of the device hardware. However, the virtual machine often contains bugs, and there are also certain features that cannot be emulated on a desktop computer, e.g. making voice calls or retrieving geolocation data.

In general, emulators will be closer to the native experience, so if you have a choice you should choose an emulator over a simulator.

iOS SIMULATORS

There are a number of iOS simulators that you can use to test your apps on a variety of iOS devices.

Web-Based Simulators

There are a few web-based testing solutions such as those found at www.testiphone.com/
and http://iphone4simulator.com/. (See Figure 2-5.) While these options are good
for quick testing, they are not overly reliable and should not be depended upon for more
robust testing efforts.

Figure 2-5: testiphone.com and iphone4simulator.com provide free in-browser testing for iPhone.

iphone4simulator.com is designed and developed by Ritesh Manchanda

Apple iOS Simulator

Apple provides the iOS Simulator, a simulator, with its iOS SDK. It allows you to run, test, and debug iOS applications locally on your Mac. You can use the simulator, shown in Figure 2-6, to simulate iPhone and iPad across a variety of device and iOS versions.

The iOS Simulator is included with Xcode, which can be downloaded from the Mac AppStore. While this simulator works well, it only runs on Mac, so Windows users will need to pursue another option.

iOS Simulators on Windows

Although Windows users cannot use the official iOS Simulator, there are other solutions that provide iOS testing capabilities in Windows. Most notably is iBBDemo2, a free simulator that you can download here: www.puresimstudios.com/ibbdemo/.

As shown in Figure 2-7, iBBDemo2 provides a decent amount of iOS emulation support, providing simulators for both iPhone and iPad, as well as support for various browser features such as orientation changes and zoom/scale.

Figure 2-6: The official iOS Simulator provides a number of testing capabilities.

21

Figure 2-7: iBBDemo2 provides respectable iOS simulation in any platform.

Source: Blackbaud, Inc. www.blackbaud.com

iBBDemo2 is far from perfect, yet it does provide a decent look into how websites and web-based applications display on iOS devices.

iBBDemo2 is a cross-platform AIR app, so it also works in Linux.

ANDROID EMULATOR

The official Android emulator is not only free but also works in several operating systems. To get the emulator, first download the Android SDK: `http://developer.android.com/sdk/`.

Setting Up Android Devices

Unlike the iOS Simulator, the Android emulator forces you to manually create a testing environment for each device you want to test. While this can be cumbersome, it does allow you to create a unique emulator to test any of the numerous devices built on the Android platform.

The first step in setting up a device emulator is to download one of the Android packages in the SDK's list of available packages, as shown in Figure 2-8.

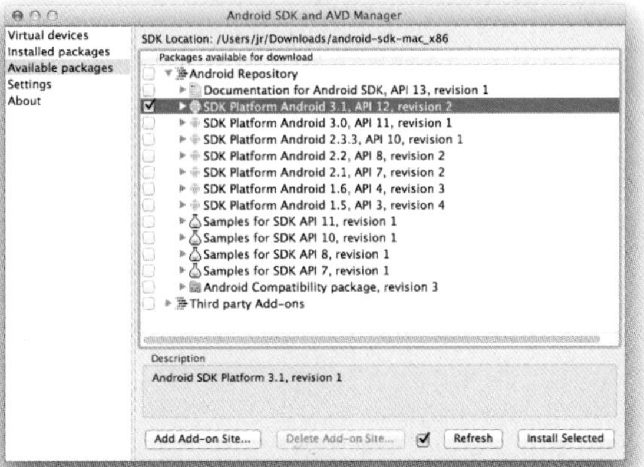

Figure 2-8: Install one of the Android packages.

Then, create an AVD (Android Virtual Device) by entering the appropriate settings in the Virtual Devices tab, as shown in Figure 2-9.

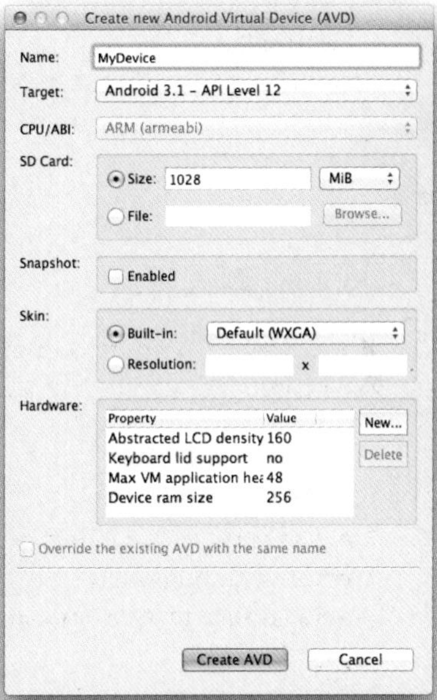

You can adjust a variety of device settings, such as the dimensions, LCD pixel density, and size of the SD card. You can find a list of relevant device settings here: `http://mobile.tutsplus.com/tutorials/android/common-android-virtual-device-configurations/`.

If you want to skin the emulator to match the given device, there are a wide variety of skins available throughout the Internet. One set is available here: `http://teavuihuang.com/android/`.

Figure 2-9: Create a virtual device corresponding to the device you want to emulate.

Testing with the Android Emulator

While setting up the individual device emulators can be time-consuming, the actual testing of web pages is simple. Just open the appropriate emulator and navigate to whichever page you want to test, as shown in Figure 2-10.

Figure 2-10: Testing a web page with the Android emulator.

DEBUGGING iOS AND ANDROID ISSUES

There are a couple tools you can use to debug WebKit Mobile, although compared to desktop testing suites, they are rather limited.

Within iOS, the developer tools in iOS Safari provide a certain amount of debugging support. Debugging Android browser is a bit more complicated, but can be accomplished using the debugging tools in the Android SDK.

iOS Safari's Developer Tools

The native debugging tools in iOS Safari can provide some quick insight into development issues in iOS web apps.

First you need to enable the debug console by going to Settings → Safari → Developer → Debug Console.

While this debug console does not provide nearly the same amount of functionality as the developer tools in Desktop Safari, it can provide some clarification of any errors you receive.

You also can use the debug console to display any console messages you create in JavaScript using `console.log()`, as shown in Figure 2-11.

Figure 2-11: The iOS Safari debug console provides the location of runtime errors as well as a brief description of the issue. It also displays console logs.

Android Browser Debugging With LogCat

While the Android SDK provides a number of debugging tools, these are mostly geared toward native app developers. Fortunately, it does provide one utility that you can use in conjunction with the Android browser to debug web apps.

That is the LogCat utility, which outputs application logs. When combined with the Android browser, you can view runtime errors as well as output text from JavaScript using `console.log()`.

For more information on using LogCat, see the Android SDK documentation: `http://developer.android.com/guide/developing/debugging/debugging-log.html#startingLogcat`.

BEYOND WEBKIT BROWSERS

In all likelihood you are not developing for WebKit browsers exclusively. This means that you have to get set up to test across a number of other environments as well.

With non-WebKit browsers, the same testing principles apply: test multiple versions on multiple platforms.

FIREFOX

Fortunately, installing multiple versions of Firefox is relatively simple using different user profiles. However, it is somewhat difficult to stay on top of the latest version of the browser. This is because the Mozilla team is committed to releasing a new version of Firefox every 6 weeks.

Installing Multiple Firefoxes

Installing multiple versions of Firefox is easy in Mac OS X using the MultiFirefox utility. MultiFirefox allows you to run multiple versions of Firefox side by side on the same machine, and also manages the user profiles for each version separately. Download MultiFirefox from `http://davemartorana.com/multifirefox/`.

It is also a good idea to test Firefox in Windows. Although it is a bit more complicated to install multiple versions in Windows, you can still do so manually following these instructions: `www.mouserunner.com/FF_Tips_Multiple_Fx.html`.

Debugging Firefox

Debugging Firefox is very easy using the Firebug addon. Firebug includes a DOM inspector, JavaScript console, resource tracker, as well as a variety of other useful tools. Install Firebug here: `http://getfirebug.com/`.

INTERNET EXPLORER

Getting set up to test on everyone's favorite browser is actually not as difficult as you may think. Although you will most likely experience your largest debugging headaches in IE, testing on multiple versions of IE is relatively easy.

Multiple IEs

Prior to IE9, you could test IE 6, 7 and 8 on a single machine using Multiple IEs. This machine had to be running Windows XP, but other than that the process was fairly straightforward after installing Multiple IEs (`http://tredosoft.com/Multiple_IE`), IE7 Standalone Mode: (`http://tredosoft.com/IE7_standalone`) and IE8.

Testing IE9 and Lower in Windows 7

However, IE9 made testing multiple versions of IE more complicated. This is because IE9 does not run in XP, which means that you cannot use Multiple IEs to test it.

Fortunately you can still test all the older versions of IE you need on a single machine by setting up virtual machines in Windows 7 using XP Mode. This is relatively easy, simply follow the instructions here: `http://ieblog.members.winisp.net/images/InstallingXPMode.htm`.

IETester

Another option for testing IE is IETester. This tool allows you to test IE5.5 – 10 on XP, Vista or Windows 7. Although this is not a completely accurate representation of using older versions of IE, it is fairly close in terms of the rendering and JavaScript engines. However keep in mind that IETester only simulates IE and can occasionally cause serious testing problems.

Download IETester here: `www.my-debugbar.com/wiki/IETester/`.

Debugging IE

There are a couple tools you can use to debug issues in IE. First, you can use DebugBar, which includes a DOM inspector, JavaScript console and a variety of other tools: `www.debugbar.com`.

Additionally, you can install Firebug Lite on your website. Firebug Lite is a JavaScript-based debugging suite that works in all browsers. The only disadvantage is that it actually has to be included in the pages you want to debug. Download Firebug Lite here: `http://getfirebug.com/firebuglite`.

OPERA

Considering Opera's limited market share, you probably only need to test the latest version of this browser. However, if you would like to install multiple versions, you can do using multiple profiles. Follow the instructions here: `http://my.opera.com/separate-blog/2009/06/10/installing-multiple-opera-builds-with-separate-profiles-on-mac`.

You can debug Opera using Dragonfly, which includes a DOM inspector, JavaScript console, resource tracker and a variety of other tools. Download Dragonfly here: `www.opera.com/dragonfly/features/`.

OTHER MOBILE BROWSERS

The default iOS and Android browsers (IOS Safari and Android Browser) both run WebKit. However, these platforms also allow users to install alternative browsers.

This means that if you are targeting these devices, you may want to also test these browsers. The main browsers to pay attention to are Firefox Mobile and Opera Mini.

Firefox Mobile is only available as a fully featured browser on Android, and can be downloaded from the Android Market. Learn more about Firefox Mobile here: `www.mozilla.com/en-US/mobile/`.

Opera Mini can be installed on both iOS and Android platforms, through their respective app stores. Learn more about Opera Mini here: `www.opera.com/mobile/`.

SUMMARY

Taking an hour or two to properly set up your environment streamlines development efforts and ends up saving a lot of time in the long run.

Often, thorough testing includes checking not only the latest version of every browser you support, but also one or two previous versions. Additionally, it is a good idea to test on multiple operating systems.

When it comes to mobile development, cross-platform testing becomes much more complicated, since there are a wide variety of devices that often contain different nuances. To test all of these devices, you will most likely need to rely on emulators and simulators.

However be careful to select accurate emulation tools, or you may end up spending time debugging issues that don't actually exist, or not debugging issues that do.

When deciding which browsers and platforms to test, you should pay attention to your user base. If you have analytics detailing which browsers and operating systems are favored by your users, you will be in an excellent position to decide which environments to focus on.

Finally, testing different environments and determining where bugs exist is only half the battle. After discovering issues, debugging tools such as JavaScript consoles and DOM inspectors make tracking down and resolving bugs significantly easier.

CSS3 SUPPORT
IN WEBKIT

3 ADVANCED STYLING WITH CSS3

CSS3 INTRODUCES A WIDE variety of new styling options that you can use to create rich graphical web pages. These attributes provide a new level of control, making element styling more intuitive and less reliant on images.

In this chapter you learn how to render entire web pages using pure CSS. The rendering techniques covered include generating graphics with rounded corners, gradients, drop shadows, and custom fonts. Because pure CSS reduces the need for images you can create web pages with improved performance and highly maintainable page styling.

You learn how to animate elements with CSS3 transition and keyframes, allowing you to avoid JavaScript animation. CSS3 animations are not only easy to use, but are also typically faster than JavaScript alternatives (and are even hardware accelerated on certain devices). You also learn how to use 2D and 3D transforms to rotate, scale, and skew elements in up to three dimensions. These visual effects create a richer user experience and combine easily with CSS animations. Finally you learn about a variety of more experimental CSS3 properties, such as image masks, which you can use to control the transparency of elements, as well as other properties such as text-strokes, reflections, and WebKit marquee.

USING CSS3 TO RENDER GRAPHICS WITHOUT IMAGES

With the plethora of styling options available in CSS3, it is now easier than ever to render graphical web pages without using images. While it may seem easier to use images, the rewards of rendering graphics with CSS3 are too attractive to be ignored. Most importantly, avoiding images provides a substantial performance boost for your websites. Besides reducing download times and HTTP requests for users, it also saves bandwidth and requests for your web server. Additionally, sites rendered in CSS3 are much easier to maintain because you can make visual changes quickly in stylesheets, rather than opening Photoshop comps to make changes and export new images.

CSS3 styling is easy to reuse across multiple elements. For instance, if you need several buttons with different text, you can either use a single CSS snippet, or cut out new images for each one (and any additional buttons that may arise in the future). This issue is magnified when combined with maintenance issues: if the styling changes, would you rather change a single style rule or export every redesigned button?

Additionally, graphics rendered in CSS3 are much better for interactive elements, which typically need a variety of states. For instance, UI elements such as buttons often need as many as four different styles: basic, disabled, hovered, and active. Rather than use four different images, it is much easier to tweak four CSS styles (not to mention the performance advantages).

If you take into account the performance improvements, as well as the support for CSS3 across modern browsers, the rewards of this approach make it an attractive solution for all websites. This section explores a real-world scenario of creating button graphics using pure CSS as shown in Figure 3-1. You'll learn how to exploit a variety of CSS3 attributes to make a visually appealing graphic that rivals those built with graphics programs such as Adobe Photoshop.

Figure 3-1: In this chapter you learn how to build this button using CSS3 and no images.

BASIC SETUP

Before adding the more advanced attributes, you first need to set up some basic markup and CSS styles. Begin with some very simple markup:

```
<a href="#" class="button">Contact Us</a>
```

Next, add some basic CSS:

```
.button {
    display: inline-block;
    padding: 10px 45px;
    background-color: #007236;
    color: #FFF;
    font-family: Arial, sans;
    font-size: 45px;
    text-decoration: none;
    border: 2px solid #004B23;
}
```

This snippet adds basic styling to the button. It applies `display: inline-block` as well as some padding to make the button larger. Then it applies some basic colors and font styling, and adds a border around the image. Although these styles are an important foundation, the button is not yet looking very impressive, as shown in Figure 3-2:

Figure 3-2: The Contact Us button with basic styling

Now add some basic styles to darken the colors when the user places his or her mouse over the button:

```
.button:hover {
    background-color: #00501E;
    border-color: #003517;
}
```

> The `:hover` pseudo-class styles elements on mouseover.

Finally, add some styles to further darken the colors when the user clicks the button:

```
.button:active {
    background-color: #00451A;
    border-color: #00280F;
}
```

> The `:active` pseudo-class styles elements on click. It is especially important for mobile devices, which generally do not use a mouse and therefore have no mouseover state.

BORDER RADIUS

Rounded corners can easily be added using the `border-radius` attribute:

```
.button {
    -webkit-border-radius: 10px;
    border-radius: 10px;
}
```

This snippet applies a `border-radius` of `10px` to all corners of the button, as shown in Figure 3-3:

Figure 3-3: The button with rounded corners

You may be wondering why there are two versions of the `border-radius` defined in this snippet. They are included to support older versions of WebKit as well as the latest releases.

The first, `-webkit-border-radius`, uses a browser-specific extension indicating that although the attribute is supported, it is not fully supported according to the W3C CSS3 specifications. It is a common practice among browsers to use special prefixes to ensure that buggy implementations do not end up adversely affecting future, improved implementations.

Fortunately, `border-radius` is fully supported in the current release of WebKit. Thus, the extensionless attribute is included here as well, to target both older and newer versions of WebKit. It is a good practice to include the extensionless attribute, even if it is not yet supported, to future-proof your CSS against later releases.

Other browser extensions will be covered in Chapter 5.

Different Border Radii for Each Corner

The `border-radius` attribute is quite versatile and allows for a variety of more advanced implementations. For instance, the previous snippet applies the same border radius to all corners of the button, but you can also define a separate radius for each individual corner (see Figure 3-4). You can either use a separate property for each (such as `border-top-left-radius`) or define them all at once using shorthand:

Figure 3-4: This button has a different border radius applied to each corner.

```
border-radius: 10px 20px 0 5px;
```

This defines all four corners clockwise from the top-left—so the top-left is `10px`, the top-right is `20px`, the bottom-right is `0px`, and the bottom-left is `5px`.

Similar to other CSS shorthands, if you leave any of these values off, they will simply repeat. For instance `10px 20px` is equivalent to `10px 20px 10px 20px`, and `10px 20px 0` is equivalent to `10px 20px 0 20px`. Be careful, though, because a shorthand can yield unexpected results with the deprecated `-webkit-border-radius` syntax, so it may be best to avoid shorthands with border radius.

Elliptical Corners

In addition to individual corner definitions, `border-radius` also supports elliptical corners; that is, rounded corners that are shaped like ovals instead of circles (see Figure 3-5). While there are a couple ways to define elliptical corners, the easiest is the slash syntax:

Figure 3-5: This button uses an elliptical border radius.

```
border-radius: 12px / 20px;
```

This defines an elliptical corner with two radii: a horizontal radius of 12px and a vertical radius of 20px. Elliptical corners are a great way to define more interesting shapes using CSS and they work well with the button graphic.

To better understand elliptical corners, take a look at Figure 3-6.

To define a separate elliptical border for each corner, simply start with all the horizontal values and use a slash to separate the vertical values:

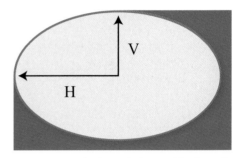

```
border-radius: 12px 20px 25px 15px / 20px
    15px 12px 25px;
```

This defines separate elliptical values for each corner. You can use any combination of shorthands here, so long as they are separated by a slash.

Figure 3-6: Horizontal and vertical values are defined using the slash syntax: `border-radius: H / V`.

Fixing Border Radius Bleed

When using `border-radius` with a colored border, you may notice the background color leaking out around the edges of the rounded corners, as shown in Figure 3-7. This is due to issues with the rounded corner rasterization, which occurs when shapes are turned into pixels for screen display.

Figure 3-7: The white background color is bleeding around the rounded corners of this element. This is mostly seen with 1px wide borders that have a lot of contrast against the background color.

Fortunately, you can easily alleviate this visual issue using CSS:

```
.button {
    -webkit-background-clip: padding-box;
    background-clip: padding-box;
}
```

The `background-clip` attribute provides more precise control over background overflow.

Although the corner rasterization is still not completely clean, using `background-clip` greatly reduces the amount of bleed around the edges. (See Figure 3-8.)

Figure 3-8: There is less corner bleed in this element, thanks to `background-clip`.

GRADIENTS

The next step for this stylized button is replacing the flat background color with a gradient to simulate three dimensionality and lighting. Fortunately, you can take advantage of CSS3 gradients, which are both versatile and easy to use. Start by defining a basic gradient for your button's `background-image`:

```
.button {
    background-image: -webkit-gradient(
        linear,
        left top,
        left bottom,
        from(#007231),
        to(#004B23)
    );
}
```

> *Note that this is applied to* `background-image`, *not* `background-color`. *Be careful with the syntax, and make sure not to leave a hanging comma after the last value.*

This snippet defines a linear gradient for the button, starting from the top and going to the bottom (see Figure 3-9).

Figure 3-9: The button with a linear gradient.

Manipulate the `left top` and `left bottom` values as needed to create horizontal or diagonal gradients (e.g. from `left top` to `right bottom`). You can also use percentage values to create gradients at a variety of angles, or those that don't extend completely to the edges of the element (e.g. `left 20%` to `left 80%`).

> *When using gradients it's always a good idea to define a basic* `background-color` *as a failsafe for non-supportive browsers.*

Color Stops

Now the gradient background looks decent, but can still be improved using color stops. Color stops allow you to add additional colors to the gradient, which you can use to add more depth and enrich the 3D effect of the button:

```
.button {
    background-image: -webkit-gradient(
        linear,
        left top,
        left bottom,
        from(#007231),
```

```
        to(#004B23),
        color-stop(0.3, #00893B)
    );
}
```

Here a `color-stop` has been added to the button to introduce a lighter shade of green at 30% (`0.3`) down from the top of the element. As shown in Figure 3-10, this provides the button a more three-dimensional appearance. You can use any number of color-stops in your gradient, and even avoid the `from()` and `to()` declarations if you'd prefer only color-stops.

Figure 3-10: A more complex gradient using an off-center color-stop

Now that you've created this gradient, make sure to define additional gradients for the `:hover` and `:active` states of the button:

```
.button:hover {
    background-image: -webkit-gradient(
        linear,
        left top,
        left bottom,
        from(#005E27),
        to(#003719),
        color-stop(0.3, #007531)
    );
}
```

```
.button:active {
    background-color: #00451A;
    border-color: #00280F;
    background-image: -webkit-gradient(
        linear,
        left top,
        left bottom,
        from(#004F1D),
        to(#00280F),
        color-stop(0.3, #006627)
    );
}
```

> The CSS3 gradient generator at `http://gradients.glrzad.com/` is very useful for building more complex gradients.

Radial Gradients

In addition to the linear gradient used in the example above, CSS3 also supports radial gradients. Radial gradients use a similar syntax, however defining the starting and ending position is a bit more complex. For the start and end points, you not only define the position, but also the radius of the gradient at that point. For instance:

```
background-image: -webkit-gradient(
    radial,
    50% 50%,
    20,
    50% 50%,
    100,
    from(#007231),
    to(#004B23),
    color-stop(0.3, #00893B)
);
```

This radial gradient is centered around the middle of the element (50% 50%). It starts with a 20px radius and ends with a 100px radius, as shown in Figure 3-11.

Figure 3-11: This button has a radial gradient.

You can use percentages or pixels to adjust the *x* and *y* position of the gradient, however make sure to leave the px off from any pixel measurements (e.g. 10 50 specifies an origin 10px to the left and 50px from the top of the element).

In general you should keep the starting and ending positions the same, and adjust only the radius. However in certain situations you may want to adjust all these values. Fortunately there's a very nice tool you can use to help you visualize and create different gradients: www.westciv.com/tools/radialgradients/.

Newer Gradient Syntax

Newer versions of WebKit support the W3C's recommended syntax for gradients. This is basically a simplified version of the original WebKit system, with the main difference being that there are two separate declarations for linear and radial gradients: -webkit-linear-gradient and -webkit-radial-gradient.

This syntax does away with the from() and to() declarations, allowing you to define any number of stops that will render in the order they are declared:

```
background-image: -webkit-linear-gradient(
    #007231,
    #00893B 30%,
    #004B23
);
```

Here a linear gradient is defined with the newer syntax. This gradient starts with #007231, then has a color stop for #00893B at 30%, and ends with #004B23.

To adjust the angle of the gradient, simply pass a degree value in as the first argument:

```
background-image: -webkit-linear-gradient(
    45deg,
    #007231,
    #00893B 30%,
    #004B23
);
```

This creates a 45° gradient.

While the newer syntax is simpler, it's still usually a good idea to use the older -webkit-gradient, since this is supported by more versions of WebKit.

Repeating Gradients

By default, basic gradients stretch to the edges of the element, however newer versions of WebKit include another type of gradient: -webkit-repeating-linear-gradient. This uses the same syntax as -webkit-linear-gradient, however color stops are defined with pixels:

```
background-image: -webkit-repeating-linear-gradient(
    blue,
    green 10px,
    white 20px
);
```

This repeating linear gradient with three color stops, shown in Figure 3-12, will render blue-to-green from 0 to 10px, then green-to-white from 10px to 20px, and repeat this pattern across the entire element. Note that there is no need to define a pixel value on the first color stop, since it defaults to 0.

Figure 3-12: This button has a repeating gradient.

You can also create solid stripes by adjusting the color stops appropriately. For instance this will create a red and white striped pattern, as shown in Figure 3-13:

Figure 3-13: This repeating gradient produces a striped background by creating a red-to-red gradient from 0 to 5px and then a white-to-white gradient from 5px to 10px.

```
background-image: -webkit-repeating-linear-gradient(
    red,
    red 5px,
    white 5px,
    white 10px
);
```

In addition to linear gradients, you can create repeating radial gradients using -webkit-repeating-radial-gradient. However, as with the newer gradient syntax, repeating gradients are not widely supported.

39

FONT FACE

The button styling is coming along well, but would improve substantially with a better font. While the list of native fonts available in most browsers is pretty limited, embedding a more unique font is easy using @font-face. First download the font Ballpark (www.fontsquirrel.com/fonts/Ballpark). Then upload the TTF of this font to your web server, and include a declaration for the new font in your stylesheet:

```
@font-face {
    font-family: 'Ballpark';
    src: url('ballpark_weiner-webfont.ttf') format('truetype');
}
```

Now attach this font to the font-stack in the button. This code applies the custom Ballpark font to the button, with an Arial fallback for non-supportive browsers. (See Figure 3-14.)

Figure 3-14: The Ballpark font

```
.button {
    font-family: Ballpark, Arial;
}
```

Font Face Licensing

While @font-face is very useful for embedding custom fonts, it is important to be aware of certain licensing concerns when using this technique. Unlike image implementations, @font-face embeds the font directly in the web page so that users can download the source file.

Unfortunately, most font licenses prohibit this type of use, so even if you have the rights to use a typeface on your computer, it does not necessarily mean you have the right to use it with @font-face. Make sure any typeface you use with @font-face is licensed for embedding within documents (it will usually have a special section that says @font-face compatible).

When to Use Font Face

If performance is your primary concern, @font-face may do more harm than good, depending on how frequently the font is used. If you're rendering only a single button, you'd probably be better off simply using an image. However, if you plan to use a font on a number of different buttons or elsewhere on your site, @font-face becomes much more advantageous performance-wise.

> You should consider whether you even need a custom font at all, or whether it would be alright to use a commonly available face that the user wouldn't have to download.

40

Font Face File Formats

Although modern WebKit browsers like Chrome and Safari support a variety of font file types, this example uses the TrueType (TTF) version because it is the most compatible across browsers. If you are only concerned with modern browsers, you can use the WOFF version, which uses a compressed TrueType font with a smaller file size.

Modern WebKit browsers also support the SVG file format. This format is typically much larger than TTF or WOFF, but it is useful because it is the only format that works on iOS devices such as iPhone and iPad. As you can see, determining the optimal file format to use with @font-face can get quite complicated. Fortunately there's a simple solution that serves the best format to each browser, which you learn about in Chapter 5.

TEXT AND BOX SHADOWS

The button is mostly styled, yet you can add some more depth to the appearance using a couple shadow methods available in CSS3.

Text Shadows

Adding a text-shadow to the button can help the text stand out better against the background and improves legibility, as shown in Figure 3-15:

Figure 3-15: A charcoal gray text-shadow is added to the Contact Us text.

```
.button {
    text-shadow: 2px 2px 2px #333;
}
```

The text-shadow attribute accepts several values—the horizontal offset, the vertical offset, how many pixels to blur the shadow, and the color. For instance, text-shadow: 1px 3px 2px #333 creates a gray shadow that is 1px to the right and 3px down from the text, with 2px of blurring. The text-shadow attribute also accepts multiple values:

```
text-shadow: 2px 2px 2px #333, 1px 3px 5px #AAA;
```

> Multiple sets of text-shadow values are separated with a comma. Note that the first value appears on top of the other shadows.

text-shadow is also often used to create an embossed or inlaid effect. For an embossed effect, try a text-shadow of 1px 1px 1px #333. This creates a solid 1px shadow on the bottom right of your text, causing a raised, embossed appearance. For an inlaid effect, try a text-shadow of -1px -1px 1px #333. This produces a solid 1px shadow on the top left of your text, creating an etched, inlaid look.

Box Shadows

Box shadows are essentially the same as text shadows except they apply to the element, not to the text. The following code creates a drop-shadow for the entire button (see Figure 3-16):

Figure 3-16: This box shadow is offset 1px to the right and 3px down, and has a blur of 8px.

```
.button {
    -webkit-box-shadow: 1px 3px 8px #333;
    box-shadow: 1px 3px 8px #333;
}
```

This snippet defines two box shadows, one with the -webkit extension, and one without. That's because older versions of Chrome and Safari did not fully support box-shadow according to the W3C specifications. Similar to text-shadow, the box-shadow attribute can accept multiple values:

```
-webkit-box-shadow: 1px 3px 8px #333, 3px 5px 10px #AAA;
```

> Multiple box-shadow values are separated with a comma. As with text shadows, the first value appears on top.

The inset keyword changes where the box shadow is rendered. Applying the inset keyword to a box-shadow causes it to render inside the element, producing an inlaid appearance:

```
-webkit-box-shadow: inset 1px 3px 8px #333;
```

Finally, box-shadow supports a spread radius parameter, which can increase or decrease the size of the shadow. Positive values make the shadow larger than the element, and negative values make it smaller:

```
-webkit-box-shadow: 1px 3px 8px 2px #333;
```

The fourth parameter here is the spread radius, which makes the shadow 2px larger than the element (which is then blurred an additional 8px).

There are a number of creative techniques that use box-shadow to render a wide variety of elements. To get some ideas, visit: www.viget.com/inspire/39-ridiculous-things-to-do-with-css3-box-shadows/.

Pulling Text and Box Shadow Values from Adobe Photoshop

When working with Photoshop comps that apply a Drop Shadow layer style, it is relatively easy to calculate the exact values you need for text and box shadows. For instance take a look at the drop shadow shown in Figure 3-17.

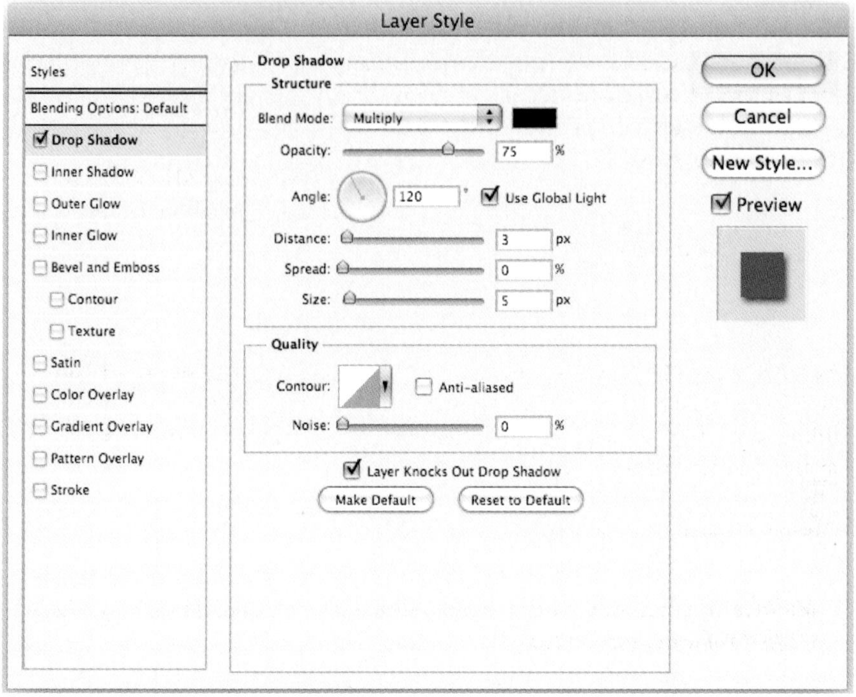

Figure 3-17: A Drop Shadow layer style from Photoshop

The blur value is the easiest to determine because you can take it directly from the Size value—in this example, the blur should be set to 5px. The offsets are a little more complicated. You may want to approximate them, but if pixel-perfect accuracy is a priority, you can generate the exact values using the distance and angle.

In this example, the angle is 120°, which is 30° to the left of 90°. You can use that information to determine the ratio of horizontal to vertical offset needed for your text or box shadow. Simply divide the angle by 90°, making 30° equivalent to 1/3 horizontal and 2/3 vertical. Multiply these ratios by the 3px in the distance value, to get an offset of 1px 2px, thus making your CSS:

```
text-shadow: 1px 2px 5px #333;
```

Because 120° falls in the second quadrant of a graph, both of these offset values are positive. However, as shown in Figure 3-18, this is different in each quadrant.

If the drop shadow includes a spread percentage, you can add it with the spread radius parameter. You will have to approximate the spread from Photoshop because the values do not line up well. Finally, the color can be pulled directly from the color value of the shadow. This color is also influenced by the Opacity value, but to incorporate opacity you'll need to use RGBa transparency.

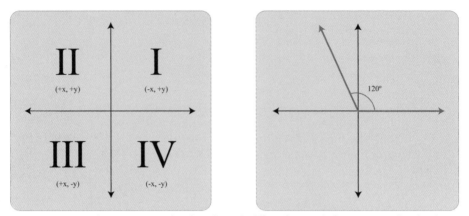

Figure 3-18: A 120° angle uses positive x and y values. This is a bit different from standard geometry — in Photoshop the angle refers to the light source, but in CSS you are positioning the shadow.

RGBa TRANSPARENCY

While the `text-shadow` looks decent, you may notice that the charcoal gray is washing out the green to a certain extent. To get around this, you could apply a black shadow (which would look too harsh) or a green shadow (which would look too green). The optimal solution is to apply a semitransparent black shadow, which will darken the background more subtly.

Fortunately, CSS3 introduces RGBa colors, which provide control over the transparency of colors. RGBa allows you to define opacity values directly on colors, and may be used with any attributes that accept a color value.

Although CSS has supported `opacity` for some time, RGBa provides more precise control over transparency. While the `opacity` attribute is applied to the entire element (and any of its descendants), RGBa transparency is applied only to a specific color attribute, as shown in Figure 3-19.

Figure 3-19: The top element has been styled with RGBa and the bottom with opacity.

Applying an RGBa color to your `text-shadow` is simple:

```
.button {
    text-shadow: 2px 2px 2px rgba(0, 0, 0, .5);
}
```

This snippet uses the same `text-shadow` as the previous example, except with an RGBa color value. The first three values in RGBa are the red, green, and blue values (from 0 to 255), and the final value (alpha) is a decimal representing how opaque you want your color. This example uses black (`0, 0, 0`) that is 50% opaque (`.5`).

It's also a good idea to apply an RGBa value for your box-shadow, in case you want to render the button over background colors:

```
.button {
    -webkit-box-shadow: 1px 3px 8px rgba(0, 0, 0, .6);
    box-shadow: 1px 3px 8px rgba(0, 0, 0, .6);
}
```

Now both the text and box shadows use subtler RGBa colors, and the button styling is complete, as you can see in Figure 3-20.

Figure 3-20: After adding RGBa transparency to the button shadows, the styling is complete.

> *In addition to RGBa, WebKit also supports HSLa (hue, saturation, lightness and alpha), which can be helpful if you are converting Photoshop comps that specify colors in this manner.*

CSS3 ANIMATIONS

Animations are one of the most powerful new tools available in CSS3. They provide an intuitive interface for adding animation to your website using pure CSS, thus reducing the need to rely on JavaScript or JavaScript libraries such as jQuery.

Using the CSS3 animation attributes transition and keyframe, you can easily animate a variety of CSS attributes—including any property that involves dimensions or color (that is anything that can be declared with a pixel or hex value). CSS3 animations are quite versatile, and provide options not only for controlling the duration of animations, but also for refining the motion through easing functions (which make animations appear more natural). Additionally, CSS3 animations are typically faster and smaller than JavaScript alternatives, and many attributes are hardware accelerated (which you learn more about in Chapter 12).

USING TRANSITIONS

The simplest CSS animation attribute is transition. Applying a CSS transition to an element establishes an animation that is triggered whenever a specified state change occurs. For instance, here's a button that changes color on :hover:

```
.button {
    background-color: #46aec9;
}

.button:hover {
    background-color: #1d6d82;
}
```

45

Without transition, the color changes immediately whenever the user places his or her mouse over the button. Adding transition will make the change smoother. This snippet uses the -webkit browser extension as well as the extension-less attribute for future-proofing:

```
.button {
    -webkit-transition: background-color 1s ease;
    transition: background-color 1s ease;
}
```

The basic `transition` attribute accepts three properties: the attribute to animate, the duration of the animation, and a timing function. So in this example, the `background-color` changes smoothly over one second using a natural easing function.

Transitions for Multiple Attributes

CSS3 transitions can also be used with multiple attributes:

```
-webkit-transition: background-color 1s ease, width .5s ease;
```

Multiple attributes are separated with a comma. Alternatively, to apply the same transition to all the attributes of the element, either leave the attribute declaration off, or use the `all` keyword. This transition will be applied to all attributes:

```
-webkit-transition: all 1s ease;
```

Although the shorthand attribute is generally easier to use, you can also define these components individually. This is useful if you want to define multiple values for certain properties:

```
-webkit-transition-property: background-color, width;
-webkit-transition-duration: 1s, .5s;
-webkit-transition-timing-function: ease;
```

In this example, the `background-color` transitions over `1s` and the `width` transitions over `.5s`; and both use the `ease` timing function.

Transition Delay

In addition to the duration of the animation, CSS3 transitions also have a property that can be set to delay the onset of the animation. You can either set this with `-webkit-transition-delay`, or include it in your shorthand declaration. This transition incorporates a two-second delay:

```
-webkit-transition: background-color 1s ease 2s;
```

This causes the animation to wait two seconds before firing. Be careful when using delays in the shorthand syntax: the duration value always comes before the delay.

Transition Timing Functions

Without timing functions, CSS3 transition animations occur linearly, meaning that for each millisecond of the transition, an equal amount of change occurs. While this looks smoother than an immediate change, it does not provide the most natural motion and that's where timing functions come in.

There are a variety of timing functions available. You've already used ease, which starts the animation off smoothly and ends with a slow finish. Other options include ease-in, which eases into the animation and then proceeds linearly, and its inverse, ease-out. You can also use ease-in-out, which eases both into and out of the animation (similar to ease, except more linear in the middle).

Additionally, you can define your own timing function. This particular function is equivalent to ease:

```
-webkit-transition-timing-function: cubic-bezier(0.25, 0.1,
    0.25, 1.0);
```

To establish custom timing functions, you must set the points of a Bezier curve, as shown in Figure 3-21.

Fortunately you can build your own timing functions without any geometry knowledge at all. There's an excellent tool (http://cssglue.com/cubic), shown in Figure 3-22, that allows you to create your own Bezier curves. This tool provides an intuitive interface that allows you to adjust and test your own timing functions.

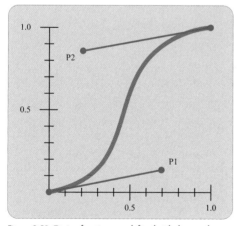

Figure 3-21: Timing functions are defined with the x and y coordinates of two points on the Bezier curve: cubic-bezier (P1(x), P1(y), P2(x), P2(x)).

47

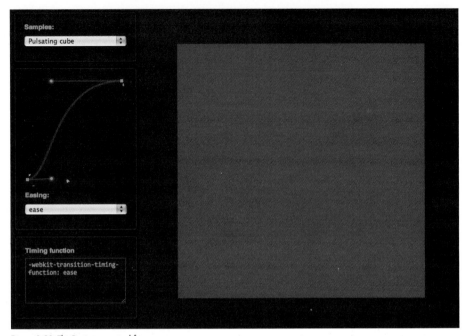

Figure 3-22: The Bezier curve tool from `http://cssglue.com/cubic`

Figure credit: Mark McKay

Properties That Can Use a Transition

While transitions can be used with a variety of CSS properties, they cannot be used everywhere. Basically, a CSS3 transition can be applied to any property that is defined with either a numeric or color value. You can use a transition with properties such as `width`, `height`, `margin`, `padding`, `color`, `background-color`, `border-width`, `border-color`, and `border-radius`, but don't expect to animate a dotted border into a solid one, or ease into underlined text.

Transition has its limits, but it can also be applied to a number of less obvious attributes such as `opacity`, `font-size`, `letter-spacing`, and `z-index`. Additionally, there are certain places you might expect to able to use transitions, but cannot. For instance, even though the W3C specifications allow for transitions of CSS gradients, this is not implemented in WebKit at the time of this writing.

Ways to Trigger Transitions

CSS3 transitions trigger animation whenever an property is changed. Frequently, this occurs on mouseover using the `:hover` pseudo-class, but there are a couple of other techniques. You can trigger a transition on mousedown using the `:active` pseudo-class, although that will stop animating if the user stops holding the click.

Another useful pseudo-class for transitions is :focus. This can be applied to trigger a change in a form element while that element is receiving input—when the cursor is in a text input, for instance. Likewise you can use the :checked pseudo-class for check boxes and radio buttons to trigger transitions when activated.

Combining Transitions with JavaScript

In addition to pseudo-classes, you can also trigger a CSS3 transition using JavaScript. For example, if you apply a class that changes a CSS attribute on an element that has a transition, the change will animate smoothly. This is because the transition applies to any CSS attribute that changes, so it doesn't matter whether the change occurs via CSS or JavaScript.

You may be wondering why you would use CSS transitions if you are already using JavaScript. After all, couldn't JavaScript supply the animation as well? There are a variety of reasons why it makes sense to combine the two. First, CSS3 transitions are very intuitive and often easier to apply than JavaScript alternatives. CSS transitions are also well-optimized and better from a performance perspective.

Finally if you use JavaScript with transitions, you can even apply an event listener to track when the transition function completes. In WebKit, this listener is webkitTransitionEnd, and it is applied the same way as any other event listener. For instance JavaScript can be used to track when a transition animation completes:

```
function myTransitionEndFunction() {
    alert('Transition complete!');
}

var el = document.getElementById('myElement');

el.addEventListener('webkitTransitionEnd', myTransitionEndFunction);
```

This script attaches a listener to an element that executes myTransitionEndFunction() when the transition completes. However, this fires once for every transition that occurs, so it can cause problems if you're animating a number of properties on a single element such as using the all keyword. Additionally, this event fires whenever the animation stops, even if it doesn't reach its end (if the user stops hovering before the animation completes, for example).

USING KEYFRAMES

Transition is excellent for creating smoother attribute changes, but keyframes allow you to build more complex animations and also to trigger those animations without relying on pseudo-classes or JavaScript. Keyframes are essentially visual stopping points, between which fluid animations occur. For instance if you have keyframes for three colors: red, yellow and blue, the animation would first animate a color transition between red and yellow, followed by a transition between yellow and blue. Although the syntax is more complicated than basic transitions, the added level of control provided by keyframes is well worth it.

With keyframes, you first define an animation:

```
@-webkit-keyframes my-animation {
    from {
        opacity: 0;
    }
    to {
        opacity: 1;
    }
}
```

The most basic keyframe animation involves a `from` and `to` declaration, which you can use to define any CSS properties you want to animate between.

Keyframe animations can be used on all the same attributes as transition.

Next, apply this animation to any element. With this snippet, the animation named earlier can now be attached to elements using CSS.

```
.button {
    -webkit-animation: my-animation 2s infinite;
}
```

The basic `-webkit-animation` attribute accepts three parameters, first the name of the animation function you defined using `@-webkit-keyframes`, next the duration of the animation, and finally the number of times to repeat the animation (which can either be an integer, or the keyword `infinite`).

Creating More Complex Animations

A simple animation is built with two keyframes: a start and a finish. But it is also possible to define more complex animations with any number of stops. The following animation uses three keyframes: a beginning, middle and an end. It uses percentage values instead of the `from` and `to` keywords (which are just shorthand for `0%` and `100%` respectively):

```
@-webkit-keyframes my-animation {
    0% {
        opacity: 0;
    }
    50% {
        opacity: 1;
    }
    100% {
        opacity: 0;
    }
}
```

This animation starts with an `opacity` of `0`, animates to `1`, and then back to `0`. Because two of these values are the same, you can shorten the syntax by combining them. The `0%` and `100%` keyframes use the same CSS so they can be combined with a comma:

```
@-webkit-keyframes my-animation {
    0%, 100% {
        opacity: 0;
    }
    50% {
        opacity: 1;
    }
}
```

Additional Keyframe Options

Keyframe animations are very versatile and provide a number of additional parameters you can customize. You can use any of the timing functions, such as `ease`, `ease-in` or your own custom `cubic-bezier` function. To apply a timing function, either use the individual `-webkit-animation-timing-function` or simply add it to the shorthand. This animation uses the `ease` timing function for more natural motion. The timing function is applied between all the keyframes of your animation:

```
-webkit-animation: my-animation 2s infinite ease;
```

You can set up a delay using `-webkit-animation-delay`:

```
-webkit-animation-delay: 5s;
```

This will delay the first instance of the animation by five seconds. There's no delay on any subsequent iterations of the animation. You can also define the delay with the `-webkit-animation` shorthand, just make sure it falls after the duration. In a shorthand animation declaration with a delay, the delay always falls after the duration, so this animation has a duration of `2s` and a delay of `5s`:

```
-webkit-animation: my-animation 2s 5s infinite;
```

Finally, you can set the animation to alternate directions. Rather than having each iteration start from the beginning, `-webkit-animation-direction` causes the animation to alternate, running forward and then backward:

```
-webkit-animation-direction: alternate;
```

This causes the animation to alternate directions with each iteration. It can also be added to the `-webkit-animation` shorthand.

Using Multiple Animations

Although it is possible to animate multiple attributes with a single keyframe animation, often you may want to apply a number of different animations to the same element. This comes in handy when animating different attributes over different durations, or reusing an animation you defined elsewhere. To define multiple animations, simply separate them with a comma:

```
-webkit-animation: first-animation 2s infinite,
    second-animation 5s infinite;
```

CSS3 TRANSFORMS

CSS3 introduced a number of exciting visual effects that can be accomplished using the transform attribute. A wide variety of effects can be generated using that single attribute: rotation, translation, scaling and skewing are just some of the options.

These effects are very useful because they can change the appearance of an element without altering the layout. For instance, you can translate an element 100px to the right, without affecting the positioning of neighboring elements. Additionally, you can combine any of these effects with CSS3 animations to create remarkable visual animations that rival those found in other graphics solutions such as Flash.

2D TRANSFORMS

The most basic and widely supported CSS3 transforms are the original set of two-dimensional transforms.

Translate

The most basic CSS transform is translate():

```
-webkit-transform: translate(50px, 100px);
```

This snippet moves the element 50px to the right and 100px down. Notice that transform still uses the -webkit extension.

CSS translations accept two parameters: the x and y values to move the element. If you leave off the y value, the renderer assumes it's zero.

While there are a number of ways to adjust the position of an element, translate() is very useful because it does not affect the layout of the page. That means you can freely adjust the visual position of an element without having to worry about the layout of other elements.

You can also specify translations using percentage values, which will be calculated based on the size of the element. For instance if you apply translate(50%, 50%) to an element that is 100px wide and 50px tall, then it moves 50px to the right and 25px down.

Rotate

Probably the most common use of CSS transforms is to rotate elements. This snippet rotates the element 30 degrees (see Figure 3-23):

```
-webkit-transform: rotate(30deg);
```

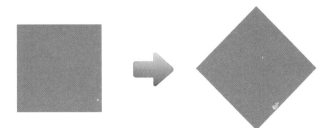

Figure 3-23: Example of an element rotated using a CSS transform

To rotate the element in the other direction, specify a negative degree value:

```
-webkit-transform: rotate(-30deg);
```

You may wonder why negative degree values are important, after all an element that is rotated -30deg looks the same as one rotated 330deg. While these two degree values appear the same statically, they behave differently when using animation. For instance, if you apply rotate(-30deg) along with a CSS3 transition, the animation will rotate 30° counterclockwise. If you use rotate(330deg), the animation will rotate 330° in the opposite direction. Although the two animations arrive at the same point, their motion is quite different.

Additionally, when using rotational transforms and animation, you can make an element spin around as many times as you want. For instance you could set rotate(720deg) to make an element spin around twice and arrive in its original position.

While rotational transforms look very smooth for elements rendered with pure CSS, you may see some pixelization issues, as shown in Figure 3-24, if you try to rotate an image. This is due to processing issues with image rasterization.

Figure 3-24: Notice the pixelization that occurs in the rotated image.

While it is difficult to avoid the pixelization issue, you can minimize its effects if you can limit the angle of the rotation. Certain angles look better than others; for instance a 90° rotation looks practically perfect, as you can see in Figure 3-25.

Figure 3-25: 90° rotations do not have pixelization issues.

While you may not want a 90° rotation, you can still limit pixelization by sticking to a number that divides evenly into 90. For instance a 45° rotation (90°/2) still looks pretty decent, and so does a 30° rotation (90°/3). However the 45° rotation looks better than the 30° rotation — in fact the larger the divisor gets, the worse the rotation looks, as shown in Figure 3-26.

0°   90°   45°   30°   20°

Figure 3-26: Notice that the 45° rotation looks better than the 30°, however both look better than the 20°.

The reason these particular rotations render better than others has to do with how browsers rasterize pixels, which are calculated based on neighboring pixels. If you stick to evenly divided numbers, the rasterization equation is much simpler.

To avoid the pixelization issue altogether, you can use an SVG image. SVG is a vectored image format that handles any type of transformation very well. You learn more about SVGs in Chapter 9.

Scale

Scale is another useful transform effect that you can use to change the size of an element. Simply pass an integer to multiply the element's size. This snippet doubles the size of the element:

```
-webkit-transform: scale(2);
```

Additionally, you can scale the x and y values differently. This triples the width of the element and doubles the height:

```
-webkit-transform: scale(3, 2);
```

You can even flip an element by passing a negative value. This flips the element horizontally, while keeping its height intact:

```
-webkit-transform: scale(-1, 1);
```

Passing negative values into `scale()` is particularly useful because it is one of the few ways to flip elements using CSS.

Skew

Skew is another useful transform property that you can use to make elements appear to lean in a certain direction. Skewing (see Figure 3-27) is similar to rotating, except the ends stretch rather than twist.

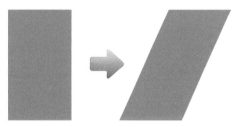

Figure 3-27: Skewing stretches an element at an angle.

The skew property accepts a degree value. For example, this skews the element -45° horizontally:

```
-webkit-transform: skewX(-45deg);
```

You can also skew an element vertically using `skewY()`:

```
-webkit-transform: skewY(30deg);
```

To skew both values at the same time, simply pass them into `skew()` separated by a comma. This skews the element -45° horizontally and 30° vertically:

```
-webkit-transform: skew(-45deg, 30deg);
```

Matrix

If you want more precise control over CSS transforms, you can use matrices. While very difficult to calculate, matrices provide a level of control that is unparalleled in the other transform properties.

You might want to avoid the mathematical headaches associated with building your own transform matrices. But if you'd like more information, visit `www.useragentman.com/blog/2011/01/07/css3-matrix-transform-for-the-mathematically-challenged/`.

Setting the Transform Origin

By default, CSS transforms are centered around the middle of the element, but this can be modified using `-webkit-transform-origin`. This attribute accepts the same syntax as `background-position` and, as shown in Figure 3-28, sets the origin of the transformation to center around the bottom right corner of the element:

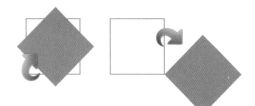

```
-webkit-transform-origin: bottom right;
```

You can also set the `-webkit-transform-origin` using pixels or percentage values.

Figure 3-28: The element on the left is rotated around the center (default), and the object on the right is rotated around the bottom right corner.

3D TRANSFORMS

In addition to the flat two-dimensional transforms mentioned earlier, WebKit also introduced an array of three-dimensional transforms that can add some nice visual flare to your projects. These transforms not only adjust the x and y values of elements, but also the z value, creating a depth effect and the illusion of perspective. Just like 2D transforms, these 3D transforms combine easily with CSS animations to build stunning visual effects.

Setting Up Perspective

Before you use 3D transforms, you must first set up the perspective by attaching `-webkit-perspective` to an ancestor of the element you want to transform. This defines the amount of perspective to use. It can be attached to the document body, or any ancestor of the element you want to transform:

```
body {
    -webkit-perspective: 500;
    perspective: 500;
}
```

Adjusting the `-webkit-perspective` value alters the level of depth used by 3D transforms. Lower values produce a more pronounced effect, and higher values produce a more subtle effect. In general, you want to use a value somewhere between `500` and `1000`. Also, pay attention to where you attach `-webkit-perspective` because the dimensions of this element will determine the center point of your transforms. For instance, if it's in the document body, the perspective will be calculated based on the overall window size.

3D Rotate

Now that you've established the perspective, you can start applying 3D transforms, such as 3D rotations. To rotate around the x-axis, use `rotateX()`. This snippet rotates the element 60° around the x-axis, as shown in Figure 3-29:

Figure 3-29: Because the rotation occurs around the horizontal axis, the element will appear to flip vertically.

```
-webkit-transform: rotateX(60deg);
```

Rotate around the y-axis using `rotateY()`. This will rotate the element 60 degrees around the y-axis, as shown in Figure 3-30:

```
-webkit-transform: rotateY(60deg);
```

To define a rotation that occurs over a number of axes, use `rotate3d()`:

```
-webkit-transform: rotate3d(0,1,1,60deg);
```

`rotate3d()` accepts an x, y and z value, which it uses to calculate the plane used for the rotation. So in this example, a 60° rotation occurs around a diagonal plane in between the y and z axes. (See Figure 3-31.)

Figure 3-30: Elements seem to flip horizontally when rotation occurs around the vertical axis.

3D rotations are particularly nice when combined with CSS3 animation. For instance, you can use `rotateY(180deg)` with a CSS transition to make an element appear to flip over.

3D Translate

You can use `translateZ()` for 3D transforms with translation:

```
-webkit-transform: translateZ(100px);
```

`translateZ()` moves the element closer and further away from the user. Unlike `translateX()` and `translateY()`, it cannot accept a percentage value. Although `translateZ()` by itself doesn't look much different from a basic two-dimensional `scale()`, it can be useful when combined with other 3D transforms. You can also define 3D translations using `translate3d()`, which accepts x, y, and z parameters.

3D Scale

Figure 3-31: This element has been rotated around a diagonal plane.

You can scale objects along the z-plane using 3D scale transforms:

```
-webkit-transform: scaleZ(2);
```

57

Again, `scaleZ()` is not overly useful by itself. It becomes more important when combined with other 3D transforms. Similarly, you can define 3D scaling using `scale3d()`, which accepts x, y, and z parameters.

3D Matrix

You can also define three-dimensional matrices using `matrix3d()`. This provides a level of control not available in the other 3D transforms. However, 3D matrices are harder to calculate than their 2D counterparts because you have to define 16 matrix values instead of six. Thus it is probably best to stick to the basic 3D transforms, unless you are passionate about matrix geometry.

Setting the Origin for 3D Transforms

To adjust the transform origin in three dimensions simply use the `-webkit-transform-origin` attribute, this time defining three values:

```
-webkit-tansform-origin: 50% 50% 0;
```

The `-webkit-transform-origin` can accept up to three values (x, y, and z). Here the transform will be centered horizontally and vertically, but occur at the front of the z axis (closer to the user). The origin for 3D transforms is calculated based on the ancestor with `-webkit-perspective`.

Backface Visibility

Finally, 3D transforms introduce a new attribute, `-webkit-backface-visibility`, which controls whether the back of an element is visible after it rotates. By default, a flipped element shows a reversed version of itself, but you can also hide this backface. This hides the element's backface, so it disappears if flipped over:

```
-webkit-backface-visibility: hidden;
```

OTHER CSS3 PROPERTIES

There are a variety of other miscellaneous properties introduced in CSS3, and new experimental attributes are still being released.

BORDER IMAGES

One useful new feature is `border-image`, which enables you to decorate the borders of elements with images. Although the usage of `border-image` is a bit complicated, the stylistic advantage of custom borders is well worth the effort.

The first step is creating an image to use for the borders. Rather than use a separate image for each corner and edge, `border-image` allows you to define a single composite image that will be cut up to define all the necessary borders, as shown in Figure 3-32:

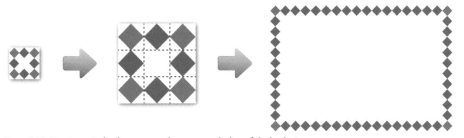

Figure 3-32: Your image is sliced to generate the corners and edges of the border image.

Next set a `border-width` and define a `-webkit-border-image`, setting the points at which to cut up your image (also known as a "9-slice"):

```
.border-image {
    -webkit-border-image: url('my-border-image.png') 3 round;
    border-width: 3px;
}
```

This creates a border image, defining the source image and how to slice it. Make sure you include a `border-width`, or the border won't be visible.

`-webkit-border-image` accepts a couple parameters, starting with the path to your composite border image. Next it takes specifications for how to slice the image. Here it is set to 3, which indicates that it should cut in 3px from each edge. You can also define this value with percentages, or define each slice separately. The final parameter indicates whether to `stretch`, `round`, or `repeat` the image along the edges. `stretch` scales the image along the edges, and `repeat` tiles it. `round` is a combination of the two: it tiles the image, but also stretches it a bit so that it fits an even number of times (with no partial tiles). Currently, WebKit treats `round` the same as `repeat`, but you can still use `round` for future-proofing.

MASKS

Another extremely useful CSS3 attribute introduced by WebKit is `-webkit-mask`. Masks allow you to control the transparency of images and elements like never before. To define a mask, first create a

Figure 3-33: The transparency in this PNG will be applied to the element.

transparent PNG image, as shown in Figure 3-33. Then `-webkit-mask` causes the element to take on the PNG's transparency:

```
-webkit-mask: url(path-to/mask.png);
```

By default, `-webkit-mask` repeats the masking image across the element, but you can control the repeating, as well as the position of the mask using the same syntax as `background-repeat` and `background-position`:

```
-webkit-mask: url(path-to/mask.png) repeat-x left bottom;
```

When adjusting the mask's repeat and position, anything outside of the repeated area will be left transparent. You can stretch the mask to the edges of the element with the `-webkit-mask-box-image` property:

```
-webkit-mask-box-image: url(path-to/mask.png);
```

One clever use of `-webkit-mask` is to combine it with a CSS gradient. Because CSS gradients are treated as background images, it makes sense that they can be used with `-webkit-mask`.

The trick is to apply the gradient using RGBa colors to give the image some transparency. This gradient will be applied to the element as a mask:

```
-webkit-mask: -webkit-gradient(
    linear,
    left top,
    left bottom,
    from(rgba(0,0,0,1)),
    to(rgba(0,0,0,0))
);
```

Because gradients stretch to the edges of the element, there is no need to use this with `-webkit-box-image`. There are a variety of gradients you can use to create image masks. Besides straight linear gradients, you can experiment with angled and even radial gradients (see Figure 3-34).

Figure 3-34: Both linear and radial gradients can be used with `-webkit-mask`.

TEXT STROKES

Text strokes are another interesting new CSS3 attribute introduced by WebKit. Previously, borders could be applied around only a square or rounded rectangle element. Now `-webkit-text-stroke` allows you to add a decorative border to the text itself. This snippet adds the 2px wide stroke around text as shown in Figure 3-35:

Smashing WebKit

Figure 3-35: Text strokes are a visually pleasing way to add some extra text styling without relying on images

```
-webkit-text-stroke: 2px orange;
```

Also, to make fonts appear smoother, simply apply a 1px transparent stroke around the text, as shown in Figure 3-36:

```
-webkit-text-stroke: 1px transparent;
```

BOX REFLECT

`-webkit-box-reflect` is another interesting CSS3 attribute. It's used to create a reflection of an element. Although not extremely versatile, it can provide a nice visual effect in the right situation as Figure 3-37 shows.

To use `-webkit-box-reflect`, simply pass the direction for the reflection: `below`, `above`, `left`, or `right`. This creates a reflection beneath the element:

```
-webkit-box-reflect: below;
```

`-webkit-box-reflect` also accepts an offset parameter, which creates a space between the element and the reflection:

```
-webkit-box-reflect: below 10px;
```

Finally, you can apply a mask to the reflection to control its transparency:

```
-webkit-box-reflect: below 10px url(path-
   to/mask.png);
```

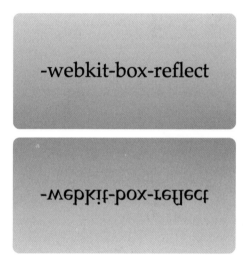

Figure 3-36: The bottom word has a transparent text-stroke. Notice that the font appears smoother.

Figure 3-37: A reflection created with `-webkit-box-reflect`

WEBKIT MARQUEE

In the '90s, a lot of websites made use of the <marquee> tag to show scrolling content. While marquees are typically associated with antiquated design patterns, there are certain situations where they can be used tastefully to create a better user experience. However, the <marquee> tag has a slew of performance problems and has even been deprecated in HTML5.

Luckily, WebKit provides a solution in the form of the versatile `-webkit-marquee` CSS property. To utilize marquee styling, you need to define a few attributes. First, define `white-space: nowrap` so the text stays on one line. Next add `overflow: -webkit-marquee`, and finally make sure to apply a `width` to the element so it is smaller than the text it contains. Here's a basic scrolling marquee:

```
.marquee {
    white-space: nowrap;
    overflow: -webkit-marquee;
    width: 100px;
}
```

Advanced Options For WebKit Marquee

The default `-webkit-marquee` creates a marquee that scrolls from right to left, but you can reverse the direction by setting `-webkit-marque-direction`:

```
-webkit-marquee-direction: forwards;
```

`-webkit-marquee-direction` can also be used to set up vertical marquees. Simply set it to `up` or `down` (and make sure to define a `height` and remove the `white-space: nowrap`). You can also set the marquee to reverse direction whenever it reaches an end instead of scrolling through the text in the same direction each time:

```
-webkit-marquee-style: alternate;
```

This causes the marquee to scroll back and forth instead of looping.

Additionally, you can set the speed of the animation:

```
-webkit-marquee-speed: 50;
```

To control the speed of the animation, you can also use the keywords `slow`, `normal`, and `fast`. Finally, you can control the number of times that the marquee animation repeats:

```
-webkit-marquee-repetition: 5;
```

This causes the marquee to stop after 5 iterations. By default it is set to `infinite`.

BACKGROUND CLIP

You saw `background-clip` used earlier to limit the amount of background bleed shown behind rounded corners. But this attribute is useful for a variety of other purposes as well.

`background-clip` adjusts where the background of an element is displayed. By default, it is set to `border-box`, which means that the background is rendered all the way to the edges of the border. But that can cause problems, as shown in Figure 3-38, if you are using a border with a transparent RGBa color.

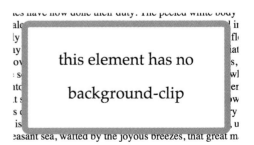

Figure 3-38: Even though the border is semitransparent, it renders as opaque due to the element's background color.

Fortunately, `background-clip` can be used to solve this problem:

```
-webkit-background-clip: padding;
background-clip: padding-box;
```

> Notice the difference in syntax between the older `-webkit-background-clip` and the current `background-clip`.

Setting the `background-clip` to `padding-box` causes the background to stop rendering at the padding instead of the border (see Figure 3-39).

You can also set `background-clip` to stop rendering the background at the edge of the content area:

```
-webkit-background-clip: content;
background-clip: content-box;
```

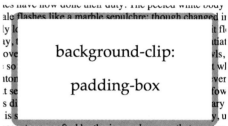

Figure 3-39: With `background-clip` set to `padding-box`, the RGBa color in the border renders correctly.

This code prevents the background from rendering in any areas with padding. Again, notice the difference syntax in the `-webkit-background-clip`.

Besides `padding-box` and `content-box`, `background-clip` can also be set to `text` to clip the background around the text of the element. This can be used to create a variety of text effects, such as text gradients.

To accomplish this effect, set the `background-clip` to `text`, set the `-webkit-text-fill-color` to `transparent`, and then attach a gradient background:

```
.gradient-text {
    -webkit-background-clip: text;
    background-clip: text;
    -webkit-text-fill-color: transparent;
    background-image: -webkit-gradient(
        linear,
        left top,
        left bottom,
        from(#F7941D),
        to(#ED1C24)
    );
}
```

When setting `background-clip: text` and `-webkit-text-fill-color: transparent`, the gradient background fills only the text of this element.

DATA URIS

Although not explicitly a part of CSS3, you can use data URIs in CSS to build faster websites.

Data URIs allow you to embed images directly in your web pages and stylesheets. While the user still has to download the image in the form of raw data, it speeds up your site because it avoids an extra HTTP request for the image file. This not only saves time on the user's end, but it also saves your web server the added processing time of the file lookup.

Using data URIs is simple. First, encode the image as raw data—for this you can use the base64 generator at this URL: www.motobit.com/util/base64-decoder-encoder.asp.

Once you have the raw data, embed it directly in your stylesheet using this syntax:

```
background-image: url("data:image/png;base64,iVBORw0KGgoAAAA...
    UhEUgAAABgAAAAYCAMAAADXqc3KAAADU5ErkJggg==");
```

> *The raw file data is embedded directly in the stylesheet. Make sure to change the* image/png *to the correct file format, and to avoid any line breaks or spaces in the raw data.*

Data URIs can be used anywhere you use a url(), so they can also be used with @font-face declarations. However this is generally not advisable if you are using multiple font formats to support various browsers.

SUMMARY

The wide variety of new properties introduced in CSS3 creates new opportunities to render visually stunning websites without the use of images. Avoiding images has three main benefits: faster load times, easier development and improved maintainability.

Besides basic styling, CSS3 introduces a number of other features that can be used to create more dynamic websites. CSS3 transition and keyframes provide animation capabilities that were previously confined to JavaScript. These native animation solutions not only are easy to use but also reduce the need for bandwidth-heavy JavaScript files.

Furthermore, 2D and 3D transforms allow you to manipulate elements like never before, and can be combined with CSS animation to create striking effects using basic DOM elements.

Best of all, as you learn in Chapter 5, most of the CSS3 properties discussed here can be supported across a wide spread of the browser market, including native implementations in modern browsers, and rock-solid fallbacks for older versions.

4 IMPROVED SELECTION WITH CSS3

IN ADDITION TO a wide variety of advanced styling options, CSS3 also provides a number of opportunities to better select elements on the page. These advanced selection methods not only make CSS3 development easier, but also allow you to reduce the amount of markup required for proper styling. By targeting elements with more robust selection techniques, you can avoid attaching a number of structural classes that were previously necessary in your markup, and thereby reduce the file size of the HTML that you serve to your users.

In this chapter you learn techniques to better select elements in CSS using selectors that target the element's HTML attributes as well as position in the DOM. You also learn how to select

elements based on other traits, such as whether it is the first of its type, or the third child of its parent element. Furthermore, you learn how to use more advanced selectors, such as whether an element is *not* selected by a given selector, and even how to use selectors to inject content into the page.

Finally, you learn how to use media queries to adjust styling based on the dimensions of the user's screen or even the orientation of mobile devices. These media queries allow you to not only create web pages that respond to the dimensions of the browser window, but also to target specific device specifications with special styling.

CSS3 SELECTORS AND PSEUDO-CLASSES

CSS3 adds a number of more advanced selectors and pseudo-classes that allow for more intuitive element selection. These techniques enable you to better target CSS to elements based on their attributes and position in the DOM, as well as change style rules for different UI states and even the language of the user.

ATTRIBUTE SELECTORS

CSS attribute selectors provide you the capability to select elements using more intuitive rules than those based simply on DOM structure and node type. These selectors can be used to target elements with specific HTML attributes, and have been available since CSS2. Additionally, CSS3 adds a variety of powerful options to attribute selectors, making selecting HTML attributes easier than ever.

Basic Attribute Selectors (CSS2)

First introduced in CSS2, attribute selectors are very effective for selecting elements in a variety of situations. For instance, you can use attribute selectors to target any links that have a title attribute:

```
a[title] { ... }
```

This selector targets all links that have a title, regardless of what that title may be (and will work even if the title is empty). But attribute selectors can also target specific values; for instance, here's how you style all the links that point to a specific URL:

```
a[href="http://jonraasch.com/"] { ... }
```

Attribute selectors can also be useful for styling form elements. For example you can select different types of input elements:

```
input[type="text"] { ... }
input[type="checkbox"] { ... }
input[type="radio"] { ... }
input[type="submit"] { ... }
```

Advanced Attribute Selectors (CSS3)

CSS3 introduced a variety of more robust options to attribute selectors that enable you to find not only specific attribute values, but substrings of those values as well.

For instance, you can use substring targeting to take the URL selection example used earlier one step further and select all the links in a given domain rather than just the links to a specific URL:

```
a[href^="http://jonraasch.com/"] { ... }
```

This finds all links that *start* with the URL http://jonraasch.com/ using the operator
^=. You may be familiar with the ^ operator from regular expressions. In fact, more regex
operators are available to attribute selectors. For instance you can use the $ operator to target
attributes that end in a given string.

There are many situations in which regex operators can be useful; for example, say you want
to target all img elements that reference an image that ends in .png:

```
img[src$=".png"] { ... }
```

Here the $ operator selects all the PNG images on the page. In addition to selecting strings
that begin or end with a given value, you can use the * operator in attribute selectors to target
substrings in any position. Here's an example:

```
img[alt*="web"] { ... }
```

This snippet selects any alt text that contains the string web, regardless of where this
substring falls within the text.

The attribute substring selectors can also be useful for setting up wildcards for standard
selectors such as id and class names. While it wouldn't make much sense to use an attribute
selector to select for a specific id, it might work to select all id values that contain a certain
string. For instance here's how you select all form input elements that start with the id
contact-form-:

```
input[id^="contact-form-"] { ... }
```

The selector now chooses all ids that start with this string, thus targeting elements with ids such
as contact-form-name, contact-form-email, contact-form-submit, and so on.

Combining Attribute Selectors

In certain situations it can be useful to combine multiple attribute selectors on a given
element. Fortunately you can use any number of attribute selectors by including each in
separate brackets.

For example, here's how to target all links that point to a given URL *and* open in a new window:

```
a[url="http://jonraasch.com/"][target="_blank"] { ... }
```

STRUCTURAL SELECTORS

One of the more familiar uses of CSS selectors involves targeting elements based on the
structure of the DOM. Selecting descendant elements is a common practice in CSS development. For instance you can target all li elements that descend from a ul using this selector:

```
ul li { ... }
```

While selecting descendant elements is extremely useful, many developers fail to take advantage of the variety of additional structural selectors available in CSS. Take a look at some of these more advanced selectors to improve your element selection abilities in CSS.

Child Selector

Despite being relatively underused, certain structural selectors have been available in CSS for some time. One of them is the child selector, which was made available in CSS 2.1.

The child selector differs from standard descendant selectors because it targets the *direct descendant* of a given element as opposed to *all descendants*. This can be extremely useful when attempting to select elements more specifically.

The previous example found all `li` elements that descend from a `ul`. That's helpful, but it can create problems with multiple nested `li` elements. For instance, take this markup:

```
<ul class="main-list">
    <li>
    <ul class="sub-list">
        <li>Secondary list item</li>
    </ul>
    </li>
</ul>
```

If you use a basic descendant selector, such as `ul.main-list li`, you end up not only targeting the `li` elements that are direct descendants of `main-list`, but also those that descend from `sub-list`.

Here's where the child selector becomes useful:

```
ul.main-list > li { ... }
```

The preceding code targets direct descendants using the > selector, ensuring that the style rules are applied to only those elements that are direct children of the `main-list`.

Besides providing more specific DOM selection, the child selector is faster than standard descendant selectors. This has to do with how browsers evaluate CSS selectors: from right to left. In the list item example, the rendering engine starts on the right of the selector, determining whether a given node is a list item. If you use a standard descendant selector, the CSS engine has to check every ancestor element all the way up to the body and HTML elements. However, because the child selector is used, it has to check only the direct parent element, which is considerably faster.

You learn more about selector performance in Chapter 12.

Adjacent Sibling Selector

Another structural selector that has been available since CSS 2.1 is the adjacent sibling selector. This combinator enables developers to target elements that occur right next to each other in the DOM. Here's an example:

```
<div class="text-block">
    <h2>Title</h2>
    <p>Paragraph 1</p>
    <p>Paragraph 2</p>
</div>
```

You could easily target both paragraphs in this snippet using a standard descendant selector:

```
div.text-block p { ... }
```

However, if you prefer to style only the paragraph that directly follows the h2, you can instead use an adjacent sibling selector:

```
div.text-block h2 + p { ... }
```

This selector styles only the p elements that are directly adjacent to an h2, thereby avoiding the second paragraph. The syntax is a bit tricky, since it is crucial that the p *follow* the h2 in the DOM. That's because this selector targets only the next sibling in the DOM, not the preceding one.

General Sibling Selector

CSS3 completes the DOM structure targeting introduced in CSS 2.1, by adding a third structural selector: the general sibling selector. Unlike the adjacent sibling selector, this combinator targets *all* siblings that follow a given element:

```
div.text-block h2 ~ p { ... }
```

This block of CSS targets all paragraphs that are siblings of an h2, as opposed to just the next sibling. Much like the adjacent sibling selector, this combinator targets only those siblings that fall *after* the h2.

Why You Can't Use Parent Selectors

Considering the usefulness of structural selectors, it migh t seem confusing that a parent selector is not included in the CSS3 spec. After all, there has been a child selector since CSS 2.1, and a parent selector would certainly be useful in many situations.

However, parent selectors have not been adopted by either the W3C or major browsers, since they would create a large performance bottleneck. This performance issue is caused by the way in which CSS engines parse the DOM and apply style rules.

Rather than wait for the entire page to load, browsers begin evaluating styling rules as soon as any elements are available. This improves perceived performance, allowing WebKit to begin rendering the page as soon as possible. To accomplish this, the engine must evaluate and style each element as soon as it is read.

When each new element is added to the DOM, its ancestors have already been evaluated, since they exist before the element in the document. Thus, the CSS engine is able to apply any descendant and child selector rules based on these elements. However, when a new element is added, it is by definition empty. So WebKit is unable to determine what elements it might eventually become a parent of, since it initially has no child nodes.

It is certainly possible that WebKit may in the future allow for parent selectors. But the performance costs are currently too high to make this feasible. For proper parent selectors to be possible, WebKit would have to reevaluate every ancestor node, every time a new element is added to the DOM, which would slow rendering down considerably.

STRUCTURAL PSEUDO-CLASSES

In addition to the structural selectors explored earlier, CSS3 introduces a variety of structural pseudo-classes that can be useful when selecting different parts of the DOM. Pseudo-classes differ from selectors since they further qualify a selector, by targeting a characteristic different from the element's name, attributes or content.

You may already be familiar with pseudo-classes, if you use the :link, :hover, :visited, and :active pseudo-classes to target different states of links. Like other pseudo-classes, these provide further qualification to standard selectors based on their state, rather than enable you to select an element outright.

First- and Last-Child Pseudo-Classes

Two of the most useful methods for targeting the DOM structure are the first-child and last-child pseudo-classes.

Introduced in CSS 2, the first-child pseudo-class selects an element only if it is the first child of its parent element.

Here's an example:

```
<div class="text-block">
    <p>Paragraph 1</p>
    <p>Paragraph 2</p>
    <p>Paragraph 3</p>
</div>
```

Here you can style only the first paragraph using this CSS block:

```
div.text-block p:first-child { ... }
```

Notice how the `:first-child` pseudo-class is attached to the p and not the div. This is because it is a pseudo-class, not a selector, so it is meant to *clarify* a selection rather than select an element itself.

If you want to target *any* `first-child` of your text-block, you could simply use the star selector (which selects any element):

```
div.text-block *:first-child { ... }
```

The child selector isn't used here, so this example finds *any* `first-child` that is contained within `div.text-block`, whether it is a `first-child` of one of its descendants. So if you want to make sure to target *only* the `first-child` of your text-block, you should instead use:

```
div.text-block > *:first-child { ... }
```

Similarly, CSS3 introduced the `last-child` pseudo-class to target the `last-child` of a given element. So to select the `last-child` of your text-block, you should use this selector:

```
div.text-block > *:last-child { ... }
```

Nth-Child Pseudo-Class

In addition to the `last-child` pseudo-class, CSS3 also introduced an even more flexible way to target individual children of an element: the `nth-child` pseudo-class. This class is extremely versatile and allows you to select child nodes in a wide variety of ways.

First you can use the `nth-child` pseudo-class to select the second paragraph in your text-block:

```
div.text-block p:nth-child(2) { ... }
```

Here you can change the value of `nth-child` as needed for different elements.

You can use `nth-child` to select all odd or even children:

```
div.text-block p:nth-child(odd) { ... }
div.text-block p:nth-child(even) { ... }
```

You can even set up your own rules to select different children based on a mathematical expression. For instance, you could target every third child (meaning the third, sixth, ninth, and so on):

```
div.text-block p:nth-child(3n) { ... }
```

Or to select every child after every third child (the fourth, seventh, tenth, and so on), you could use:

```
div.text-block p:nth-child(3n+1) { ... }
```

You can target only the third and higher children:

```
div.text-block p:nth-child(n+3) { ... }
```

Or the third and lower children:

```
div.text-block p:nth-child(-n+3) { ... }
```

While the flexibility of nth-child expressions is very useful, writing these expressions can be a bit confusing. To better understand an nth-child expression, it helps to run through the available options for the n value, starting with 0. So in the last example, (-n+3), the first node it selects is the third (-0 + 3), then the second (-1 + 3), then the first (-2 + 3), and then it stops targeting since there is no "zeroeth" child.

Only-Child Pseudo-Class

Another useful selection technique added in CSS3 is the only-child pseudo-class, which selects elements that are the only descendant of their parent node. For instance you can use this to select only those list items that do not have any siblings:

```
li:only-child { ... }
```

This selector chooses li elements only if they are an only child, and is essentially shorthand for:

```
li:first-child:last-child { ... }
```

Empty Pseudo-Class

Additionally, it is possible to use the empty pseudo-class to select elements that have no child nodes. For instance:

```
p:empty { ... }
```

This CSS block selects all paragraphs that are empty. Bear in mind that this refers to nodes that not only are empty of other HTML elements, but also empty of any text. In fact, even if an element contains only a space, it will not be selected with this pseudo-class because the space still counts as a text node.

Of-Type Pseudo-Classes

Another useful pseudo-class is related to the first-child pseudo-class . This is first-of-type, which selects the first child that fits the specified element type. For instance you can select the first paragraph within a given div:

```
div.text-block > p:first-of-type { ... }
```

This is different from `first-child` because it will select the first paragraph in `div.text-block` even if it is not the first element.

The `first-of-type` selector can be used to pick the first element that fits any criteria, not just the node name. For instance you can select the first paragraph in your `div` with the class name `text-paragraph`:

```
div.text-block > p.text-paragraph:first-of-type { ... }
```

In addition to the `first-of-type` selector, there is also `last-of-type`, `nth-of-type`, and `only-of-type`, all of which work similarly.

OTHER PSEUDO-CLASSES

Besides the structural pseudo-classes, there are a number of additional pseudo-classes that you can use to better control CSS selection and create more dynamic documents.

Negation Pseudo-Class

The `negation` pseudo-class is another powerful tool introduced by CSS3. It targets all elements *except* those that have certain qualities.

For instance, you can select all images, except those that are contained in a link:

```
img:not(a img) { ... }
```

You simply place a normal CSS selector within the `:not()` pseudo-class. This block targets any element except those that match the negated selector. The `negation` pseudo-class is extremely versatile, so you can use any selector you want here, even more complex CSS3 selectors and pseudo-classes.

For instance you can select all images that do not include an `alt` attribute:

```
img:not([alt]) { ... }
```

Here you can combine the `negation` pseudo-class with an attribute selector. You could also select all images that are not a first child:

```
img:not(:first-child) { ... }
```

However, that could also be accomplished by simply using an `nth-child` pseudo-class:

```
img:nth-child(n+1) { ... }
```

> *With the variety of selection techniques available in CSS3, it is important to realize that there are many ways to select the same element, and you should always take care to opt for the simplest method.*

Target Pseudo-Class

The `target` pseudo-class provides a particularly interesting option for CSS styling because it allows developers the capability to style a block when a link is clicked. Unlike the `:active` pseudo-class, this unique method styles a *different* element from the anchor element that is actually clicked, and can even be triggered without using anchor elements at all.

Using the `target` pseudo-class can be a bit confusing, so here it is shown with some markup:

```
<a href="#block1">Highlight block 1</a>
<a href="#block2">Highlight block 2</a>
<a href="#block3">Highlight block 3</a>

<div id="block1">This is block 1</div>
<div id="block2">This is block 2</div>
<div id="block3">This is block 3</div>
```

This code sets up three links that point to different hashes, as well as three associated `div`s. Notice how each hash link corresponds to the different id of each of the blocks. These are used to highlight each block with the `:target` pseudo-class.

Here's how you would set up the CSS to add a border around each active block:

```
div:target { border: 1px solid red; }
```

Now the target highlighting CSS is complete. When each block is clicked, it will highlight the appropriate block of text. In fact, the text blocks can be highlighted even without the links simply by routing to the corresponding URL in the browser (for example myurl.html#block1).

For longer sections of text, the `target` pseudo-class can be combined with internal page links so that when a link is clicked, the browser scrolls to the appropriate section of the page and highlights the appropriate block of text.

To accomplish that, you simply need to add some named anchors to the previous markup (and some additional text to your text blocks to see the effect):

```
<a href="#block1">Highlight block 1</a>
<a href="#block2">Highlight block 2</a>
<a href="#block3">Highlight block 3</a>

<a name="block1"></a>
<div id="block1">... add a long section of text for block 1 ...</div>

<a name="block2"></a>
<div id="block2">... add a long section of text for block 2 ...</div>

<a name="block3"></a>
<div id="block3">... add a long section of text for block 3 ...</div>
```

Now when any of these links is clicked, the browser scrolls down to the correct portion of the page and highlights the corresponding block of text. And just like the first example, this technique works if the user clicks a link on the page or browses directly to the appropriate hash URL.

UI State Pseudo-Classes

UI state pseudo-classes are very useful for building more attractive and dynamic form elements.

One of these techniques, the `focus` pseudo-class, has been around since CSS 2.1. This pseudo-class allows you to style form elements differently when the element is active (e.g. when the user is actively entering data into the field). For instance you can add a red border to any input elements that are in focus:

```
input:focus { border: 1px solid red; }
```

CSS3 adds some UI pseudo-classes that are helpful when styling forms. First the `:checked` pseudo-class can be used to style check boxes and radio buttons that are checked (and the `:indeterminate` pseudo-class can be used to style those that are unchecked):

```
input:checked { ... }
input:indeterminate { ... }
```

This snippet styles both checkboxes and radio buttons, but you can combine this with an attribute selector if you want to style each differently:

```
input[type="radio"]:checked { ... }
input[type="checkbox"]:checked { ... }
```

Additionally, CSS3 includes a method to style form elements differently whether they are enabled or disabled:

```
input:enabled { ... }
input:disabled { ... }
```

Form elements are enabled by default, but this state can be changed by applying the `disabled` HTML attribute (which prevents the field from receiving input of gaining focus).

> *Because this depends on the* `disabled` *attribute, it can also be accomplished using an attribute selector.*

Language Pseudo-Class

The language pseudo-class can be used to localize styling for different languages. Many sites include the `lang` value in their HTML declaration:

```
<html lang="en">
```

The language pseudo-class allows you to style content differently based on whichever language is flagged in the markup. For instance you can style your paragraphs differently for English and French:

```
p:lang(en) { ... }
p:lang(fr) { ... }
```

The `lang` attribute can also be applied to any element, not just the `<html>` tag, so it is possible to have multiple languages in a single HTML document. In this case, the `:lang` pseudo-class references whichever language is most specific to the given element.

> *The* `lang` *pseudo-class is useful both for accounting for differences between left-to-right and right-to-left languages, as well as adding* `line-height` *to prevent accents from overlapping in certain languages.*

TEXT AND CONTENT BASED PSEUDO-ELEMENTS

In addition to pseudo-classes and selectors that affect actual elements, there are a few text-based pseudo-elements that affect the text-content contained within elements.

First-Letter and First-Line

First you can use the `:first-letter` and `:first-line` pseudo-elements to style the first letter and line of text blocks differently. In certain situations this can be quite useful because otherwise it can be a difficult problem to solve (particularly `first-line`). Here's how you style the first letter and line within all paragraphs on a page:

```
p:first-letter { ... }
p:first-line { ... }
```

Before and After

Additionally, you can use the `:before` and `:after` pseudo-elements to add content to your pages. These elements add a specified text string to either the beginning or end of a text block, which can be very useful for adding extra styling with text instead of images. For instance you can add a `&raquo` (») to the beginning of all your list elements:

```
li:before {
    content: "&raquo;";
    padding-right: 5px;
}
```

Notice how this uses the `content` attribute to add the given content, and that you can also apply additional styling to this text element.

The `:before` and `:after` pseudo-elements can also be used with images. For instance you can add a smiley face GIF to the end of each paragraph:

```
p:after {
    content: url(../path_to/smiley.gif);
    padding-left: 5px;
}
```

This image appears inline after the text in your paragraph.

Styling Text Selection

Finally, you can even use CSS pseudo-elements to style the text selection on your pages. Despite being a relatively underused technique in CSS, this is a subtle way to create a better user experience and a more seamlessly styled environment.

Here's the code for styling your text selection to use a green background and yellow text:

```
::selection {
    background-color: green;
    color: yellow;
}
```

Be careful with the syntax here; it uses two colons instead of one.

Here the `::selection` pseudo-element is applied to the entire document, but you could restrict its scope to certain elements if you want to style the text selection differently in different parts of the page. For instance, you can apply this style to only paragraphs:

```
p::selection { ... }
```

It's also important to note that while the `::selection` pseudo-element is useful, the styling options it provides are fairly limited. You can use it to style only the background and text colors of the selected text, but not to add borders, margins or other more complex styling.

If you want a little extra control, you can adjust the opacity by defining the colors using RGBa (but bear in mind that certain versions of WebKit already style the background color of the text selection with a little transparency).

MEDIA QUERIES

Media queries are a powerful technique that allows you to build websites that respond to different aspects of the device being used to display their pages. With media queries, you can style pages differently based on the dimensions of the display device. This technique is extremely useful for creating truly flexible layouts that expand and contract depending on the size of the user's screen.

In the mobile arena, media queries provide the convenient opportunity to style content differently based on the device orientation (that is, whether it is being held vertically or horizontally).

Beyond dimensions and orientation, media queries can be used to accommodate different aspect ratios, resolutions, and color display abilities. These additional media queries can be helpful in certain specific situations, and can also be used as hacks to cater styling to specific devices.

USING MEDIA TYPES

Media queries build upon the CSS media type, which was first introduced in CSS2.1. Initially, media types were designed primarily to allow developers to style content differently for display on the screen or when being sent to the printer. Because websites often contain a considerable amount of information that is irrelevant when printing a document, print stylesheets were introduced as a way to save ink and printing time.

In most cases, print-specific styles are defined in a separate stylesheet, using the media attribute in the markup:

```
<link rel="stylesheet" type="text/css" media="screen" src="screen-styles.css" />
<link rel="stylesheet" type="text/css" media="print" src="print-styles.css" />
```

The previous example included two stylesheets, `screen-styles.css` that is used to display the page on the screen, and `print-styles.css` that is used when printing the document.

As an alternative to the HTML `media` attribute, specific media types can be flagged inline within a single stylesheet, using a media type declaration:

```
@media print {
    * { margin: 0; }
}
```

Media types can also be flagged while using the `@import` syntax, for example:

```
@import url(stylesheet.css) screen;
```

Besides `screen` and `print`, there are several additional media types such as `handheld`, `braille`, `tty`, `tv`, `projection`, `embossed` and `speech`. However, support for these options is spotty and depends not only on the browser but the device manufacturer. For instance, the `handheld` media type has been largely ignored by handheld manufacturers in an effort to display more feature-rich pages and prevent developers from creating stripped-down mobile pages for their devices.

You learn more about how media queries work in mobile devices in Chapter 10.

Finally, to include a stylesheet in all devices, simply flag the media type as `all`.

USING MEDIA QUERIES

Media queries expand on the media type syntax, providing additional options you can use to further adjust web pages to accommodate different display devices.

Media queries can simply be appended to a standard media type declaration by adding the media query in parentheses separated by `and`:

```
@media screen and (orientation: landscape) {
    /* style rules here */
}
```

These can be used in any of the media type syntaxes described earlier. For instance to reference an external stylesheet in the HTML:

```
<link rel="stylesheet" type="text/css" media="screen and (orientation: landscape)"
href="screen-landscape-styles.css" />
```

You can also combine multiple media queries:

```
@media screen and (orientation: landscape) and (min-device-width: 420px) { ... }
```

Additionally, you can use a `not` keyword to negate a result:

```
@media not screen and (orientation: landscape) { ... }
```

This negates the result of this media query, meaning if the media query would normally be true, it is now false. Thus this rule will be applied only if the media type isn't screen *and* the orientation isn't landscape (as opposed to if either criteria isn't true).

Finally, if you want to apply a media query to all media types, there is no need to use the `all` keyword. For instance these two queries produce identical results:

```
@media (orientation: landscape { ... }
@media all and (orientation: landscape) { ... }
```

CREATING FLEXIBLE LAYOUTS WITH MEDIA QUERIES

One of the most widespread uses of media queries is to alter styling to better accommodate different screen sizes. By styling pages to respond to the user's screen size, you can finally stop debating which resolutions to support and have the best of both worlds: content that looks good on small devices and maximizes the extra space available on larger ones.

In the past, CSS developers could use percentage widths to build flexible layouts, but that was relatively underused because it was quite cumbersome and limited. Issues arose when a screen was too large or too small. Additionally, percentage widths don't combine well with fixed widths, which caused many problems. For instance, images with percentage widths tend to look pixelated.

Fortunately media queries provide the tool developers need to build truly flexible layouts. They provide an added level of control that can be used to resize portions of layouts intelligently, and hide and show additional content as needed.

Different Stylesheets for Different Window Sizes

Now let's include three stylesheets—a different one for small, medium, and large layouts:

```
<link rel="stylesheet" type="text/css" media="screen and (max-width: 420px)"
href="small-styles.css" />
<link rel="stylesheet" type="text/css" media="screen and (min-width: 421px) and (max-
width: 1223px)" href="medium-styles.css" />
<link rel="stylesheet" type="text/css" media="screen and (min-width: 1224px)"
href="large-styles.css" />
```

This markup used the `min-width` and `max-width` instead of `min-device-width` and `max-device-width` because it's more concerned with the actual window size rather than the overall screen size.

The first stylesheet will be used with extremely small browser windows, which will mainly target smart phones but is also included for users who have resized their desktop browser windows to be extremely small. In both cases the amount of available real estate is limited, so it makes sense to treat both situations equally from a styling perspective.

The second stylesheet applies to normal sized windows, and will mainly be included for normal desktop and tablet browsing experiences. The third stylesheet affects larger windows and should include styles to maximize the extra space available in those situations.

These media queries will style the page when it loads, but you may be wondering what happens when a user resizes his window. Fortunately media queries are very robust and will adjust on the fly as the window changes dimensions.

This markup applied three distinct stylesheets to three situations, but you may prefer to use one base stylesheet (for instance the medium styles), and then apply extra styling to overwrite any of those styles for small and large window sizes.

In fact, using separate stylesheets provides no performance advantages because WebKit will download all three stylesheets no matter the window size. This allows the renderer to quickly switch between media queries as users resize their window; however, it has the downside of adding some often unnecessary HTTP requests.

If you are concerned with performance, it is actually best to apply all your media queries inline in a single stylesheet, using a media type declaration:

```
@media screen and (max-width: 420px ) { ... }
@media screen and (min-width: 421px) and (max-width: 1223px) { ... }
@media  screen and (min-width: 1224px ) { ... }
```

What To Change In Flexible Layouts

Now that you've included different stylesheets, you have to decide which styles to change in each. For most style rules, optimizing for the available real estate should be a fairly straight-forward process of resizing the layout and hiding or showing any less essential page elements.

Furthermore, in extremely small windows, like those used on mobile devices, it is usually best to stick to a single column layout and avoid multiple columns. If the additional columns are secondary, nonessential content, it is probably best to simply hide them. Otherwise reposition indispensible columns beneath the main content.

In extremely large windows, it is usually best to avoid filling the entire window with the page content unless the site is very text-heavy. Instead use the media queries to expand the layout to a reasonable size, and then consider using a larger background image to better fill the negative space in larger window sizes.

DETECTING SPECIFIC DEVICES

In most cases it's best to use media queries to style pages according to general criteria about the user's screen size, device orientation, and so on. However you can also exploit the versatility of media queries to create hacks to target more specific devices.

For instance, iPad has a width of 768px, so you can target iPad using an appropriate media query:

```
@media only screen and (device-width: 768px) { ... }
```

While useful for targeting certain specific devices, these media queries are by no means perfect and may end up targeting other devices. For instance, the iPad media query will target other devices with the same `device-width`.

You will learn more about device detection using media queries in Chapter 10.

SUMMARY

Taking advantage of CSS3's new selection tools not only makes styling web pages easier but also reduces the amount of markup needed for theming. Since these selectors allow you to target specific elements, they eliminate the need for extraneous classes and ids previously required for styling. This streamlines CSS development and reduces the file size of markup that is served to the user.

Additionally, CSS3 media queries allow you to create flexible layouts that respond dynamically the dimensions of the browser window. These media queries ensure that web pages take full advantage of the screen dimensions, whether large or small.

5

CROSS-BROWSER SUPPORT FOR CSS3

ALTHOUGH IT IS difficult to support every possible environment, it is important to support at least 95% of the browsers used by your site's visitors (98% in some cases). Fortunately, a large percentage of CSS3 attributes are now available in all modern browsers, and there are a number of fallback solutions that allow you to style elements reasonably well in non-supportive browsers.

If you have detailed analytics data about your site's usage, it will be easy to discern which browsers to target, otherwise look to historic market share data.

Supporting a large percentage of browsers is important, but it is not always necessary to support each browser in exactly the same way. Often it is acceptable to allow older browsers to gracefully degrade to less visually appealing implementations while making sure that all users are still able to access the same content. You'll have to decide whether you're comfortable with that sort of compromise (although with most CSS3 features you won't have to compromise at all).

When making this decision, it's good to be optimistic. Rather than focusing on what's missing from older browsers, think of what's gained by newer ones. Although it is important to support older browsers, there is no sense in holding back newer browsers from reaching their full potential. In this sense, it is sometimes better to conceptualize it as "progressive enhancement" as opposed to "graceful degradation."

In this chapter you learn the correct syntax for using CSS3 attributes that are supported in non-WebKit browsers. Whenever possible you also learn techniques that allow you to recreate CSS3 styles in non-supportive browsers. Often, for older versions of Internet Explorer, this means using a proprietary filter. In other cases you learn JavaScript and jQuery backup techniques that work in all non-supportive browsers: from older versions of IE to Firefox and even WebKit.

Finally you learn about the feature-detection library Modernizr, and how to combine it with CSS backup solutions to create bulletproof CSS3 implementations.

BASIC CSS3 STYLES IN ALL BROWSERS

With the release of IE9, a wide variety of CSS3 attributes finally became available in all modern browsers. This means that a number of CSS3 attributes can easily be supported for a large percentage of users. Additionally, many backup techniques provide decent solutions for non-supportive browsers.

> To determine which features are available in which browsers, look at the tables on
> www.caniuse.com.

CROSS-BROWSER BORDER RADIUS

border-radius is currently supported in all modern browsers without browser extensions. However, it's a good idea to include fallbacks for older versions of Mozilla and WebKit:

```
.button {
    -webkit-border-radius: 12px / 20px;
    -moz-border-radius: 12px / 20px;
    border-radius: 12px / 20px;
}
```

If you'd like to be extra-careful, include fallbacks for old versions of Opera (`-o-border-radius`) and extremely old versions of Safari / Konqueror (`-khtml-border-radius`). Considering the market shares of these deprecated versions, though, it is probably unnecessary.

Border Radius in Non-Supportive Browsers

While these CSS3 fallbacks cover a large portion of the browser market, IE has only supported `border-radius` since IE9. Unfortunately, supporting `border-radius` without CSS3 is quite difficult, and the variety of hacks available for non-supportive browsers are all buggy. These hacks work in certain basic situations, but cause problems when combined with other complex styles (not to mention the issues that will arise when using other IE hacks).

It is probably best to allow rounded corners to gracefully degrade to square corners in older versions of IE, but this is a decision you'll have to make based on your design.

With a considerable percentage of users running older versions of Internet Explorer, you may decide that rounded corners are crucial. In that case you can use a basic image implementation for IE6 through 8, and still use CSS3 styling for all other users. Alternatively you can try out one of the various JavaScript or CSS hacks, but be prepared to handle a number of bugs associated with these approaches.

CROSS-BROWSER GRADIENTS

Fortunately, CSS gradients are one property that is relatively easy to support for the majority of browsers. Between browser-specific CSS3 syntax and some proprietary MS filters, you can get very good market penetration using CSS alone. For older unsupportive browsers, image fallbacks are a reasonable solution for gradients that are design-critical.

CSS Gradients in Firefox

As of Firefox 3.6, CSS3 gradients are also available in Mozilla, although the syntax is a little bit different from — and simpler than —the original WebKit syntax. For a basic linear gradient:

```
background-image: -moz-linear-gradient(
    #007231,
    #004B23
);
```

You'll notice a couple differences in the syntax here. The `linear` parameter has been taken out of the parentheses and placed into the gradient declaration. There's also no need for the `from()` and `to()` parameters used by WebKit—the Mozilla version assumes these based on the order of the color parameters.

The previous CSS assumes a top-to-bottom gradient, but you can pass a degree value into the first parameter:

```
background-image: -moz-linear-gradient(
    90deg,
    #007231,
    #004B23
);
```

While there are a variety of ways to define the angle of the gradient, degrees is the most intuitive. Here you used 90deg, which declares a bottom-to-top gradient. Likewise you can use 0deg for left-to-right or 180deg for right-to-left gradients.

Color stops are a little easier to use in the Mozilla version as well. Simply add as many colors as you want, and Mozilla accommodates them:

```
background-image: -moz-linear-gradient(
    #007231,
    #00893B,
    #004B23
);
```

Here Mozilla spreads the three colors equally across the element. To define a position for any of the color stops, simply add a percentage value to any of these parameters:

```
background-image: -moz-linear-gradient(
    #007231,
    #00893B 30%,
    #004B23
);
```

This snippet adds a 30% to the second color stop. This color will be placed 30% of the way into the gradient, with the other two colors staying locked to the ends.

Mozilla also supports radial gradients, which are defined using -moz-radial-gradient():

```
background-image: -moz-radial-gradient(
    #007231,
    #00893B 30%,
    #004B23
);
```

By default the gradient is centered in the element, but you can also adjust its position, and even change its shape using -moz-radial-gradient(). See the Mozilla docs for more information: https://developer.mozilla.org/en/CSS/-moz-radial-gradient.

You may find it confusing that Mozilla uses a different syntax than WebKit, but Mozilla actually supports the correct syntax as defined by the W3C recommendations. WebKit pioneered CSS gradients before W3C specifications were declared, so it uses its own original syntax. Fortunately WebKit is already up to speed with the correct syntax, and current versions of Chrome and Safari support `-webkit-linear-gradient()` and `-webkit-radial-gradient()`.

CSS Gradients in IE

Although IE9 doesn't support CSS3 gradients, it is quite easy to create linear gradients in all versions of Internet Explorer, even IE6. For some time, IE has supported a proprietary filter that can be used to create background gradients:

```
filter: progid:DXImageTransform.Microsoft.gradient(
    startColorstr=#EFB67B, endColorstr=#DB7306);
```

This gradient renders from top to bottom, but you can create a horizontal gradient by setting the `gradientType` to 1:

```
filter: progid:DXImageTransform.Microsoft.gradient(
    startColorstr=#EFB67B, endColorstr=#DB7306,
    gradientType=1);
```

While this filter renders CSS gradients, it has a number of drawbacks. First, it supports only horizontal or vertical gradients, and cannot be used for angled or radial gradients. Additionally, the Microsoft filters are notoriously slow and buggy. So using this filter causes performance issues for IE, which already runs slower than other browsers. Furthermore, it may cause problems if used dynamically or combined with other filters, so make sure to always test IE filters thoroughly.

Finally, IE will support CSS3 gradients as of IE10, so it is a good idea to future-proof your code with the IE10 declarations:

```
background-image: -ms-linear-gradient(
    #007231,
    #004B23
);
```

> IE10 also supports `-ms-radial-gradient`.

CSS Gradients in Opera

Although Opera support may not be high on your list, CSS3 gradients can be supported in Opera as well. Current releases of Opera support linear gradients via a browser extension:

```
background-image: -o-linear-gradient(
    #007231,
    #004B23v
);
```

Opera supports linear gradients with the same syntax as Firefox. Unfortunately, radial gradients are still unsupported as of Opera 12.1, but will eventually become available using `-o-radial-gradient()`.

CSS Gradients in Other Non-Supportive Browsers

Considering the gaps in CSS gradient support, you should always define a default `background-color` as a fallback when working with gradients. Besides providing a fail-safe for non-supportive browsers, a background color makes corrections during rendering less conspicuous.

In addition to a default background color, you can also use an image as a fallback for non-supportive browsers. Simply define a normal `background-image` first, and then define the gradient `background-image` afterward:

```
background-image: url('path_to/my_gradient.png');
background-image: -webkit-gradient(
    linear,
    left top,
    left bottom,
    from(#007231),
    to(#004B23),
    color-stop(0.3, #00893B)
);
background-image: -moz-linear-gradient(
    #007231,
    #00893B 30%,
    #004B23
);
background-image: -o-linear-gradient(
    #007231,
    #00893B 30%,
    #004B23
);
```

> Be careful with the order when working with gradients. CSS3 gradients have to be last so they overwrite the regular image in supportive browsers.

Non-supportive browsers ignore the gradient, and supportive browsers ignore the regular image (which means it won't waste HTTP requests or download time).

One downside with the basic image solution is that the image will not stretch to the edges of the element. So this backup works perfectly for any elements that have set dimensions, but falls a bit short for those with dimensions that vary dynamically.

CROSS-BROWSER FONT FACE

Custom fonts are not only supported by modern browsers, but by a large percentage of older browsers as well. However, while these browsers all support custom fonts via the same `@font-face` declaration, the supported file formats differ from browser to browser.

Believe it or not, Internet Explorer was the first browser to allow the embedding of fonts via `@font-face`, which has been available since IE4. To get around font-licensing issues, Microsoft invented a proprietary font format called Embedded Open Type (EOT) and released a conversion tool called Web Embedding Fonts Tool (WEFT): `www.microsoft.com/typography/WEFT.mspx`.

Unfortunately, in typical Microsoft fashion the EOT file format is not open source, and thus could not be used by any other browsers. It took some time before the other browsers caught up, but now there is `@font-face` support in all modern browsers, which use a variety of different font formats. TrueType Font (TTF) is the most widely supported, and the compressed Web Open Font Format (WOFF) is an emerging standard that is supported by all modern browsers. Certain fringe formats are also useful, such as Scalable Vector Graphics (SVG), which is the only format supported by iOS and thus necessary for iPhone and iPad support.

Bulletproof Font Face Support

It may seem difficult to navigate the various formats needed to support `@font-face` across different browsers and devices, but there is an effective syntax that has been refined several times. First introduced in 2009, Paul Irish's Bulletproof Syntax (`http://paulirish.com/2009/bulletproof-font-face-implementation-syntax/`) accommodated all the formats needed for supportive browsers and devices of the time. Hacks used in this syntax eventually caused problems for Android, so after a few iterations, a better syntax emerged, known as the Fontspring Syntax:

```
@font-face {
    font-family: 'MyFont';
    src: url('myfont.eot?#iefix') format('embedded-opentype'),
         url('myfont.woff') format('woff'),
         url('myfont.ttf')  format('truetype'),
         url('myfont.svg#svgFontName') format('svg');
}
```

Older versions of IE have problems with multiple `src` declarations, but the `?` hack in this syntax avoids those issues by fooling IE into viewing the rest of the `src` declarations as a query string. The rest of the formats are included for various devices, in an order that ensures the browser uses the best format possible. Pay attention to the SVG declaration, which requires that you include the font name in the hash string.

Font-Stacks for Non-Supportive Browsers

Once you define your custom font using @font-face, you then have to attach it to elements using the font-family attribute. When doing so, make sure to define a robust font-stack with backup fonts for non-supportive browsers:

```
.button {
    font-family: Ballpark, Arial, Sans-serif;
}
```

This font-stack defines a custom font (Ballpark), as well as alternate fonts to be used in non-supportive browsers. Browsers start with the first font, then move down through the alternative fonts until one is supported.

Some designers like to use fancy font-stacks, with a hodge-podge mix of fonts that are safe to use in different environments. Even when building basic font-stacks, there are a few rules to follow. Mainly, pay attention not only to the aesthetics but also the widths of the alternative fonts. For a variety of reasons, it is a good idea to pick backup fonts with similar widths to the font you're embedding with @font-face.

If the width is too different, it can cause substantial layout differences for various users (especially if you define any layout dimensions with em). Because @font-face takes a moment to load, users may also see a flicker as the font adjusts, which will be magnified by a backup font with a significantly different width. Commonly referred to as "Flash of Unstyled Text" (FOUT), this issue has fortunately been mostly resolved by most modern browsers.

Using Font Squirrel's Font Face Generator

Font Squirrel's @font-face Generator is a tool that can help you avoid the headaches associated with generating the various file formats needed for bulletproof @font-face support. This indispensible tool allows you to upload a font file and control a wide variety of options about the formats it generates. Access Font Squirrel's generator (www.fontsquirrel.com/fontface/generator). In most cases you can stick to the default Optimal options, shown in Figure 5-1.

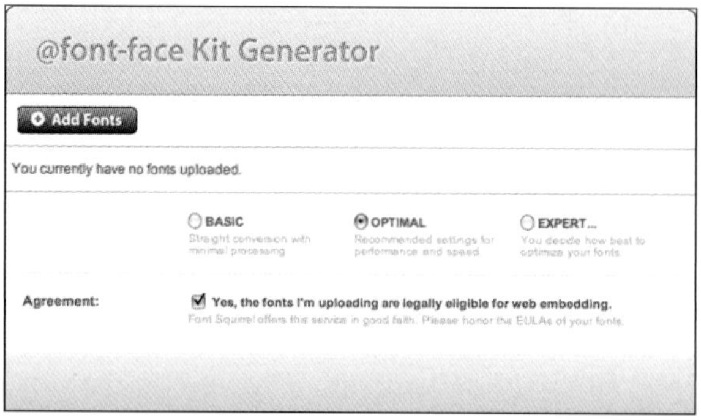

Figure 5-1: Notice the license agreement checkbox — EULAs are very important for @font-face embedding.

Source: © 2011 Font Squirrel

Figure 5-2 shows the wide variety of Expert options available to you.

A number of the settings in the Expert options can be left alone, although there are a few you may want to tweak, including the file format options.

@font-face Kit Generator

⊕ Add Fonts

You currently have no fonts uploaded.

	○ BASIC	○ OPTIMAL	⊙ EXPERT...
	Straight conversion with minimal processing.	Recommended settings for performance and speed.	You decide how best to optimize your fonts.
Font Formats:	☑ TrueType ☑ WOFF	☑ EOT Lite ☐ EOT Compressed	☑ SVG ☐ SVGZ
Rendering:	☑ Apply Hinting Improve Win rendering	☑ Fix Vertical Metrics Normalize across browsers	☐ Remove Kerning Strip kerning data
Fix Missing Glyphs:	☑ Spaces	☑ Hyphens	
X-height Matching: Resize to match the selected font's x-height.	⊙ None	○ Arial ○ Verdana ○ Trebuchet	○ Georgia ○ Times New Roman ○ Courier
Protection:	☐ WebOnly™ Disable desktop use		
Subsetting:	⊙ Basic Subsetting Western languages	○ Custom Subsetting... Custom language support	○ No Subsetting
CSS Formats:	⊙ Fontspring Syntax More information	○ Smiley More Information	○ Mo' Bulletproofer More Information
CSS Options:	☐ Style Linking Group styles under family	☐ Base64 Encode Embed font in CSS	
OpenType Options: If the features are available, the generator will flatten them into the font.	☐ Small Caps ☐ Caps to Sm. Caps	☐ Old Style Numerals ☐ Lining Numerals ☐ Tabular Numerals ☐ Proportl. Numerals ☐ Slashed Zero	☐ Stylistic Alts ☐ Style Set 1 ☐ Style Set 2
Advanced Options:	Font Name Suffix [webfont]	Em Square Value [2048]	Adjust Glyph Spacing [0] In units of the em square
PostScript Hinting:	○ Keep Existing	⊙ Font Squirrel	○ Adobe FDK
Font Tables:	☑ Fix GASP Table Better DirectWrite Rendering		
Shortcuts:	☐ Remember my settings		

Figure 5-2: Font Squirrel's Expert options for adjusting font file creation.

Source: © 2011 Font Squirrel

It's a good idea to always use at least the TrueType, WOFF, EOT Lite, and SVG options, but you also may consider including the EOT Compressed and SVGZ formats. These provide compressed versions of their respective formats, and are supported in certain browsers.

If reducing file size is a big priority, you can remove the kerning data from the fonts, as shown in Figure 5-2.

Additionally, you may want to sync the x-height matching with the other fonts in your font-stack, as shown in Figure 5-2. This can reduce layout disparities across browsers.

If you'd like to save HTTP requests and embed the fonts with a data URI, check the Base64 Encode checkbox (see Figure 5-2). That's usually a bad idea because it encodes several fonts while a given browser needs to download only one.

You can add extra spacing to the font, by adjusting the glyph spacing value in the Advanced Options section (see Figure 5-2).

CROSS-BROWSER TEXT AND BOX SHADOWS

Although still unsupported in IE9, text shadows have been supported in all other browsers for some time. In fact, even multiple text shadows are supported in Chrome, Safari, Firefox 3.5+ and Opera without any browser extension:

```
text-shadow: 2px 2px 2px #333, 4px 4px 4px #555;
```

Additionally, box shadows are supported in all modern browsers, including IE9. While most modern browsers do not require any browser extensions, they are still needed in older versions, as well current releases of iOS Safari and Android Browser. So to safely support the largest percentage of users, simply include all the extensions:

```
-webkit-box-shadow: 1px 3px 8px rgba(0, 0, 0, .6);
-moz-box-shadow: 1px 3px 8px rgba(0, 0, 0, .6);
box-shadow: 1px 3px 8px rgba(0, 0, 0, .6);
```

Text and Box Shadows in IE

Although IE9 supports box shadows, they are not supported in earlier versions, and no currently released versions of IE support text-shadow.

IE does provide certain proprietary filters that can be used to create both text and box shadows, but these are very buggy, so only use them with extreme caution.

The simplest filter for text and box shadow degradation is the Shadow filter:

```
.button {
    filter: progid:DXImageTransform.Microsoft.Shadow(
        color=#777777, direction=135, strength=5);
```

```
    zoom: 1;
}
```

The `Shadow` filter accepts a few parameters:

- The `color` property accepts any hex value, but not shorthand hex values such as #777.
- The `direction` accepts an integer to set the angle of the shadow.
- The `strength` property accepts a pixel value as an integer, which is the number of pixels to blur the shadow along.

While the `Shadow` filter stays attached to the element, the `DropShadow` filter provides more control over the positioning:

```
.button {
    filter: progid:DXImageTransform.Microsoft.DropShadow(
        color=#777777, OffX=5, OffY=5);
    zoom: 1;
}
```

The parameters of the `DropShadow` filter are basically the same, except the `OffX` and `OffY` values determine the position of the shadow, which can be used to create a shadow that is disconnected from the parent element. Unfortunately there is no way to control the blur radius with this filter.

Besides looking pretty bad, these filters have additional downsides. First, they only work with elements that "have layout," which is why `zoom: 1` is applied in these snippets.

Next, the shadow offsets the layout of the element, in this case making it 5px larger than it would be otherwise (because of the `Strength` and `OffX` / `OffY` properties). This can cause issues when used as a backup for `box-shadow` or `text-shadow`, which do not affect layout.

Finally, if these filters are used for a `text-shadow`, they cannot be applied to an element with a background, or it will render as a `box-shadow`. To support the `text-shadow` in an element with a background, you need an additional wrapper for the text.

All things considered, it is usually best to avoid the `Shadow` and `DropShadow` filters, unless you are willing to deal with a variety of issues.

CROSS-BROWSER RGBA TRANSPARENCY

All modern browsers support RGBa color values, and all browsers except IE have supported it for several versions. It is still a good idea to define a backup hex or RGB color when using RGBa:

```
.myRGBa {
    background-color: rgb(82, 151, 167);
    background-color: rgba(82, 151, 167, .5);
}
```

Notice that the RGBa color comes second, allowing it to overwrite the RGB color in supportive browsers.

Alpha Transparency in IE6-8

While opaque `rgb()` colors are a decent backup for all non-supportive browsers, you can provide much better RGBa support in older versions of IE.

The IE solution involves a hack using the Microsoft gradient filter:

```
.myRGBa {
    background-color: transparent;
    filter: progid:DXImageTransform.Microsoft.gradient(
        startColorstr=#7F5297A7, endColorstr=#7F5297A7);
    zoom: 1;
}
```

The gradient filter accepts color values with alpha transparency, so it can be used to emulate RGBa colors when both the starting and ending colors are the same. The syntax for the colors is a bit strange—the filter accepts hexadecimal color values, starting with a hexadecimal alpha value. So here, an alpha value of 0.5 converts to 7F.

> To generate an alpha hex value, multiply your decimal value by 256, subtract 1, and convert to base16.

This hack also applies a transparent background color, which is essential for avoiding the static background color you applied as a backup. This causes problems for other browsers, so make sure to apply this hack only for IE6-8. To do so you can either use a browser conditional, or define the transparency with an attribute hack for IE6-8:

```
.myRGBa {
    background-color: rgb(82, 151, 167);
    background-color: transparent\9;
    background-color: rgba(82, 151, 167, .5);
    filter: progid:DXImageTransform.Microsoft.gradient(
        startColorstr=#7F5297A7, endColorstr=#7F5297A7)\9;
    zoom: 1;
}
```

Old non-IE browsers will get the flat RGB color. IE6-8 will get the transparent background and filter (due to the \9 hack). All other browsers will get the RGBa color.

While this trick is useful for supporting RGBa `background-color`, it cannot be used to support any of the other attributes to which RGBa colors can be applied. For these you have to use an opaque fallback color.

This technique also has a couple of drawbacks associated with the Microsoft filter. It can be used only on elements that "have layout," so make sure to add zoom: 1 to any element that uses this. Microsoft filters are notoriously slow, so this technique comes with some performance disadvantages.

CROSS-BROWSER BORDER IMAGES

While difficult to support in some browsers, border images are fortunately also available in Firefox and Opera. You can implement a cross-browser border-image solution by including the appropriate browser extensions:

```
-webkit-border-image: url('my-border-image.png') 3 round;
-moz-border-image: url('my-border-image.png') 3 round;
-o-border-image: url('my-border-image.png') 3 round;
border-image: url('my-border-image.png') 3 round;
```

Unfortunately, border images are not available in IE9, or in older versions. You might consider gracefully degrading to plain CSS2 borders in non-supportive browsers. If degradation is not an option, you'll have to support the borders using background-image and a sliding-door technique to accommodate different sized content (www.alistapart.com/articles/slidingdoors/).

CROSS-BROWSER BACKGROUND CLIP

95

background-clip is available in all modern browsers, and most browsers do not even need a special extension. It's still a good idea to use the -moz and -webkit prefixes to accommodate older versions of these browsers:

```
-webkit-background-clip: padding;
-moz-background-clip: padding-box;
background-clip: padding-box;
```

Note the slightly different syntax in the old -webkit-background-clip, which uses padding instead of padding-box.

CROSS-BROWSER DATA URIS

Data URIs not only can be used across all modern browsers, but there is a technique that makes raw file data possible even in older non-supportive versions of IE.

Across most browsers you can use data URIs with the same syntax you used for WebKit:

```
background-image: url("data:image/png;base64,iVBORw0KGgoAAAA...
UhEUgAAABgAAAAYCAMAAADXqc3KAAADU5ErkJggg==");
```

Although IE9 supports data URIs without restrictions, in IE8 they can be used only with files that are up to 32kb in size.

Raw Image Data in IE6 and IE7

IE6 and IE7 do not support data URIs at all. However, you can still use raw image data in older versions of IE, by taking advantage of MIME HTML (MHTML).

MHTML is an antiquated file type that allows you to embed multipart files within a single document. Although not normally used in modern web development, it's perfect for allowing raw image data in equally antiquated versions of Internet Explorer.

The first step is to include MIME data as a comment in your stylesheet:

```
/*
Content-Type: multipart/related; boundary="MYSEPARATOR"

--MYSEPARATOR
Content-Location: image1
Content-Transfer-Encoding: base64

iVBORw0KGgoAAAANSUhEUgAAABgAAAAYCAMAAADXqc3KAAAD....U5ErkJggg==
--MYSEPARATOR
Content-Location: image2
Content-Transfer-Encoding: base64

iVBORw0KGgoAAAANSUhEUgAAABgAAAAYCAMAAADXqc3KAAAA....U5ErkJggg==
--MYSEPARATOR--
*/
```

When including the MIME data, there are a couple syntactical issues to note:

- Make sure you define a boundary and then use the boundary exactly as it's being used in this example; with `--MYSEPARATOR` before each new image and `--MYSEPARATOR--` at the end of the MIME data.
- Each block of image data has a different name defined after `Content-Location`. You'll use these to reference the particular image.

Next include the image in your stylesheet, pointing to an MHTML reference:

```
/*
The MIME data from above goes here
*/

.image1 {
    background-image:
```

```
            url(mhtml:http://mysite.com/styles.css!image1);
}

.image2 {
    background-image:
        url(mhtml:http://mysite.com/styles.css!image2);
}
```

This snippet references the images as MHTML, pointing to the same URL as the stylesheet. You must use an absolute link to the stylesheet, and include the name of the image you defined with `Content-Location` in the MIME data.

Use this only with IE6 and 7 because it causes problems for other browsers that do not support MHTML. It's best to include this in a separate stylesheet for IE6 and 7, using browser conditionals:

```
<!--[if lte IE 7]>
<link rel="stylesheet" type="text/css" href="ie7-styles.css" />
<![endif]-->
```

Alternatively, you can use the star hack (`*background-image`) to define the attribute for only IE6 and 7. However, since you are also using data URIs to define these images for other browsers, this becomes a performance issue because you are then including the data twice in the same stylesheet. So use the star hack only when defining really small images.

97

CSS3 ANIMATIONS IN ALL BROWSERS

While unsupported in IE9, CSS3 transition is supported in both Firefox 4 and Opera 10.5 using special browser prefixes. Thus you can define a cross-browser safe transition:

```
-webkit-transition: background-color 1s ease;
-moz-transition: background-color 1s ease;
-o-transition: background-color 1s ease;
transition: background-color 1s ease;
```

TRANSITIONS IN NON-SUPPORTIVE BROWSERS

Transition support is relatively new and is still not available in any versions of Internet Explorer. While transition tends to degrade gracefully to an immediate style change as opposed to an animation, it is possible to provide a near-perfect backup solution for non-supportive browsers.

Although it cannot be accomplished with pure CSS, transition backups can be easily achieved using JavaScript, for instance with the JavaScript library jQuery.

Detecting Transition Support

The first step to creating your transition backup is determining when it is necessary—after all, it is important to use native CSS3 animations whenever possible. You could create a list of browser versions that do not support transition, but that would be time-consuming and it would also be perpetually incomplete because new versions and browsers come out frequently.

Thus it is always better to use feature detection to check if transition is supported in the browser and then apply the backup if it is not.

The jQuery support object is used to determine whether the browser supports various features. While there is currently no transition detection included in the jQuery core, you can easily extend the support object for transition:

```
$.support.transition = (function(){
    var thisBody = document.body || document.documentElement,
    thisStyle = thisBody.style,
    support = thisStyle.transition !== undefined ||
        thisStyle.WebkitTransition !== undefined ||
        thisStyle.MozTransition !== undefined ||
        thisStyle.MsTransition !== undefined ||
        thisStyle.OTransition !== undefined;

    return support;
})();
```

This detects whether the body element can have a transition style applied, checking all the various browser extensions.

After extending the support object, you can reference the object anywhere in your JavaScript:

```
if ( ! $.support.transition ) {
    // what to do if transition isn't supported
}
```

Creating a Backup Animation with jQuery

You can recreate transition animations using the jQuery `animate()` method. For instance, if you are using transition to change the dimensions of an object on `:hover`:

```
$(function() {

if ( ! $.support.transition ) {
    var defaultCSS = {
```

```
            width: 200,
            height: 50
    },
    hoverCSS = {
            width: 300,
            height: 75
    };

    // loop through each element
    $('.element').each(function() {
        var $thisElement = $(this);

        $thisElement.hover(function() {
            // execute this on mouseover
            $thisElement.css(defaultCSS)
                .animate(hoverCSS, 500, 'swing' );
        }, function() {
            // execute this on mouseout
            $thisElement.animate(defaultCSS, 500, 'swing' );
        });
    });
}
});
```

Note that this script starts with `$(function() {})`*—this is to ensure that the element has loaded on the page before the script executes.*

Here you used a number of techniques to recreate the transition:

1. You define the `defaultCSS` and `hoverCSS` for the two different states of your element.

2. You loop through each element that has the transition, applying a `hover()` event to call the various animations.

3. You use the `animate()` method to recreate the components of the transition animation. You simply pass in the CSS styles you want to change, and then set the duration of the animation to whatever you use in your transition.

   You can even use a timing function; for instance the previous example uses `'swing'`, which is similar to `ease` in CSS3. In addition to `'swing'`, the jQuery core also offers `'linear'`, and you can use a jQuery plugin, such as jQueryUI, if you need more specific timing functions.

4. The mouseover event first attaches the `defaultCSS`, before animating to the `hoverCSS`. Without this style change, there would be problems with the native `:hover` styles that are applied for browsers that support CSS3 transition. These styles have to be overwritten with jQuery, so they don't flicker before the animation begins.

KEYFRAME ANIMATIONS IN NON-SUPPORTIVE BROWSERS

Cross-browser keyframe support is pretty lacking. Although it has been supported in Safari, Chrome for several versions, there is no support in sight for Opera or IE. It is fortunately supported in Firefox 5+, using a similar syntax to WebKit-based browsers. However make sure to use the correct browser extension for Firefox: `-moz-animation` and `@-moz-keyframes`.

Luckily, you can easily support keyframes in all browsers using a similar jQuery backup to the one you applied for transitions.

Detecting Keyframe Animation Support

Again, it is better to use feature detection rather than browser sniffing to determine when to apply the backup solution.

Start by first extending the jQuery support object to detect animation support:

```
$.support.animation = (function(){
    var thisBody = document.body || document.documentElement,
    thisStyle = thisBody.style,
    support = thisStyle.animation !== undefined ||
        thisStyle.WebkitAnimation !== undefined ||
        thisStyle.MozAnimation !== undefined ||
        thisStyle.MsAnimation !== undefined ||
        thisStyle.OAnimation !== undefined;

    return support;
})();
```

Creating a Backup Animation with jQuery

If the browser doesn't support animation, set up your keyframe animation by chaining together different jQuery `animate()` methods for each keyframe. Define these in a recursive function, so that you can loop the animation infinitely:

```
$(function() {

if ( ! $.support.animation ) {
    // custom animation to recreate 3 keyframes
    function myAnimation($obj) {
        // first keyframe
        $obj.animate(firstStyles, 500, 'swing', function() {
            // second keyframe
            $obj.animate(secondStyles, 500, 'swing',
```

```
        function() {
          // third keyframe
          $obj.animate(thirdStyles, 500, 'swing',
            function() {
              // looping back to the beginning
              myAnimation($obj);
            });
        });
      });
  }

  $('.element').each(function() {
    myAnimation( $(this) );
  });
}
});
```

Make sure to define firstStyles, secondStyles, *and* thirdStyles *with whichever CSS you need.*

Notice how this takes advantage of the capability to chain together jQuery animations. The last argument in each of these animate() methods triggers the next function to execute after the animation completes. After completing the three different keyframes, the function calls itself again, causing the animation to loop infinitely.

101

CSS3 TRANSFORMS IN ALL BROWSERS

While 3D transforms are relatively unsupported, 2D transforms are supported in all modern browsers. Although only recently introduced to Internet Explorer, transforms can even be accommodated in older versions of IE by taking advantage of MS filters.

No browser currently supports transform perfectly according to the W3C specifications, but you can create a cross-browser friendly transform declaration using a number of browser extensions:

```
-webkit-transform: rotate(45deg);
-moz-transform: rotate(45deg);
-ms-transform: rotate(45deg);
-o-transform: rotate(45deg);
transform: rotate(45deg);
```

The different transform effects are all supported across modern browsers: rotate(), translate(), scale(), skew(), and even matrix().

All modern browsers also allow you to adjust the `transform-origin`:

```
-webkit-transform-origin: bottom right;
-moz-transform-origin: bottom right;
-ms-transform-origin: bottom right;
-o-transform-origin: bottom right;
transform-origin: bottom right;
```

SUPPORTING TRANSFORMS IN OLDER VERSIONS OF IE

IE9 supports some CSS3 transforms, but older versions are still left out. Fortunately you can still support all the 2D transforms in older versions of IE all the way down through IE5.5.

Be aware that the MS filter that accommodates transforms is very difficult to use because it relies on matrices. This is great if you're trying to provide graceful degradation for a transform matrix; however, it is quite difficult to calculate the correct values for the other CSS3 transforms.

To get an idea of the complexity of this filter, simply look at this backup for `rotate(15deg)`. This MS filter is the same as `-webkit-transform: rotate(15deg)`:

```
filter: progid:DXImageTransform.Microsoft.Matrix(
    M11=0.9659258262890683, M12=-0.25881904510252074,
    M21=0.25881904510252074, M22=0.9659258262890683,
    sizingMethod='auto expand');
```

> *If you want to dig into the math required to generate your own matrices, go to* www. useragentman.com/blog/2011/01/07/css3-matrix-transform- for-the-mathematically-challenged/.

There are a number of tools that can help you generate the matrix values you need to support transforms in older versions of IE. If you're using `rotate()`, simply head to www.css3 please.com and customize the `.box_rotate` style.

Alternatively, there are a number of JavaScript solutions you can implement to handle the IE transforms. One such script is the Transformie plugin for jQuery, available here: www. transformie.com.

Transformie supports most CSS3 transforms, with the exception of `translate()`. You can accommodate `translate()` using the basic CSS `position` attribute.

Transformie has one other downside: it doesn't work with `transform-origin`. You can also get around this by using the `position` attribute.

CROSS-BROWSER SUPPORT FOR 3D TRANSFORMS

At the time of this writing, 3D transforms are available only in Safari 4+ and Chrome 12+. They are rumored to be supported in IE10, although it may be some time before you can use these transforms across a reasonable portion of the browser market.

That said, it is possible to imitate the effects made with 3D transforms by combining 2D transforms such as `skew()` and `rotate()`. While these backup solutions have to be handmade to fit your particular situation, 3D transform-like effects can thus be achieved in any browser that supports 2D transforms.

For an example of a 3D transform effect accomplished using a 2D transform hack, see this URL: `http://hacks.mozilla.org/2009/06/3d-transforms-isocube/`.

CROSS-BROWSER SUPPORT FOR CSS3 SELECTORS AND PSEUDO-CLASSES

Although some CSS3 selectors are not available in older browsers, support has been improving and most selectors are now available across all modern browsers.

CROSS-BROWSER SUPPORT FOR SELECTORS

Fortunately, even the advanced attribute selectors have been around for some time, and are supported by most browsers (except IE6). So unless IE6 support is critical, feel free to use both the CSS2 and CSS3 attribute selectors in cross-browser projects.

Although cross-browser support for structural selectors isn't perfect, most are usable for all major browsers except IE6. First, the child selector works perfectly in IE7+. Next, the adjacent sibling selector works in IE7+, however doesn't update correctly in IE7 and IE8 if content is added dynamically (e.g. if an element is placed before an element using JavaScript). Finally the general sibling selector works with only a few minor bugs in older IEs: in IE7 it fails if there is a comment between the siblings, and in IE8 it only applies to the first 298 elements in range.

CROSS-BROWSER SUPPORT FOR PSEUDO-CLASSES AND PSEUDO-ELEMENTS

Although the structural pseudo-classes are all fully supported by modern browsers, support in older versions of IE is spotty. The `first-child` pseudo-class works in IE7+, but it has issues in IE7 and 8 when content is added dynamically with JavaScript. None of the other structural pseudo-classes discussed in Chapter 4 are available in IE6, 7, or 8, although they are all supported by IE9.

Other pseudo-classes such as :not and :target are supported in all modern browsers, but are not available in older versions of IE. The :lang pseudo-class is available throughout modern and older browsers.

There are a variety of JavaScript solutions that can be implemented to support these pseudo-classes in older versions of IE. One such project is IE9.js, which upgrades IE6, 7, and 8 to be compatible with many of the features in IE9. Although it is not as perfect as native browser support, this script can fix most styling issues with a single JavaScript include. Visit http://code.google.com/p/ie7-js/ for more information.

The first-line and first-letter pseudo-elements have existed for a while in CSS and are supported by all major browsers (even IE6). The before and after pseudo-elements work in all major browsers except IE6 and IE7. Text selection styling works in all modern browsers, but is not supported in IE6, 7, or 8.

> In Firefox, text selection requires a browser-specific extension:
> ::-moz-selection

JQUERY SUPPORT FOR CSS3 SELECTORS

Although cross-browser support is spotty for some CSS3 selection tools, you can use all the CSS3 selectors and pseudo-classes in jQuery. This means that when it really counts, you can apply any styles you need.

Detecting CSS3 selector support is a bit tricky, so you may want to simply use the $.browser object to determine which browser is being used. For instance, because you know the child selector is not supported in IE6, you could detect for IE6, and then apply any necessary styles. For example, this uses the jQuery browser object to determine if the user is using IE6 or lower, and then applies a style using a child selector and the css() method:

```
if ( $.browser.msie && $.browser.version < 7 ) {
    $('ul > li').css('color', 'red');
}
```

If you prefer to avoid browser-sniffing, you can use a more robust approach by checking if the style has been applied to the element:

```
if ( $('ul > li').css('color') != 'rgb(255, 0, 0)'  ) {
    $('ul > li').css('color', 'red');
}
```

However, there are a couple things to be aware of when using this technique. First make sure that you are selecting the right element. With a general selector like `ul > li`, you may be selecting an element that has been styled with another, higher priority style.

Then, the style value returned by `css()` may not always be what you expect. For instance, in this example, you apply the color using the keyword `'red'`, however must check for the string `rgb(255, 0, 0)` because that's how the browser will normalize this color keyword.

CROSS-BROWSER SUPPORT FOR MEDIA QUERIES

Although all modern browsers support media queries, they are disappointingly not supported by older versions of IE. Fortunately, in most cases, the styling applied in media queries is nonessential, and sites will render decently without extra adjustments.

However, it is important to ensure that any situation-specific rules included in media queries do not get implemented in these older browsers. This can be tricky because all major browsers *do* support media types even if they don't support media queries. Here's an example:

```
<link rel="stylesheet" type="text/css" media="screen and (max-width: 420px)"
  href="small-styles.css" />
```

Browsers that support media queries will apply this stylesheet only to smaller windows; older browsers will simply read the `screen` media type and apply it for all window sizes. This can cause major problems in non-supportive browsers because these styles are not meant for all users.

Fortunately you can use the `only` keyword to hide these rules from any older browsers that do not support media queries:

```
<link rel="stylesheet" type="text/css" media="only screen and (max-width: 420px)"
  href="small-styles.css" />
```

Here modern browsers will still apply the media query correctly, but older browsers will view this stylesheet as having the media type `only`, and therefore will not include the stylesheet.

> However, make sure to omit the keyword and any stylesheets you want to load in nonsupportive browsers.

USING MODERNIZR FOR FEATURE DETECTION

Throughout this chapter you've learned a variety of backup techniques to support different CSS3 features in non-supportive browsers. Clearly it is important to know when to apply these backups to ensure that the backup solutions are used only in non-supportive browsers. After all, you don't want to overwrite any of the native CSS3 implementations with a less-effective backup solution.

Although in most cases non-supportive browsers can be handled using either the order of CSS attribute declarations or various hacks, you may consider using the Modernizr library to assist your feature detection.

Modernizr is a JavaScript solution that implements a variety of CSS feature detections at the stylesheet level. You can download the library here: `www.modernizr.com`.

Even though Modernizr uses JavaScript, you can take advantage of its feature detection with CSS alone. That's because Modernizr attaches a variety of classes to the root `<html>` element, which you can then leverage in your stylesheets as needed.

For instance, to detect support for `border-image`, you can first apply a class for supportive browsers:

```
.borderimage .element {
    -webkit-border-image: url('my-border-image.png') 3 round;
    -moz-border-image: url('my-border-image.png') 3 round;
    -o-border-image: url('my-border-image.png') 3 round;
    border-image: url('my-border-image.png') 3 round;
}
```

These styles will only be applied to the `.element` in browsers that support `border-image`. This works because Modernizr applies the class `.borderimage` to the root `<html>` element in supportive browsers.

Next you can apply a backup solution for non-supportive browsers using the `.no-border-image` class:

```
.no-borderimage .element {
    border: 1px solid orange;
}
```

Although Modernizr is useful, bear in mind that it will be ineffective if the user has turned off JavaScript. Additionally, the script requires not only a few extra kilobytes, but also some extra processing time, so you should avoid using Modernizr if you can adequately style non-supportive browsers without it.

SUMMARY

While you probably prefer to develop only for modern browsers like Safari and Chrome, the reality is that most projects need cross-browser support across a wide variety of environments. Although a number of these other browsers support modern features, in some places cross-browser support is certain to be lacking.

In these situations, consider whether the feature is even necessary for older browsers. Certain bells and whistles are great to include as progressive enhancement, but are not "mission critical" to include in every browser. Typically, the features that are not commonly supported are visual improvements rather than essential elements for the site's content.

If a feature is deemed important enough to build fallbacks, make sure to thoroughly consider your options. Although certain IE filters and JavaScript fallback scripts may seem like miracles, they are often more like snake oil: creating more problems than they solve. In dire situations like these, remember that you can always resort to using basic background images to recreate a lot of the visual styling.

III

HTML5 SUPPORT IN WEBKIT

6

HTML5 MEDIA TAGS

MEDIA TAGS ARE one of the most useful features introduced by HTML5. These tags enable you to embed media elements such as audio and video directly in the browser, which means that you can create rich interactive websites without relying on third-party plugins such as Flash, Silverlight or QuickTime.

HTML5 media tags have a number of advantages over third-party plugins:

- They are easier to use because they can be accessed directly using native browser methods.
- They are generally faster because they don't depend on loading an external application.

- They make debugging easier because they reduce the potential points of failure to only the browser itself.

In this chapter you learn how to use the HTML5 video and audio tags to embed rich media on your websites. You learn a bit about the different file formats that can be used with each, and also how to interface with these elements dynamically using JavaScript. Then, you tie it all together by creating custom controls for HTML5 media elements. Finally, you learn how to create a Flash fallback for non-supportive browsers.

WHY USE HTML5?

Using HTML 5—and avoiding third-party plugins—provides a variety of advantages. HTML5 is completely open-source, while third-party plugins such as Flash Player are a closed-source "black box." Although these plugins work well primarily, using them is always a matter of blind faith because you have to trust that the plugin does the right thing. When the plugin behaves differently than you expect, it's difficult to debug because you are limited by the debugging tools provided by the software vendor, and can never determine exactly where the code is failing.

In addition to introducing an extra point of failure, third-party plugins also introduce performance issues. Native browser methods generally outperform third-party plugins, if only because there is no need to instantiate an external application. Furthermore, HTML5 runs in the browser, which means that the browser can takes steps to optimize it directly, both through software optimizations and hardware acceleration.

HTML5 works natively in any browser that supports it, but third-party plugins work only if the user has installed the plugin (and a recent enough version for whatever you need to accomplish). While it is true that more users currently have Flash Player installed than an HTML5 compatible browser, third-party plugins introduce an additional versioning issue because you must depend on users having both a current enough browser and a current enough plugin. Not to mention the fact that these plugins can't be installed on certain devices, such as iPhone and iPad. Considering the popularity of these devices and the rise of HTML5-compatible browsers, it is likely that the scales will soon reverse, and more users will be able to use HTML5 than Flash at some point in the near future.

Furthermore, native browser methods like HTML5 are simply more natural and easy to use. You can interface with HTML5 media elements using the same techniques you use for the rest of your website. This not only makes development more intuitive, but it removes the gap between Flash and HTML portions of a project, streamlining both development and maintenance issues. For instance, to pause a video using JavaScript, would you rather create a gateway between JavaScript and ActionScript, or would you rather just pause the video?

Finally, new third-party plugins are being created all the time. It is not uncommon for an interactive site to use multiple plugins, such as Flash, Silverlight, and Java applets. Opting instead to use native browser methods reduces this segmentation and puts an end to plugin wars. Besides, third-party plugins are constantly going in and out of favor, for instance Real Player was very popular in the late 1990s and early 2000s, but has since fallen into disuse. On the other hand, you can count on browsers supporting HTML5 into the distant future.

HTML5 VIDEO

The HTML5 video tag is extremely easy to use. The syntax is the same as an image tag; simply point to the file you want to display:

```
<video src="myvideo.mp4"></video>
```

Just like with image tags, it's a good idea to specify dimensions for your video. This can be done either via CSS, or attached as attributes to the video element:

```
<video src="myvideo.mp4" width="480" height="320"></video>
```

When specifying dimensions, you don't need to worry too much about the ratio of width to height. If it doesn't match up with the video, your browser simply centers the video within that box, rather than stretching the video or messing up the proportions.

HTML5 VIDEO OPTIONS

One advantage of HTML5 video tags is that they come with a variety of native options you can leverage easily using markup. First, with a single attribute you can add video controls to your video:

```
<video src="myvideo.mp4" width="480" height="320" controls></video>
```

This quick and effortless solution adds the default browser controls to the video element. If you want a more refined or differently styled solution, you can build your own custom controls.

Autoplaying a video is also easy; simply attach the `autoplay` keyword to your video element:

```
<video src="myvideo.mp4" width="480" height="320" autoplay></video>
```

This plays the video automatically when the page loads. You can also signal the browser to preload the video instead (that is, download the video but not play it):

```
<video src="myvideo.mp4" width="480" height="320" preload></video>
```

By default the browser waits to download the video until it is played, but the preload keyword speeds up playback by starting the download immediately when the page loads. That's not always a good thing because it can tie up network resources and slow down other elements on the page. So be smart when using `preload`; if the whole point of the page is to view the video, then it's a good idea to use this keyword. Otherwise if you think that only a small percentage of users will end up viewing the video, you can also ensure that the browser does not preload the video:

```
<video src="myvideo.mp4" width="480" height="320" preload="none"></video>
```

Additionally, if you'd like the video to loop, simply pass the `loop` keyword:

```
<video src="myvideo.mp4" width="480" height="320" loop></video>
```

You can also include an image to be displayed if the video doesn't load by setting the `poster` attribute:

```
<video src="myvideo.mp4" width="480" height="320" poster="failwhale.jpg"></video>
```

Be aware that the `poster` attribute causes problems in iOS 3, so it is probably best to avoid this attribute because some users will take a while to upgrade to iOS 4 and 5.

HTML5 VIDEO FORMATS

While the basic syntax for HTML5 video is very simple, implementing it becomes more complicated because not all browsers support the same formats. In fact, even to support different WebKit-based browsers, you need to use multiple video formats.

When you hear "video format," you may be thinking of a file type such as AVI or MP4. However, those are simply containers that hold information about the playback, as well as different tracks for the audio and video that will be played.

While the type of container is important (because certain browsers can use only certain file types), it is much more important to pay attention to the codecs, which are the formats used to encode and decode the video and audio data. The codec determines a variety of features of the video, from playback quality to file size. It is also interrelated with the video container because certain file types can use only certain codecs.

Different Formats for Different Browsers

Although there are many combinations of video containers and codecs, you need only three to support all HTML5 browsers.

MP4/H.264/ACC

Encoding an MP4 with a H.264 video track and AAC audio track (MP4/H.264/ACC) results in a format that's usable in Safari and IE9, as well as iOS and Android. Although H.264 can work well for higher bandwidth/CPU devices such as desktop computers, it is especially well suited for lower bandwidth/CPU devices such as mobile phones. This makes it an ideal format for iOS/Android playback.

H.264 also works well for Safari because it can be played without the user having to install any additional software. Safari can, in fact, play anything that works with QuickTime, although special plugins are required for the other formats.

Ogg/Theora/Vorbis

Encoding an Ogg with a Theora video track and Vorbis audio track (Ogg/Theora/Vorbis) is a format that's used by Chrome, Firefox, and Opera. Older versions of Chrome (5.0 and earlier) can actually use the MP4/H.264/AAC format, however Chrome has opted to phase out H.264 support.

WebM/VP8/Vorbis

Encoding a WebM with a VP8 video track and Vorbis audio track creates a format that's used in newer versions of Firefox, Chrome, and Opera. It can also be used by newer versions of Android, although there are hardware issues with the playback so it is best to stick to the MP4/H.264/AAC solution in the interest of improving battery life.

In case you got lost in the sea of file format acronyms, Table 6-1 can help you figure out which video formats are needed where.

Table 6-1   Three Video Formats Needed to Support the Widest Variety of Users

	Safari	Chrome	iOS	Android	FireFox	IE	Opera
MP4 (H.264 & AAC)	3.0+	5.0-	3.0+	2.0+		9.0+	
WebM	*	6.0+	*	2.3+	4.0+	*	10.6+
Ogg (Theora & Vorbis)	*	5.0+			3.5+		10.5+

*Not playable natively, but can be played if the correct plugin is installed by user

Ogg/Theora/Vorbis and WebM/VP8/Vorbis Decision

You may have noticed some overlap between the Ogg and WebM formats. If you would like to cut down on video encoding, it is possible to use only two formats—MP4/H.264/AAC and either Ogg/Theora/Vorbis or WebM/VP8/Vorbis—provided that you are willing to make some compatibility compromises. If you are not concerned with older versions of Chrome, Firefox, and Opera, you may consider avoiding the Ogg/Theora/Vorbis format. Alternatively, you may consider skipping the WebM/VP8/Vorbis format; however it makes up an emerging standard, and is better for future-proofing.

115

> *Video format decisions are still very much in flux among major browsers and device manufacturers. Make sure to keep on top of which formats are used in the future as well.*

Including Different Formats In Your Markup

Using the different formats in a single HTML5 video element is easy. Simply remove the `src` attribute, and instead nest some source elements within the video tag:

```
<video width="480" height="320" controls>
  <source src="myvideo.mp4"  type='video/mp4; codecs="avc1.42E01E, mp4a.40.2"'>
  <source src="myvideo.webm" type='video/webm; codecs="vp8, vorbis"'>
  <source src="myvideo.ogv"  type='video/ogg; codecs="theora, vorbis"'>
</video>
```

There are several important things to note about this syntax:

- You only removed the `src` attribute from the video element. Other attributes such as `width`, `height`, `controls`, `autoplay`, and `preload` should all stay attached to the video element.
- Each of the source elements contains a MIME type as well as the codecs used for the video and audio encoding. Without these the video will not play.
- The syntax of the `type` value is a bit wonky. You have to use double quotes for the `codecs`, which means you need to switch to single quotes for the `type` attribute.
- The order of the source declarations is important because the browser runs through these, using the first format it supports. Thus it is a good idea to keep the WebM format, which is generally a better video format, before the OGG. The MP4 format should always come first because early versions of iPad shipped with a bug that reads only the first source format. Even if you are not concerned with older iPads, it is a good idea to place MP4 before WebM, to ensure that Android uses the more optimal MP4 format.

In addition to declaring the correct MIME type in your markup, make sure that your web server is using the proper MIME type in the HTTP Header `Content-Type` *value.*

ENCODING DIFFERENT FORMATS

While it can be a hassle to encode each video three different times, it is important if you want to support the widest variety of users. Fortunately, there are a number of free tools you can use to make video encoding simple.

Selecting which tool to use is a decision that depends on how much control you want over the output versus how easy you want the encoding process to be. If you're more comfortable with a quick out-of-the-box solution, you'll have to accept a lesser level of control. Likewise if you want to control a variety of aspects of the playback, you'll have to accept a more tedious encoding process.

If you are not familiar with video encoding, it is probably best to opt for a simpler tool. To learn more about video encoding options, read this document: `www.streaminglearningcenter.com/attachments/download/49/Encoding%20Video%20for%20HTML5.pdf`*.*

Quick and Easy Encoding with Miro Video Converter

Unless you have a compelling reason to control various aspects of the video encoding, you'll be happiest using Miro Video Converter. This open-source tool is specially geared towards converting video for HTML5 and mobile devices, and is 100% free for both Mac OSX and Windows.

Download Miro Video Converter here: www.mirovideoconverter.com.

Encoding videos with Miro Video Converter couldn't be easier, simply drag and drop the video you want to convert as shown in Figure 6-1.

Figure 6-1: Miro Video Converter provides a simple interface for encoding videos.

To encode the MP4/H.264/AAC video format, select the iPhone option from the drop-down as shown in Figure 6-2.

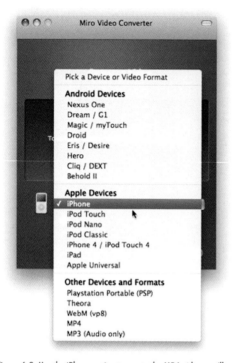

Figure 6-2: Use the iPhone option to create the MP4 video you'll need for Safari, iOS, Android, and IE9. Make sure to select iPhone and not iPhone 4 / iPod Touch 4.

There is no need to send the video to iTunes, so uncheck that check box. Then click Convert and wait for the video file to be encoded. The encoding process will take a good amount of time, anywhere from a couple minutes to even an hour or two depending on the size of your video and the processing power of your computer.

Next, select the WebM (vp8) option (see Figure 6-3) to encode the WebM/VP8/Vorbis video format.

Click Convert, and wait for this format to finish encoding.

Finally, select the Theora option (see Figure 6-4) to encode the Ogg/Theora/Vorbis video format.

Click Convert and wait for this video to encode. Now you have all the formats you need for your HTML5 video element.

While Miro Video Converter is extremely easy to use, there are unfortunately no options to customize the output. If you want more control over the video file encoding, you need to use a couple different tools.

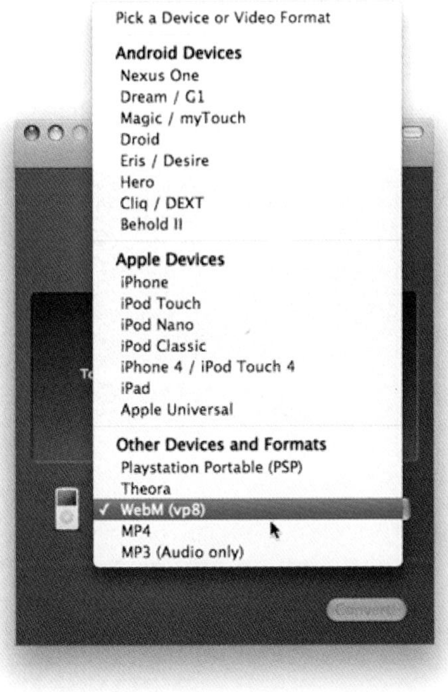

Figure 6-3: Use the WebM (vp8) option to create the WebM video for Chrome, Firefox, and Opera.

Figure 6-4: Use the Theora option to create the Ogg video for older versions of Chrome, Firefox, and Opera.

Fine-tuned MP4 Encoding with Handbrake

MP4/H.264/AAC encoding is easy using a GPL-licensed, open-source video conversion tool called Handbrake. First download and install Handbrake for Mac OSX, Windows or Linux: http://handbrake.fr/.

After Handbrake is installed, open it and select the video file you want to convert. Then navigate to the Presets menu (you may need to click the Toggle Presets button) and select the option for iPhone & iPod Touch as shown in Figure 6-5.

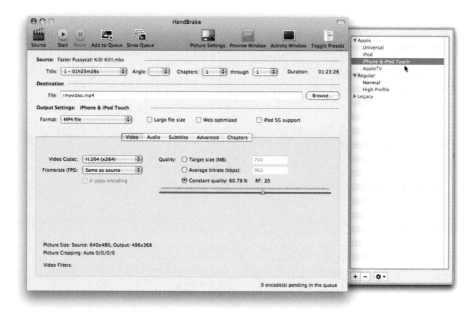

Figure 6-5: Selecting the iPhone & iPod Touch preset preloads most of the options you need.
© Copyright HandBrake Project 2011

This sets the majority of the options you'll need for your MP4, such as the codecs for H.264 and AAC. However there are a few other options you may want to customize:

- It's always a good idea to check the Web Optimized check box (see Figure 6-6) to improve performance.
- To adjust the dimensions of the video, select Picture Settings (see Figure 6-7). In MacOSX this is accessed via a button in the top bar, and in Windows it has its own tab.

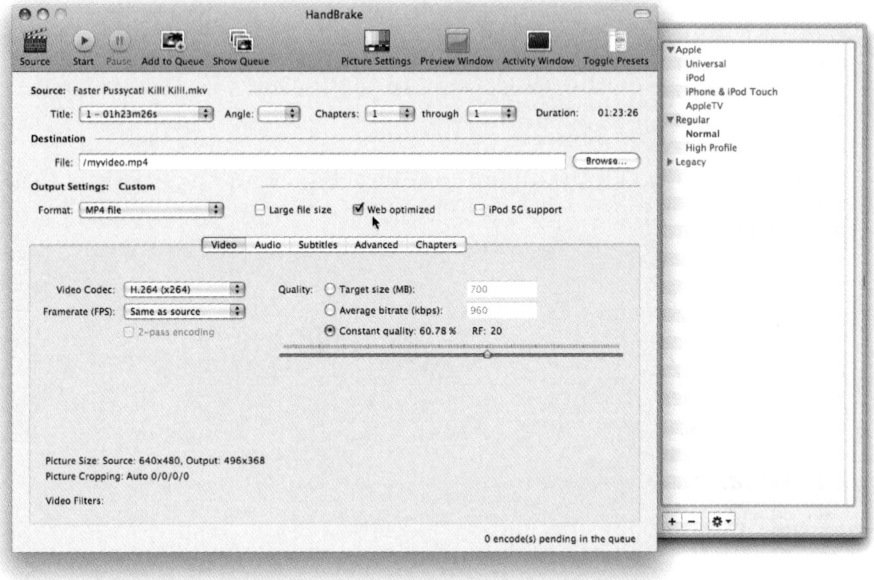

Figure 6-6: Selecting Web Optimized reorders some of the metadata for better streaming.
© Copyright HandBrake Project 2011

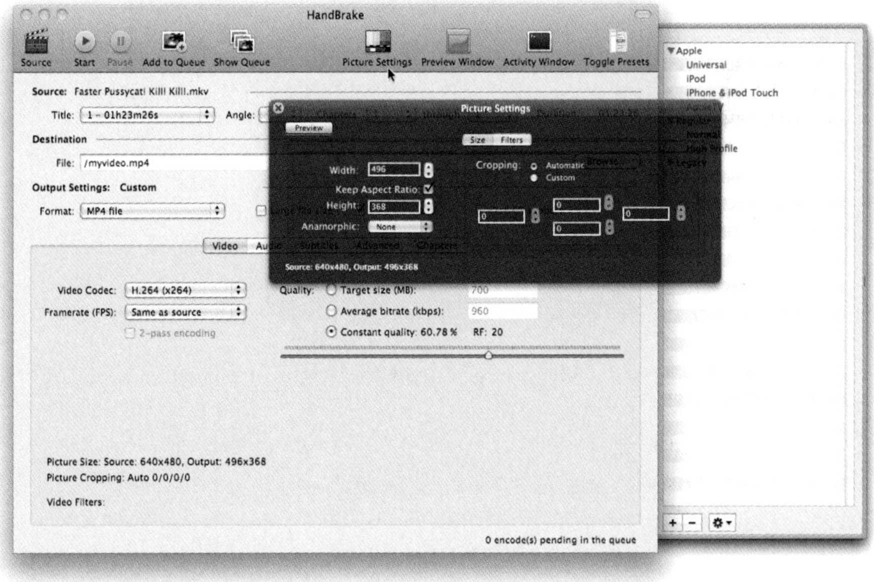

Figure 6-7: Change the video dimensions using the Picture Settings.
© Copyright HandBrake Project 2011

- Adjust the quality of the playback, by setting a target size, average bitrate, or simply a quality percentage. If you use either of the first two, it's a good idea to also check the check box for 2-pass encoding (as well as the subsequent Turbo first pass) as shown in Figure 6-8. 2-pass encoding improves the quality of the video without adding file size, and Turbo first pass speeds up the encoding without a huge loss in quality.

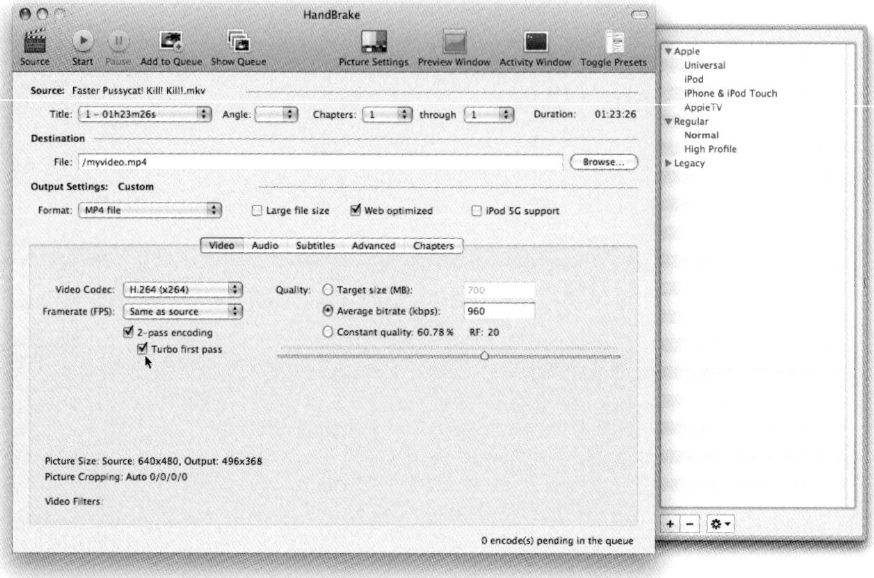

Figure 6-8: Change the video quality, select 2-pass encoding, and then select Turbo first pass.
© Copyright HandBrake Project 2011

Fine-tuned WebM and Ogg Encoding with Firefogg

The GPL-licensed, open-source tool Firefogg is a Firefox extension. You can use it for more customizable encoding of both WebM/VP8/Vorbis and Ogg/Theora/Vorbis video formats.

Get the plugin from www.firefogg.org and install it in Firefox.

After installing the Firefogg plugin, you can begin encoding by again visiting www.firefogg.org. Click the Make web video link, and you'll see a dialog for encoding your video. Don't worry, the video will not be uploaded—all the encoding occurs locally on your machine. Here's what to do:

1. Click the Select File button, shown in Figure 6-9, and navigate to the file you want to encode.

Make Web Video

Select File   >>   Options   >>   Encode   >>   Done

Please select the media file you want to encode

[Select File...]

Figure 6-9: First select the video you want to encode.

2. Select the WebM (VP8/Vorbis) format and the quality preset you want to use from the Presets drop-down, as shown in Figure 6-10.

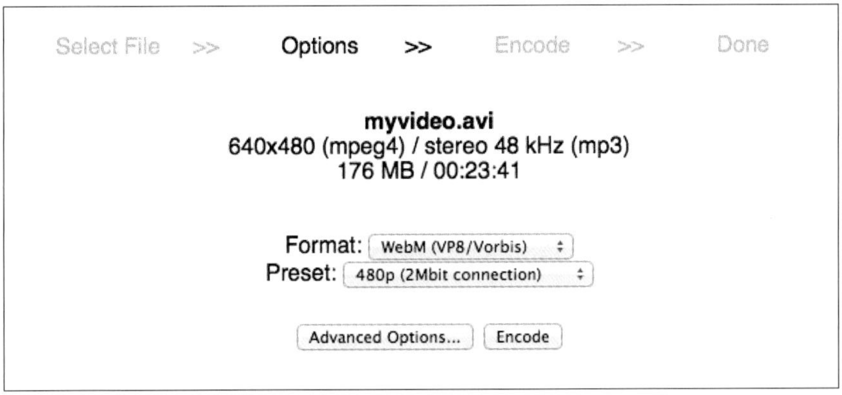

Select File   >>   **Options**   >>   Encode   >>   Done

myvideo.avi
640x480 (mpeg4) / stereo 48 kHz (mp3)
176 MB / 00:23:41

Format: [WebM (VP8/Vorbis) ‡]
Preset: [480p (2Mbit connection) ‡]

[Advanced Options...] [Encode]

Figure 6-10: The Preset drop-down allows you to pick a quality preset.

3. If you would like more fine-grained control, click the Advanced Options button. As shown in Figure 6-11, here you can customize a variety of options about the encoding, from video and audio quality to the dimensions of the playback.

123

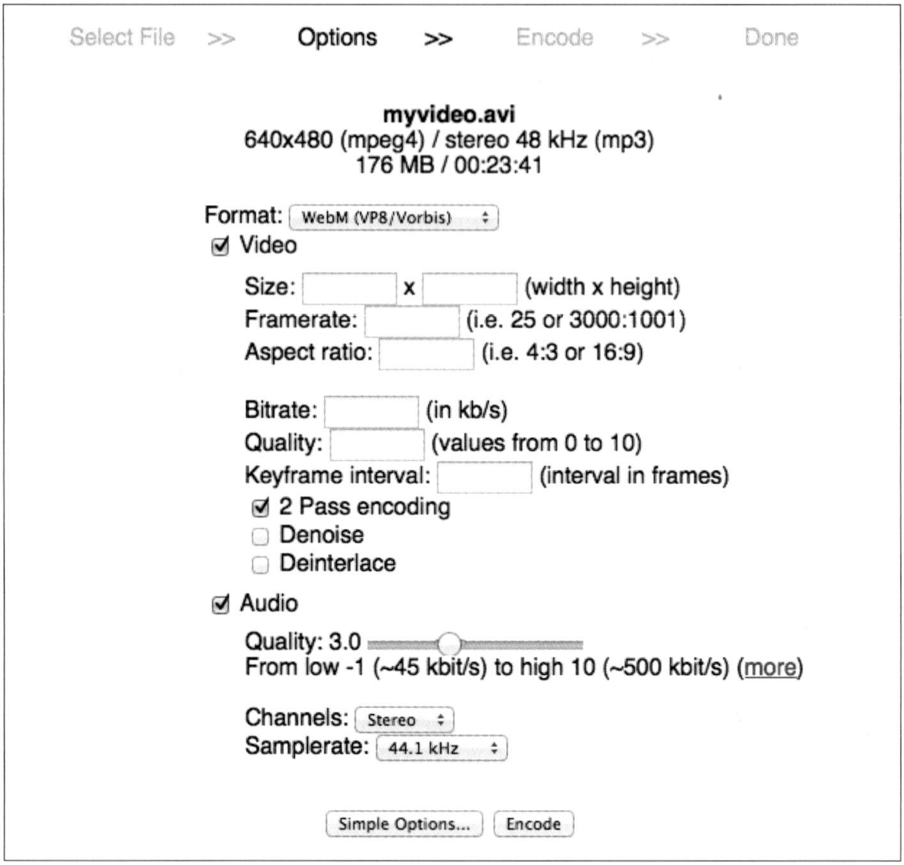

Figure 6-11: Firefogg allows you to customize a variety of options concerning the quality and dimensions of the video.

4. It is also a good idea to check Two pass encoding to improve the quality of the video encoding.

5. Click the Encode button and wait for the file to encode. As you can see in Figure 6-12, encoding can take some time depending on the size of the video and your computer's processing power.

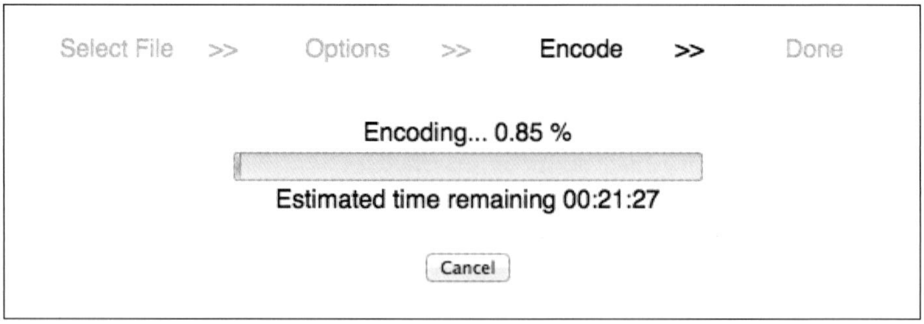

Figure 6-12: You must wait for the file to finish encoding.

Repeat the process to encode the Ogg/Theora/Vorbis format. Note that with the Ogg format you should not use two pass encoding because it doesn't improve quality (and makes the encoding process take longer).

TESTING HTML5 VIDEO ENCODING

If you are fortunate enough to have a production team that will handle the video encoding for you, there is an easy tool that you can use to ensure that the encoding has been performed properly.

MediaInfo is an open-source cross-platform tool that you can install to ascertain the codecs used in a video file. Download MediaInfo here: `http://mediainfo.sourceforge.net/`.

Once you have installed the application, simply drag the video file you want to test into it, and it will display all the information you need to know about the file, as shown in Figure 6-13.

Check the format and codecs against the standards you need, to make sure the file was encoded properly. This is a lot simpler than testing it manually in different browsers and platforms.

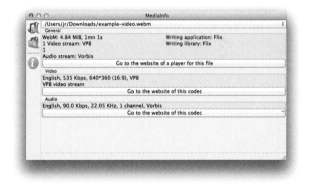

Figure 6-13: MediaInfo provides information about how a video file was encoded.

Figure Credit: MediaInfo.net SARL (France)

125

HTML5 AUDIO

The HTML5 audio element works much like `<video>`. The markup is practically identical, except that there is no need to define width and height values:

```
<audio src="mysong.mp3"></audio>
```

Similarly to video, you can pass the `controls` keyword to add native browser controls to the element:

```
<audio src="mysong.mp3" controls></audio>
```

In addition to `controls`, most of the other HTML5 video options are also available: `autoplay`, `preload`, and `loop`. The only option unavailable in audio is `poster` because there is no visual backup needed.

HTML5 AUDIO FORMATS

Like video, you need to include a variety of audio formats to support different browsers, although the file format landscape for audio is a bit simpler and you need only two formats to get decent market coverage.

In fact, if you are only concerned with WebKit, you can get away with just one format because MP3 is supported by Chrome, Safari, iOS, and Android, as well as IE9.

For cross-browser compatibility, you also need to encode an Ogg Vorbis file for Firefox and Opera. Ogg Vorbis also works in Chrome.

To better understand which formats are supported in which browsers, see Table 6-2.

Table 6-2   MP3 and Ogg Vorbis and Audio Format Support

	Safari	Chrome	iOS	Android	Firefox	IE	Opera
MP3	3.1+	6.0+	3.0+	2.0+		9.0+	
Ogg Vorbis	*	6.0+			3.6+		10.5+

*Not playable natively, but can be played if correct plugin is installed by user.

Including Different Formats in Your Markup

When you have the different formats you want to embed, simply nest both `<source>` elements within your audio element:

```
<audio controls>
  <source src="mysong.mp3"  type="audio/mp3">
  <source src="mysong.ogg" type="audio/ogg">
</audio>
```

The nested source elements work the same as those in a video element. The browser goes through the various options, playing the first format it can support (so make sure to include the MP3 format first, since it is typically smaller than Ogg Vorbis).

Pay attention to the MIME type declaration, and make sure it matches the file format. You can also include a codec in this declaration like you did with the video element earlier, although that is less important when dealing with audio.

ENCODING HTML5 AUDIO

Encoding the audio files needed for HTML5 audio is a bit easier than the video files because you only need one application for both quick and feature-rich conversion. That tool is the Switch Audio Converter, which you can download for Mac OSX or Windows here: www.nch.com.au/switch/.

While Switch is not GPL licensed, it is free for non-commercial use, and the fully licensed version is fairly affordable ($9.99 at the time of this writing). It can convert between a variety of file formats quickly and easily and provides a number of options if you want more control over the encoding.

After installing Switch, simply drag any audio files you want to convert into the application as shown in Figure 6-14.

By default, Switch is set up to export MP3 files, but you can change the output format to Ogg as well (see Figure 6-15).

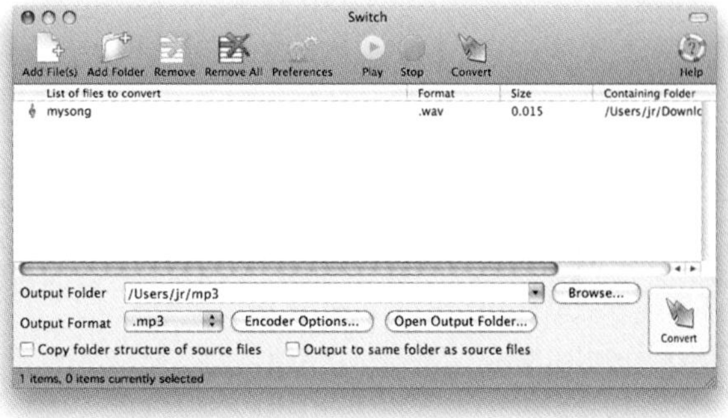

Figure 6-14: Encoding different audio files is easy using Switch Audio Converter.

Figure 6-15: Switch can output a number of different formats, but you'll only need MP3 and Ogg for HTML5 audio.

If you want just basic encoding, simply click Convert at this point (making sure to create both an MP3 and Ogg file). However Switch provides a number of more advanced options as shown in Figure 6-16. Access them by clicking the Encoder Options button.

Although the advanced options are slightly different between MP3 and Ogg encoding, both formats allow you to customize the quality (bitrate) and set to either stereo or mono (mono will reduce file size).

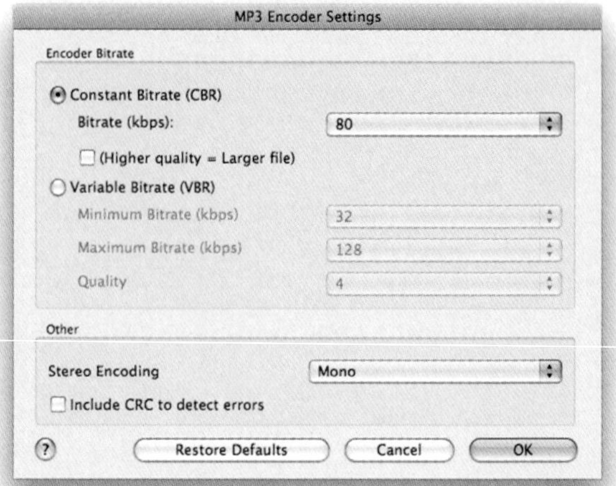

Figure 6-16: Switch allows you to customize a number of settings for the encoding.

HTML5 MEDIA TAGS AND JAVASCRIPT INTERACTION

One of the main advantages of using HTML5 media elements is that you can interface directly with them using JavaScript. This makes more advanced interaction much more intuitive than it is with third-party plugins.

JavaScript enables you to build custom functionality into your video and audio elements. This can be as simple as allowing users to click a video element to start playback, or as complex as creating fully functional controls for your media elements.

BASIC JAVASCRIPT COMMANDS

Before you can interface with your video or audio element, you must first select the node using JavaScript. This is most easily accomplished by first adding an `id` to the element:

```
<video id="my-video" width="480" height="320">
  <source src="myvideo.mp4"  type='video/mp4; codecs="avc1.42E01E, mp4a.40.2"'>
  <source src="myvideo.webm" type='video/webm; codecs="vp8, vorbis"'>
  <source src="myvideo.ogv"  type='video/ogg; codecs="theora, vorbis"'>
</video>
```

Then select the element using `getElementById()`:

```
var myVideo = document.getElementById('my-video');
```

Now you can use this variable to pass any commands you need. For instance, you can play the video using the play() method:

```
myVideo.play();
```

Or pause the video using pause():

```
myVideo.pause();
```

These commands work the same for video and audio elements.

Playing and Pausing the Video on Click

Using these basic commands, you can easily set up a simple player that plays and pauses the video when clicked.

Here's the basic onclick event:

```
myVideo.onclick = function() {
  myVideo.play();
}
```

This script causes the video to start playing after the video element is clicked. While this works well the first time the element is clicked, any subsequent clicks restart the video. Thus it makes more sense to pause the video on subsequent clicks.

One technique to accomplish this might be to set an external variable, for instance playing = false, and then use this to determine whether the video is paused. However, there's a better approach that takes advantage of the native HTML5 attribute paused:

```
myVideo.onclick = function() {
  if ( myVideo.paused ) {
    myVideo.play();
  }
  else {
    myVideo.pause();
  }
}
```

Now when the element is clicked, it will play() the video if it is paused, and pause() it if it is playing. This is a much more robust approach because it works regardless of the initial state of the video (if the autoplay attribute is set, for instance).

129

The onclick event can bind only a single event to an element. You may consider a more robust click handler such as addEventListener() and attachEvent() instead. Although it's a little more complicated, you need to use both to support all browsers.

FLASH BACKUPS FOR HTML5 MEDIA TAGS

While all modern browsers support HTML5 media tags, it is a good idea to provide a fallback solution for older browsers. Fortunately you can easily create a Flash backup for all non-supportive browsers. This backup will only be used in older browsers that do not support open HTML5 standards.

INCLUDING THE FLASH BACKUP

Including the Flash backup on your page is simple—just nest the Flash markup within the video or audio element:

```
<video width="480" height="320" controls>
  <source src="myvideo.mp4"  type='video/mp4; codecs="avc1.42E01E, mp4a.40.2"'>
  <source src="myvideo.webm" type='video/webm; codecs="vp8, vorbis"'>
  <source src="myvideo.ogv"  type='video/ogg; codecs="theora, vorbis"'>

  <object width="480" height="320" type="application/x-shockwave-flash"
    data="myflashbackup.swf">
    <param name="allowfullscreen" value="true" />
    <param name="flashvars" value="" />
    <p>Backup text in case they don't even have Flash Player</p>
  </object>
</video>
```

While this markup is pretty ugly, it won't present any problems to browsers that support HTML5 because the HTML5 video/audio specification states that any children of the video and audio elements be ignored altogether (except, of course, <source> elements). So the object and param elements are ignored in HTML5-enabled browsers and are used to embed the Flash in others.

You can even include fallback markup for browsers that don't support either Flash or HTML5 by nesting this fallback content within the Flash object. You can use this content to provide an error message, or even a link to download the video files directly.

Make sure to use valid XHTML syntax for your Flash embed.

CREATING THE FLASH FILE

There's no need to encode yet another video or audio format for the Flash fallback solution because Flash Player natively supports some of the formats you used in the HTML5 implementation.

For video, Flash Player natively supports the MP4/H.264/AAC video you encoded for Safari and iOS. For audio, Flash Player supports both MP3 and Ogg Vorbis. However Ogg Vorbis support has been introduced more recently, so it is best to stick to MP3.

While HTML5 media tags provide their own controls, you'll need to create these for the Flash solution. Either use the players available within newer releases of Flash, or look to a free script such as Flowplayer (`http://flowplayer.org/`) if you need something more robust and extensible.

SUMMARY

Opting for native HTML5 video and audio support instead of third-party plugins is advantageous for a variety of reasons. Besides being better for performance, native HTML5 media tags can be interfaced directly via JavaScript, meaning that you can easily alter these components without segmenting development efforts.

Additionally, HTML5 media does not depend on the user having installed a particular third party plugin. Some users decide not to install these plugins, and others, such as iPhone and iPad users, cannot install them without hacking their devices. Although some older browsers do not support HTML5, you can still provide a reasonable fallback for older devices. While this does force you to segment development, it is necessary if you want your content accessible by iOS users.

HTML5 video and audio is still very much an emerging standard, and is likely to change in the future. Right now, this means encoding video and audio files in a variety of formats to cover a large enough percentage of the market.

Although the optimal formats may change in the future, it is unlikely that browsers will stop supporting the formats they already use. This means that as browsers evolve, and become less reliant on third party plugins, the HTML5 video and audio support you incorporate today will still be effective into the distant future.

7

THE CANVAS ELEMENT

ARGUABLY THE MOST powerful addition to HTML5, the canvas element allows you to render visual data like never before. Using canvas, not only can you draw a wide variety of shapes and lines, but you can also transform and animate these shapes easily. Canvas also offers a number of more advanced features, from native 3D support to physics support using simple libraries, that you can leverage.

Canvas is so robust that you can use it to create rich applications directly in the browser. No longer do you need to rely on third-party plugins like Flash to build visually stunning interfaces and games.

In this chapter, you learn the basics of canvas elements, and how to draw simple shapes such as rectangles, circles, and curves. You then learn how to style these elements, both with native styling techniques and using your own images.

You also learn how to manipulate your shapes using basic transforms such as rotation and scaling, as well as how to animate canvas elements. You then go beyond basic animations to learn how to incorporate more advanced features such as physics and 3D effects.

Finally, you see a variety of impressive applications built with canvas, that I hope will inspire you to build your own rich canvas apps.

THE BASICS OF CANVAS

The first step to using canvas is including a canvas element in your markup:

```
<canvas id="mycanvas" width="200" height="150"></canvas>
```

The basic canvas syntax is simple. You define a `width` and `height` (which you can also do in CSS), as well as an `id`. The `id` is important because the majority of canvas involves interfacing with the element using JavaScript.

For non-supportive browsers, you can include fallback content within the canvas element:

```
<canvas id="mycanvas" width="200" height="150"><p>Fallback content</p></canvas>
```

The fallback content is displayed in browsers that do not support canvas. Keep in mind that older versions of Safari display the fallback content in addition to the canvas, so you may want to take steps to hide this content from Safari (using CSS that only applies to Safari) if supporting older versions is important.

DRAWING BASIC SHAPES

Now that you have your basic canvas element, it's time to start drawing. Here is where the markup stops—from now on you interface with the element using JavaScript. Select your element in the DOM:

```
var canvas = document.getElementById('mycanvas');
```

Then specify that it is a two-dimensional canvas (don't worry, you'll learn about 3D canvas later in this chapter):

```
var c = canvas.getContext('2d');
```

This method throws errors in any browsers that don't support canvas, so always check if `getContext()` is available before scripting the canvas:

```
var canvas = document.getElementById('mycanvas');

if ( canvas.getContext) {
    var ctx = canvas.getContext('2d');

    // additional canvas functionality goes here
}
```

> Make sure that this script occurs after the canvas element is loaded on the page. Either use an `onLoad` event, or place this script after the canvas element in your markup (for example at the end of your document, just above the `</body>`).

134

Drawing Rectangles

You can begin drawing two dimensional shapes on your canvas by referencing the `ctx` variable you set with `getContext()`.

Drawing shapes in canvas requires two steps: first you define the color of the object, and then you draw it:

```
var canvas = document.getElementById('mycanvas');

if ( canvas.getContext) {
    var ctx = canvas.getContext('2d');

    ctx.fillStyle = '#f60';
    ctx.fillRect(10, 15, 100, 50);
}
```

Here the `fillStyle` is set to orange using the hex shorthand value `#f60`. You can pass a variety of color values into `fillStyle`; RGB, RGBa, and HSL all work, and you can even use color keywords such as `'green'`, `'blue'`, and `'red'`.

Next `fillRect` draws a rectangle. The four values define the location and dimensions of your rectangle—horizontal position, vertical position, width and height. So `fillRect(10, 15, 100, 50)`, defines a 100×50 rectangle that is placed 10 pixels from the left and 15 pixels from the top of your canvas element, as shown in Figure 7-1.

Figure 7-1: A rectangle drawn with `fillRect(10, 15, 100, 50)`

A solid rectangle was drawn, but there are a couple other options. First you can use `strokeRect` to draw a rectangle outline:

```
ctx.strokeStyle = '#17b';
ctx.strokeRect(70, 30, 120, 80);
```

The stroke color is defined using `strokeStyle`, and `strokeRect` draws the outline. Note that the elements you draw in canvas stack based on the order in which you render them. So if you first draw the filled rectangle, and then the stroked rectangle, the latter will be on top as shown in Figure 7-2.

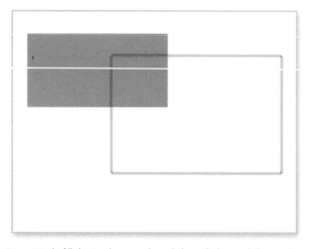

Figure 7-2: The filled rectangle appears beneath the stroked rectangle because it was rendered first.

You can also use `clearRect`, which makes anything behind it transparent:

```
ctx.clearRect(50, 25, 30, 30);
```

The order in which you render the rectangles is important for `clearRect` as well because it only clears the elements that are behind it. For instance, if you draw the `clearRect` after the `fillRect` but before the `strokeRect`, it clears only the `fillRect` as shown in Figure 7-3.

You may be wondering about the importance of `clearRect` because in this example it is the same as rendering a white `fillRect`. However, it becomes more important as your canvas becomes more complex because the canvas can have not only a background image, but also other elements that can be visible in the holes created by `clearRect`.

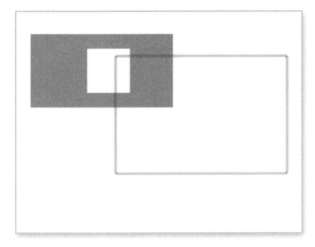

Figure 7-3: `clearRect` makes everything behind it transparent. Here the `clearRect` is rendered after the `fillRect` but before the `strokeRect`.

Drawing Lines, Triangles and Other Polygons

While drawing rectangles can be accomplished with a few simple commands, you need some additional tools to draw more complex shapes. You need to learn how to draw paths. For this you have to master a few new commands: `beginPath()`, `moveTo()`, `lineTo()`, and `fill()`. For instance, you can use these commands to draw a simple triangle:

```
ctx.beginPath();
ctx.moveTo(20, 25);
ctx.lineTo(140, 25);
ctx.lineTo(80, 90);
ctx.fill();
```

`beginPath()` starts the path, and `moveTo()` sets the starting point `(20, 25)`. This means the shape starts 20 pixels from the top and 25 pixels from the left of the canvas element.

`lineTo()` draws two lines: one to `(140, 25)` and then another to `(80, 90)`. Finally the shape is filled in by the `fill()` method. Even though only two lines are drawn, this renders a triangle. There's no need to draw a third line back to `(20, 25)` because `fill()` closes the space automatically.

By default this renders a black triangle as shown in Figure 7-4, but you can change the color using the same `fillStyle` technique you used when drawing rectangles.

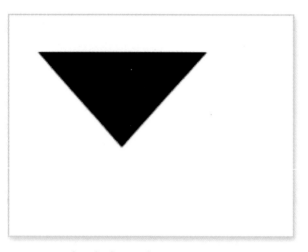

Figure 7-4: A triangle rendered using paths

You can also render outlined shapes by using `stroke()` instead of `fill()`:

```
ctx.beginPath();
ctx.moveTo(20, 25);
ctx.lineTo(140, 25);
ctx.lineTo(80, 90);
ctx.stroke();
```

However, `stroke()` doesn't draw in the third line in this shape, and instead only renders the two lines you specified, as shown in Figure 7-5.

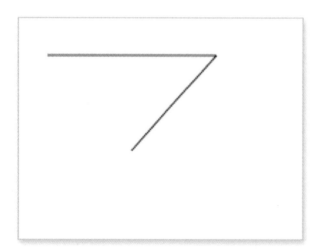

Figure 7-5: This stroked path is left open.

There are a couple commands you can use to draw the third line to close this triangle. You could add a third `lineTo()` command, pointing back to the starting point:

```
ctx.lineTo(20, 25);
```

However, `closePath()` is an easier built-in command you can use to close it off automatically:

```
ctx.beginPath();
ctx.moveTo(20, 25);
ctx.lineTo(140, 25);
ctx.lineTo(80, 90);
ctx.closePath();
ctx.stroke();
```

`closePath()` completes the last line in the triangle, as shown in Figure 7-6.

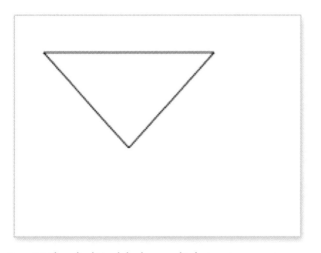

Figure 7-6: The outlined triangle has been completed using `closePath()`.

As with `fill()` earlier, this renders a black stroke by default, which you can change by setting the `strokeStyle`.

In addition to creating triangles, you can use this technique to draw polygons with any number of sides: quadrilaterals, pentagons, hexagons, stars, and so on.

Drawing Arcs and Circles

The next tool to add to your canvas arsenal is the arc, which you can use to create circles and semicircles. Drawing arcs leverages some of the same tools you used when drawing straight lines, such as `beginPath()`, `stroke()`, and `fill()`:

```
ctx.beginPath();
ctx.arc(80, 75, 50, 0, 2 * Math.PI);
ctx.stroke();
```

The syntax for `arc()` may look a bit complicated at first glance, but it's actually fairly simple.

The first two values are the coordinates for the center of the circle, in this case 80 pixels from the left and 75 pixels from the top of the canvas element. The next value is the radius of the circle (50 pixels), and the final two values are the starting and ending point of the arc in radians.

Don't worry if you don't remember arc geometry; radians are easy. There are 2Π radians in a complete circle, which is why this example uses 2 * Math.PI to draw a full circle as shown in Figure 7-7. It is important to use the Math.PI value, rather than an approximation such as 3.14, which may cause a gap in your circle.

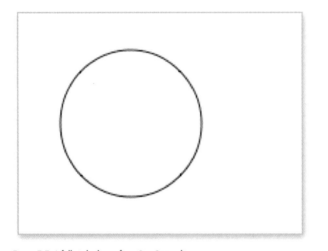

Figure 7-7: A full circle drawn from 0 to 2Π radians

To draw a half circle, you need only have 1Π radians, so use the values 0 and Math.PI:

```
ctx.arc(80, 75, 50, 0, Math.PI);
```

This draws a half circle from 0 (the right side) to Π (the left side) as shown in Figure 7-8. While the starting point doesn't matter as much with a full circle, you'll need more control when drawing semi-circles. For instance, a semicircle from 0 to Π is very different from one drawn from Π /2 to 3Π /2, even though both circles span 1Π radians:

```
ctx.arc(80, 75, 50, Math.PI / 2, 3 * Math.PI / 2);
```

This arc renders from the bottom to the top as shown in Figure 7-9.

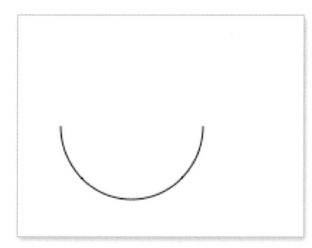

Figure 7-8: A semicircle drawn from 0 to ∏ radians

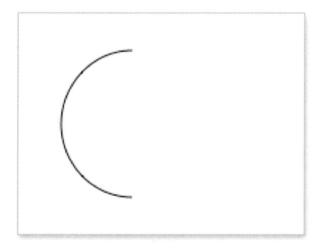

Figure 7-9: A semicircle drawn from ∏ /2 to 3∏ /2 radians

The arcs you've drawn here have rendered clockwise, but canvas can render counterclockwise arcs as well. To draw a counterclockwise arc, simply pass an additional value of `true` at the end of the `arc()` method:

```
ctx.arc(80, 75, 50, Math.PI / 2, 3 * Math.PI / 2 , true);
```

Even though this arc uses the same starting and ending point, it renders a very different curve as shown in Figure 7-10.

Figure 7-10: A semi-circle drawn counterclockwise from Π /2 to 3Π /2 radians

DRAWING COMPLEX SHAPES

In addition to basic polygons and circles, you can use canvas to render a wide variety of more complicated shapes. Between more precise controls over path curvature and the capability to create compound shapes, canvas provides the tools you need to draw any shape you can imagine.

Drawing Complex Curves

Canvas enables you to draw more complex curves, which allow you to draw any variety of shapes you want. There are two methods you can use for more complex curves: `quadraticCurveTo()` and `bezierCurveTo()`. Both of these methods work similarly to `lineTo()`, except that they draw a curved path to a given point.

The simpler of the two, `quadraticCurveTo()`, accepts four arguments:

```
ctx.quadraticCurveTo(25, 50, 60, 40);
```

The first two values are the *x* and *y* coordinates of the control point, which adjusts how curvy the line is. The second two values are the coordinates of the point that you want to draw the line to. Look at Figure 7-11 to better understand the control point in a quadratic curve.

Bezier curves provide more fine-tuned control by allowing you to define two control points:

```
ctx.bezierCurveTo(25, 50, 40, 100, 60, 40);
```

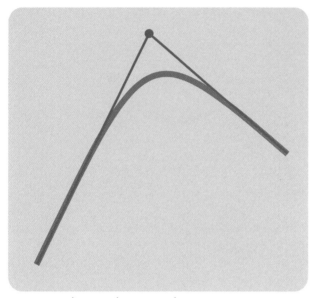

Figure 7-11: Quadratic curves have one control point.

The first two values are the coordinates of the first control point, the second two are the coordinates of the second control point, and the last two values are the coordinates of the point you want to draw the line to. Figure 7-12 shows a Bezier curve with two control points.

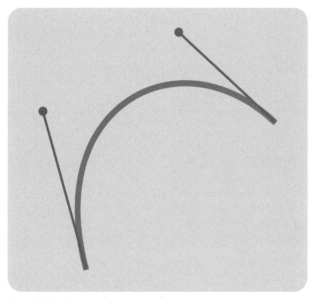

Figure 7-12: Bezier curves have two control points.

More About moveTo()

In the previous examples, you used moveTo() to change the starting point of your shapes in canvas. But that command is also very useful in building compound shapes.

When used in a series of path commands, moveTo() is basically like picking up the pen and moving it to a new location. Without moveTo(), a path is drawn between those coordinates. For instance, try drawing two circles without moveTo():

```
ctx.beginPath();
ctx.arc(50, 50, 20, 0, 2 * Math.PI);
ctx.arc(100, 100, 20, 0, 2 * Math.PI);
ctx.stroke();
```

This draws the two circles, but also includes a line from the ending point of the first arc to the origin of the second as shown in Figure 7-13.

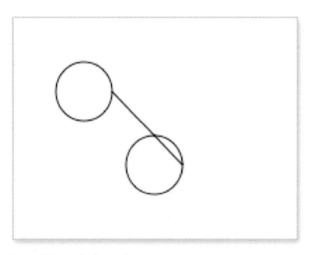

Figure 7-13: Two circles drawn without moveTo()

You can use moveTo() to move the next point in the path to line up with the starting point of the second circle:

```
ctx.beginPath();
ctx.arc(50, 50, 20, 0, 2 * Math.PI);
ctx.moveTo(120, 100);
ctx.arc(100, 100, 20, 0, 2 * Math.PI);
ctx.stroke();
```

This draws the two circles without the line in between as shown in Figure 7-14.

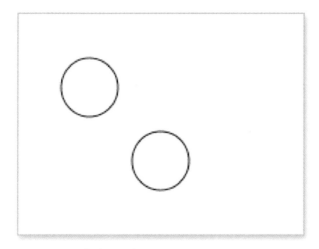

Figure 7-14: Two circles drawn with `moveTo()`

This is a little odd when working with arcs because you have to move the point to line up with the starting point of the arc (the starting point of this arc is on the right edge, so you have to use 120 for the x value, which is the center point of 100 pixels plus the 20-pixel radius). But it is important to use the correct coordinates with `moveTo()`, or else a line is drawn from whichever new point you set to the starting point of the second circle.

> *If you would like to avoid `moveTo()`, you could create the two circles separately, initiating each with its own `beginPath()`. However, there are certain advantages to including both in the same path, such as more concise code and the ability to control stroke and fill in a single place.*

Drawing Compound Shapes

While you might be annoyed that you need to use JavaScript to interface with the canvas element, there are some considerable advantages, one of which is that you can create custom JavaScript functions to generate more complex shapes. Are you always drawing a circle on top of a triangle? Then wrap that in a custom function:

```
function drawIceCreamCone(ctx, x, y, width, height) {
    var radius = width / 2;

    ctx.beginPath();
    ctx.arc(x + radius, y + radius, radius, 0, 2 * Math.PI);
    ctx.moveTo(x, y + width);
    ctx.lineTo(x + width, y + width);
    ctx.lineTo(x + radius, y + height);
    ctx.fill();
}
```

The specific code here is unimportant. What matters is that you can pass in a number of variables, such as the `ctx` object, the *x* and *y* starting points and the dimensions. Now whenever you want to draw this shape, you can simply call this function:

```
drawIceCreamCone(ctx, 30, 15, 40, 120);
```

This draws the complex shape shown in Figure 7-15.

Figure 7-15: A complex shape drawn with a custom function

You can pass any information you need into the variables of your function. In addition to offsets and dimensions, you may want to include styling information, such as the fill or stroke color.

Custom functions can be used to create a variety of useful shapes. Here's a function that draws rounded rectangles:

```
function drawRoundedRectangle(ctx, x, y, width, height, radius, color) {
    ctx.beginPath();
    ctx.moveTo(x, y + radius);
    ctx.lineTo(x, y + height - radius);
    ctx.quadraticCurveTo(x, y + height, x + radius, y + height);
    ctx.lineTo(x + width - radius, y + height);
    ctx.quadraticCurveTo(x + width, y + height, x + width, y + height - radius);
    ctx.lineTo(x + width, y + radius);
    ctx.quadraticCurveTo(x + width, y, x + width - radius, y);
    ctx.lineTo(x + radius, y);
    ctx.quadraticCurveTo(x, y, x, y + radius);
    ctx.fillStyle = color;
    ctx.fill();
}
```

STYLING THE CANVAS

`stroke()` and `fill()` are just the beginning when it comes to the wide variety of styling controls available in canvas. The canvas element is very versatile, allowing you to style elements using gradients, patterns, and even your own images and text. You also can add visual effects such as line styles and drop shadows.

These advanced styling techniques enable you to render even more stunning visual elements using canvas.

> *If you're a Mac user, there's a graphics program called Opacity that allows you to draw elements in a Photoshop-like GUI, and export HTML5 canvas code. For more information visit: `http://likethought.com/opacity/`. However, keep in mind that WYSIWYG-generated code is rarely as good as code written by hand.*

USING IMAGES

You can draw a wide variety of shapes in canvas but it is preferable to include an external image such as a photograph. Canvas not only allows you to use images, but also provides a variety of controls to customize their rendering.

Including Images

The first step to using images in canvas is to create a reference to the image in JavaScript. You can accomplish that in a number of ways, but the easiest is to simply create a new image and reference an external file:

```
var img = new Image();
img.src = 'myimage.jpg';
```

This reference pulls the image from the given URL into JavaScript. However, downloading the image takes time, so you will not be able to use it immediately in canvas. To avoid any errors related to the file loading, make sure to use an `onload` event for any canvas scripting:

```
var img = new Image();
img.src = 'myimage.jpg';

img.onload = function() {
    // canvas stuff in here
}
```

In addition to the download time, using an external image also has an additional performance drawback, which is that it requires an HTTP request. You can get around the HTTP request by using a data URI and raw image data:

```
var img = new Image();
img.src = 'data:image/png;base64,iVBORw0KGgoAA6 ... yQErkJggg==';
```

```
img.onload = function() {
    // canvas stuff in here
}
```

The data URI embeds the raw image data directly into the JavaScript, much like you used data URIs with CSS in Chapter 3. The same performance rules apply: the data URI speeds up your app if it references an image that is definitely going to be seen by the user, and in other situations performance may degrade because the user must download the image data regardless of whether the image is used.

Even with the data URI it is important to use the `onload` function, or you may encounter JavaScript errors.

If the image you want to use in canvas already exists on the page, you can save a lot of time by referencing that image. You simply need to get the DOM reference of the image; for instance:

```
var img = document.getElementById('onpage-image');
```

In addition to using `document.getElementById()`, you can also access on-page images using `document.getElementsByTagName('img')` or the `document.images` object because any browser that supports canvas also supports these JavaScript calls.

Remember, even when using an on-page image, you need to use the `onload` function in case the image has not yet downloaded.

Rendering Images

Now that you have a reference to your image, you can render it in your canvas element using `drawImage()`:

```
img.onload = function() {
    ctx.drawImage(img, 50, 25);
}
```

The basic `drawImage()` command accepts three arguments: the image reference and then the *x* and *y* coordinates of where you want to place this image. In this example, the image is placed 50 pixels from the left and 25 pixels from the top of the canvas element.

By default the image renders at its native dimensions, but you can also scale the image by passing extra arguments to `drawImage()`:

```
img.onload = function() {
    ctx.drawImage(img, 50, 25, 75, 50);
}
```

Here the last two arguments adjust the image's width and height to 75 pixels and 50 pixels, respectively.

Slicing Images

You can even crop the image by passing several more arguments to the `drawImage()` method:

```
img.onload = function() {
    ctx.drawImage(img, 10, 15, 50, 60, 50, 25, 75, 50);
}
```

The first four arguments after the image reference define how to slice the original image. The first two (`10` and `15`) define the coordinates of where to start the slice, and the second two define the dimensions of the slice. So in this example, a 50 × 60-pixel section would be cut out of the image starting 10 pixels from the left and 15 pixels from the top.

The last four values then define how to place the sliced image in the canvas, starting with the *x* and *y* coordinates and ending with the width and height of the scaled image. In this example, the sliced image would be placed 50 pixels from the left and 25 pixels from the top, and then also stretched to 75 × 50.

To get a better understanding of how image slicing works, take a look at Figure 7-16.

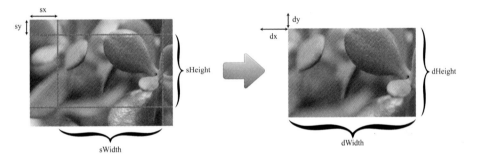

Figure 7-16: Image slicing in canvas uses `drawImage(img, sx, sy, sWidth, sHeight, dx, dy, dWidth, dHeight)`.

FILL AND STROKE STYLES

When building basic shapes you learned how to add colors to fills and strokes using `fillStyle` and `strokeStyle`. But canvas provides a variety of additional styling options you can leverage to create much more visually pleasing elements.

Linear Gradients

One technique you can use for richer visual elements is adding linear gradients. Applying a gradient in canvas involves two steps: create the gradient using `createLinearGradient()` and then add color stops using `addColorStop()`.

Gradients and color stops in canvas work similarly to those in CSS3, which you learned about in Chapter 3.

The create syntax for linear gradients, accepts the coordinates of the starting and ending points:

```
var myGradient = ctx.createLinearGradient(0, 0, 100, 100);
```

This defines a gradient starting from (0, 0) to (100, 100). These coordinates are relative to the canvas, not the element you apply the gradient to, so if you want the gradient to start at the top-left corner of an element that is positioned 25 pixels from the left and 25 pixels from the top of your canvas, you'll want to change the starting point to (25, 25).

It's important to define the gradient as a variable because you will use the variable to add color stops:

```
var myGradient = ctx.createLinearGradient(0, 0, 100, 100);
myGradient.addColorStop(0, '#FFF');
myGradient.addColorStop(1, '#000');
```

The first argument in `addColorStop()` accepts a number between 0 and 1, so this adds two color stops, one at 0% and another at 100%. These percentages refer to the distance along the gradient you defined earlier, so 0% is at the starting point (0, 0), and 100% is at the ending point (100, 100), as shown in Figure 7-17.

Figure 7-17: A linear gradient has been applied to a rectangle.

You can add any number of color stops you want; for instance, to add another color stop at 50%:

```
myGradient.addColorStop(0.5, '#F60');
```

> Color stops can accept any number of color values: hex, RGB, RGBa, HSL, HSLa, and even HTML and X11 color keywords.

Finally, after you add all your color stops, attach your gradient to either the `fillStyle` or `strokeStyle`:

```
ctx.fillStyle = myGradient;
```

This works just like the color values you used before, except with gradients you pass the variable you defined when creating the gradient.

Radial Gradients

Radial gradients work basically the same way as linear gradients. First you define the gradient using createRadialGradient(), and then you add color stops.

However, with radial gradients, you also have to define the radius of both starting and ending points:

```
var myGradient = ctx.createRadialGradient(75, 75, 0, 75, 75, 60);
```

This defines the two starting and ending points at (75, 75), with the starting point having a radius of 0 pixels and the ending point having a radius of 60 pixels. In general, you want to keep the coordinates of your starting and ending points either the same or close to one another; otherwise your gradients start looking really funky.

Finally, add your color stops and then set the radial gradient to your fill or stroke style:

```
var myGradient = ctx.createRadialGradient(75, 75, 0, 75, 75, 60);
myGradient.addColorStop(0, '#FFF');
myGradient.addColorStop(1, '#000');

ctx.fillStyle = myGradient;
```

This creates a circular white-to-black gradient as shown in Figure 7-18.

Figure 7-18: A radial gradient has been applied to a rectangle.

151

Patterns

In addition to gradients, you can also style canvas elements using patterns made from your own custom images. While the basic syntax for creating patterns is simple, it is made more complicated by the use of images. Just like when you added images directly into canvas, you need to wait for the image to load when creating a pattern:

```
var img = new Image();
img.src = 'myimage.jpg';

img.onload = function() {
    // apply the pattern here
}
```

> *Make sure to use an onload event regardless of whether you're using an external image or a data URI.*

After you've loaded your image, build a pattern using `createPattern()`:

```
var img = new Image();
img.src = 'myimage.jpg';

img.onload = function() {
    var myPattern = ctx.createPattern(img, 'repeat');

    ctx.fillStyle = myPattern;

    ctx.fillRect(25, 25, 100, 100);
}
```

`createPattern()` accepts two arguments: the reference for your image, and whether it repeats. The repeat argument accepts the same arguments as `background-repeat` in CSS: `repeat`, `repeat-x`, `repeat-y`, and `no-repeat`.

Once you've created the pattern, you can then set it to your `fillStyle` or `strokeStyle`.

Unlike gradients, `createPattern()` does not require a lot of extra information, so you can skip the variable if you want more concise code (and don't plan on reusing the pattern):

```
ctx.fillStyle = ctx.createPattern(img, 'repeat');
```

The most obvious application of `createPattern()` is to render a shape with a repeating background pattern. However, another creative use of this method involves rendering images as different shapes.

For instance, if you want a circular photo as shown in Figure 7-19, you could simply apply a non-repeating gradient to an arc:

```
ctx.fillStyle = ctx.createPattern(img, 'no-repeat');

ctx.beginPath();
ctx.arc(75, 75, 50, 0, 2 * Math.PI);
ctx.fill();
```

You can use this technique with any shapes you want: stars, triangles, and so forth. Just make sure that the image is large enough to cover the entire area of your shape because there is no way to scale the image when creating a pattern. (Actually, because your image needs to cover the entire shape, the `'no-repeat'` is inconsequential.)

Figure 7-19: A circular photo created using an arc and a non-repeating pattern

LINE STYLES

In addition to applying colors, gradients and patterns to stroke styles, canvas also provides control over the size and shape of the line itself.

Line Width

By default, any strokes you apply to canvas elements will be 1 pixel wide. But you can change that by setting the `lineWidth` value:

```
ctx.lineWidth = 5;
```

This makes any strokes 5 pixels wide. When working with `lineWidth`, pay attention to the crispness of your lines. An even value for the `lineWidth` tends to make straight horizontal and vertical lines look blurry because they're rendered with half-pixels. Opt for an odd `lineWidth` value, and your lines may appear sharper.

Line Caps

Canvas also provides control over how the caps at the end of the line are rendered. While that doesn't make a difference for continuous shapes, it is a nice way to add a visual touch to any lines with endpoints.

For instance, you can specify round endpoints using `lineCap`:

```
ctx.lineCap = 'round';
```

This creates softer, rounded endpoints for any stroke. `lineCap` also accepts two other values: `butt` and `square`. Both of these create square endpoints; `butt`, the default value, stops the line right at the end of the stroke, while `square` adds a small square cap on the end, as shown in Figure 7-20.

Butt

Round

Square

Figure 7-20: The difference between `butt`, `round`, and `square` line caps

Line Joins

In addition to styling endpoints, you can control how the corners of your lines render. For instance, you can create more rounded corners using `lineJoin`:

```
ctx.lineJoin = 'round';
```

The default value for `lineJoin` is `miter`, which creates hard, angular corners. But you can also set it to `bevel`, which rounds the corners in a less angular fashion, sort of in between `round` and `miter`. The different line join styles are shown in Figure 7-21.

Miter Limits

When you use mitered line joins, the corners can start to look weird with really sharp angles because the edges must be extended far outside of the stroke before they meet and create a hard corner.

154

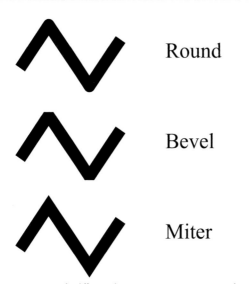

Round

Bevel

Miter

Figure 7-21: The difference between round, bevel, and miter line joins

You can control this by setting the miterLimit:

```
ctx.miterLimit = 10;
```

The miterLimit property adjusts how far outside of the path a miter can extend. Then if the angle is too sharp, a beveled join is rendered instead as shown in Figure 7-22.

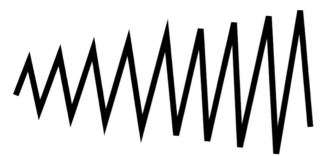

Figure 7-22: Once the angles get too sharp, beveled joins are used because of the miterLimit.

SHADOWS

You can add drop shadows to canvas elements by setting a few values. At a minimum, you need to set two values: `shadowBlur` and `shadowColor`:

```
ctx.shadowBlur = 7;
ctx.shadowColor = 'rgba(0, 0, 0, .7)';
```

`shadowBlur` defines the softness of the shadow in pixels, similar to the blur value in CSS3 `box-shadow` and `text-shadow`. The `shadowColor` value defines the color of the shadow. Although this can accept any of the color values you've used elsewhere in canvas, it's a good idea to use an RGBa or HSLa to soften the shadow with a little transparency. (See Figure 7-23.)

Figure 7-23: A canvas drop shadow has been applied to this circle.

If you don't set any other values, the drop shadow renders directly beneath the element as shown in Figure 7-23. You can adjust its placement using `shadowOffsetX` and `shadowOffsetY`:

```
ctx.shadowBlur = 7;
ctx.shadowColor = 'rgba(0, 0, 0, .7)';
ctx.shadowOffsetX = 1;
ctx.shadowOffsetY = 3;
```

Here the shadow renders 1 pixel to the right and 3 pixels down from the element, as shown in Figure 7-24.

USING TEXT

The canvas element also allows you to add text, with a variety of styling options. To draw text to the canvas, use the `fillText()` method:

```
ctx.fillText('Smashing WebKit', 10, 50);
```

The `fillText()` method accepts three arguments: the text you want to add, and the x and y coordinates of where you want to place the text. In this example, the words "Smashing WebKit" will be printed 10 pixels from the left and 50 pixels from the top of the canvas origin.

Figure 7-24: This shadow has been offset using `shadowOffsetX` and `shadowOffsetY`.

Styling the Text

Adjusting the font styling is easy; you just define any styles you want ahead of time:

```
ctx.font = 'bold 12px Helvetica';
ctx.fillText('Smashing WebKit', 10, 50);
```

The `font` declaration can accept any of the definitions available for fonts in CSS: bold, italic, font sizes, and font families. You can even use custom fonts that you've embedded with `@font-face`, which you learned about in Chapter 3. However, when using custom fonts, make sure that the font is loaded before drawing to the canvas.

Additionally, you can use any of the font size measurements available in CSS, even relative font sizes like `200%` and `1.5em` (which is calculated based on the CSS font size of the canvas element).

Positioning the Text

While styling the font is fairly straightforward, positioning the text is a little bit different from what you might be used to in CSS.

In the preceding example, the text is placed 10 pixels from the left and 50 pixels from the top of the canvas origin. By default, this means that the bottom left corner of the text will be at this position. However, you can easily adjust how the text is positioned around these coordinates.

To adjust the horizontal positioning, use the `textAlign` property. It accepts a number of values, such as `left`, `right`, and `center`.

Use the `textBaseline` property to adjust the vertical positioning. It can be set to a number of values, such as `top`, `bottom`, and `middle`.

By default `textAlign` is set to `left` and `textBaseline` is set to `bottom`. But if you want to align your text's top-right corner to the coordinates in `fillText()`,write:

```
ctx.textAlign = 'right';
ctx.textBaseline = 'top';
ctx.fillText('Smashing WebKit', 10, 50);
```

TRANSFORMATIONS

Canvas transformations work similarly to CSS3 transformations, in that they provide methods to translate, rotate, scale, and transform. The main difference is that instead of transforming a given element, you transform the canvas itself. This transformation does not affect the elements that have already been drawn to the canvas, but applies to any that are drawn after the transformation occurs. For instance, if you apply a rotation to your canvas, any elements already on the canvas stay put, and any elements you draw later are rotated.

Although this may not be intuitive, you can think about it as transforming the canvas origin. For instance, if you apply a translation that moves the canvas 50 pixels to the right, any elements you draw afterward begin at an origin that is 50 pixels to the right of the original canvas origin.

TRANSLATIONS

The simplest type of canvas transformation is the translation, which moves the canvas a set number of pixels. `translate()` accepts both an x and y value. To move the canvas 50 pixels to the right and 100 pixels down, you can write:

```
ctx.translate(50, 100);
```

This moves the canvas, so that subsequent drawing occurs with the origin 50 pixels to the right and 100 pixels down from the original canvas origin. Although you could simply change the position of your canvas drawings, `translate()` is useful for repositioning a number of drawings without having to adjust each of their positions manually.

> *Translations become crucial when combined with other canvas transformations because they allow you to control the origin of these changes.*

ROTATIONS

The rotation type of canvas transformation allows you to rotate the canvas at any angle. `rotate()` accepts a degree measurement in radians, which means that you'll probably want to take advantage of the `Math.PI` value you used earlier for drawing arcs:

```
ctx.rotate(Math.PI / 4);
```

This rotates the canvas 45° because 45° is equivalent to π/4 radians.

Although it is a bit of a hassle, converting degrees to radians isn't overly difficult as demonstrated in Figure 7-25. You just have to remember that there are 2Π radians in 360°, then multiply 2Π whatever percentage of 360° you want to rotate. For instance, 45° is 1/8 of a full circle because 45 ÷ 360 = 1/8. So multiply 2Π by 1/8 and you get Π /4.

$$\text{Radians} \; = \; 2\pi \bullet \frac{\text{degrees}}{360}$$

Figure 7-25: Formula for converting degrees into radians

With `rotate()`, the rotation always occurs around the origin of the canvas, which is by default the top-left corner. To rotate around another point in the canvas, you need to apply a translation before applying your rotation:

```
ctx.translate(50, 20);
ctx.rotate(Math.PI / 4);
```

This rotation occurs around an origin that is 50 pixels to the right and 20 pixels down from the original canvas origin. When adjusting the origin, make sure to do the translation first, or it produces unexpected results (since the translation occurs in the rotated canvas).

SCALING

Scaling is another useful transformation that you can leverage to adjust the size of the elements you draw to the canvas. `scale()` accepts two arguments: the x and y scale factors.

In general you want to keep both arguments the same; for instance, to double the size of any elements you draw:

```
ctx.scale(2, 2);
```

However, you can scale the horizontal and vertical dimensions separately. For instance you can double the width while keeping the height the same:

```
ctx.scale(2, 1);
```

You can shrink the canvas by passing in a decimal value less than 1:

```
ctx.scale(.5, .5);
```

You can even pass in negative values to mirror the canvas:

```
ctx.scale(-1, 1);
```

This flips the canvas horizontally. Because this mirroring occurs around the origin, you probably want to combine this with a translation. For example, if you have a canvas that is 200 pixels wide and you want to flip it in place, first translate the canvas 200 pixels to the right, and then apply the scaling:

```
ctx.translate(200, 0);
ctx.scale(-1, 1);
```

TRANSFORMS

The canvas element allows for precise control over the transformation matrix using `transform()`. This enables you to skew, rotate, and scale the canvas in any combination of operations that you see fit.

You pass in the same transformation matrix values you used in Chapter 3 with CSS3 transform matrices. Although these can be rather complicated to calculate, they provide a level of precision that is unparalleled in the other transformations.

SAVING AND RESTORING THE CANVAS STATE

When working with transformations, it is a good idea to also get comfortable with saving and restoring the canvas state. As with transformations, saving and restoring the canvas state does not affect elements already drawn to the canvas, but rather those that are drawn afterward.

For instance, if you save the canvas before applying a rotation and drawing an element, when you restore the canvas, it doesn't remove the rotation from the existing element, but rather ensures that any subsequent elements you draw won't be rotated.

Thus before applying any transformation, it is a good idea to save the canvas state. This makes it much easier to return to your starting point than applying a reverse transformation to undo the transformation manually.

What Gets Saved?

Saving the canvas state affects more than just translations. Basically, it saves any style that can be used when drawing elements.

In addition to translations, it saves the `fillStyle` and `strokeStyle`, as well as line styles such as `lineWidth`, `lineCap`, `lineJoin` and `miterLimit`. It also saves shadow values such as `shadowOffsetX`, `shadowBlur` and `shadowColor`, as well the `globalCompositeOperation` and current clipping path (which you learn about in the next section).

However saving the canvas state does not have any relationship to elements that have already been drawn. If you restore the canvas state, it does not undo what you have already drawn, but rather it returns the canvas to the base state for drawing the next element.

Usage Example

Saving and restoring the canvas state is simple—just use the `save()` and `restore()` methods:

```
ctx.fillStyle = 'blue';
ctx.fillRect(10, 15, 80, 40);

ctx.save();

ctx.translate(50, 20);
ctx.rotate(Math.PI / 4);

ctx.fillStyle = 'red';
ctx.fillRect(10, 15, 80, 40);

ctx.restore();

ctx.fillRect(50, 65, 80, 40);
```

In this script, a blue rectangle is drawn first, and then saved on the canvas state. Next it translates and rotates the canvas, and changes the `fillStyle` to red. Then another rectangle is drawn. Finally, after restoring the canvas state, the last rectangle drawn not only loses the translation and rotation, but it also reverts to the blue `fillStyle` set for the first rectangle, as shown in Figure 7-26.

Figure 7-26: The canvas state has been saved after the first blue rectangle was drawn. After transforming the canvas and changing the fill color to red, the canvas state has been restored before drawing another blue rectangle.

SAVING AND RESTORING MULTIPLE STATES

With canvas, you can save and restore as many states as you want. Add as many `save()` calls as you need, and then use `restore()` to restore the latest state. Then any previously saved states can be restored using additional `restore()` calls:

```
ctx.fillStyle = 'blue';
ctx.fillRect(10, 15, 120, 60);

ctx.save();

ctx.fillStyle = 'red';
ctx.fillRect(20, 25, 120, 60);

ctx.save();

ctx.fillStyle = 'green';
ctx.fillRect(30, 35, 120, 60);

ctx.restore();

// this will draw a red rectangle
ctx.fillRect(40, 45, 120, 60);

ctx.restore();

// this will draw a blue rectangle
ctx.fillRect(50, 55, 120, 60);
```

Here a blue rectangle is drawn and the canvas is saved. Then a red rectangle is drawn and the canvas saved. A green rectangle is drawn last. After the canvas state is restored, a red rectangle is drawn, because that is the most recently saved `fillStyle`. Finally, after the canvas is restored again, a rectangle is drawn in the original blue `fillStyle`, as shown in Figure 7-27.

Figure 7-27: The canvas state has been saved twice, once after drawing the first blue rectangle, and again after drawing the next red rectangle.

Unfortunately there is no way to flag a specific state to restore; you must simply keep track of how many times you have saved the canvas, and restore the appropriate number of times.

COMPOSITES AND CLIPPING PATHS

When drawing multiple shapes on the canvas, how the individual shapes are rendered is just as important as how they are combined. Fortunately, the canvas element provides a number of useful tools for creating complex combinations of shapes.

COMPOSITES

So far whenever I've shown you multiple shapes on the canvas, I've allowed them to stack up naturally on top of each other. However there are several options you can use to control how multiple shapes combine in canvas.

Adjusting Layer Ordering with Composites

By default, any shape you draw in canvas appears on top of the shapes you have drawn previously. So if you draw a blue rectangle, followed by a red circle, the circle is rendered on top of the rectangle as shown in Figure 7-28.

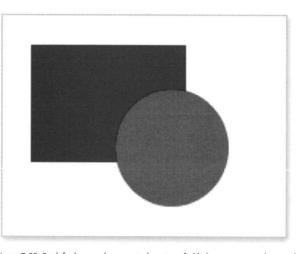

Figure 7-28: By default, new elements stack on top of old elements as you draw to the canvas.

You can change this default behavior by setting the globalCompositeOperation. For instance, to render elements in the reverse order (newest one on the bottom), you can set globalCompositeOperation to destination-over:

```
ctx.fillStyle = 'blue';
ctx.fillRect(20, 20, 110, 80);

ctx.globalCompositeOperation = 'destination-over';

ctx.fillStyle = 'red';

ctx.beginPath();
ctx.arc(120, 90, 40, 0, 2 * Math.PI);
ctx.fill();
```

Here the circle is rendered beneath the rectangle, as shown in Figure 7-29.

To render the next element above these shapes, reset globalCompositeOperation to the default value of source-over (or simply save() and restore() the canvas state as you learned earlier).

Using Composites to Clip Shapes

Composites can also be used to adjust which parts of the shapes are visible. For instance, you can cause all the shapes to render within the existing canvas content:

```
ctx.globalCompositeOperation = 'source-atop';
```

In the previous example, this clips all the content within the blue rectangle as shown in Figure 7-30.

Figure 7-29: The circle is rendered beneath the rectangle because
`globalCompositeOperation` is set to `destination-over`.

Figure 7-30: The composition operation has been set to `source-atop`, which
renders the circle only within the boundaries of the previously-drawn rectangle.

You can do the opposite and clip the existing canvas with the boundaries of the new element
as shown in Figure 7-31. Simply set the `globalCompositeOperation` to
`destination-atop`.

If you set the `globalCompositeOperation` to `source-in`, it renders the new shape in
the area that overlaps only the existing canvas content (but does not render any of the existing
content itself), as shown in Figure 7-32.

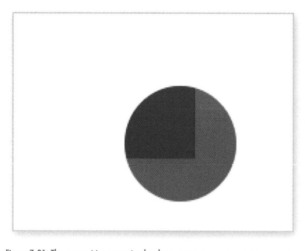

Figure 7-31: The composition operation has been set to `destination-atop`, which clips the previously drawn rectangle within the boundaries of the circle.

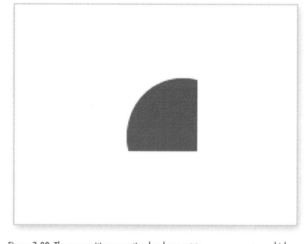

Figure 7-32: The composition operation has been set to `source-in`, which renders only the overlapping area of the circle.

You can set `destination-in` to render the existing content only in the area that overlaps the new shape, as shown in Figure 7-33.

You also can use composites to render what is outside the overlapping area. For instance, to render the new shape outside of any overlap, set `globalCompositeOperation` to `source-out` as shown in Figure 7-34.

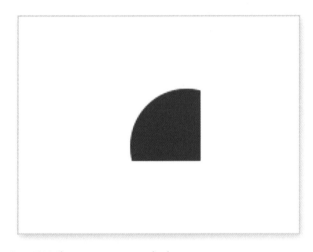

Figure 7-33: The composition operation has been set to `destination-in`, which renders only the overlapping area of the rectangle.

Figure 7-34: The composition operation has been set to `source-out`, which renders only the non-overlapping area of the circle.

Set `globalCompositeOperation` to `destination-out` to render the existing content only in the non-overlapping areas as shown in Figure 7-35.

Or if you'd rather render both shapes outside of any overlapping area, you can set `global CompositeOperation` to `xor`. The result is shown in Figure 7-36.

Figure 7-35: The composition operation has been set to `destination-out`, which only renders the non-overlapping area of the rectangle.

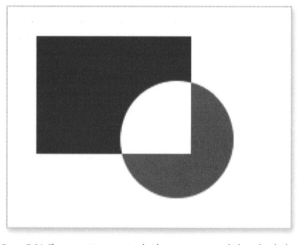

Figure 7-36: The composition operation has been set to `xor`, which renders both shapes, except for any overlapping areas.

To render the new shape in its entirety and hide any existing content as shown in Figure 7-37, set the `globalCompositeOperation` to `copy`.

Figure 7-37: The composition operation has been set to `copy`, which renders the circle and hides the previously existing rectangle.

When setting the composition operation, it is important to pay attention to where the `globalCompositeOperation` is attached in the code. In these examples it is crucial that the `globalCompositeOperation` be set after the blue rectangle is drawn, but before the red circle is drawn.

> At the time of this writing, some of the shape-clipping composites have bugs in WebKit. `source-in` is working only in the WebKit Nightlies, and `source-out` is working in the Nightlies, but has some visual issues. `destination-in`, `destination-atop`, and `copy` are not working in any WebKit. There are already bug reports so these will eventually all be fixed according to the W3C specifications, and pushed to the various WebKit browsers.

Changing the Color of Overlapped Areas with Composites

You can use composite operations to change the color overlap of shapes. With these techniques, the two colors are blended in different ways, similar to blend modes in Photoshop.

To darken the overlapping areas, simply set the `globalCompositeOperation` to `darker`. The results are shown in Figure 7-38.

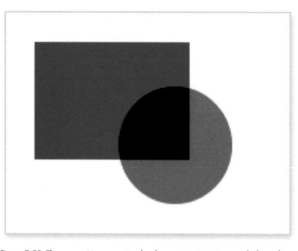

Figure 7-38: The composition operation has been set to `darker`, which combines the overlapping darkness values of both shapes.

Set the `globalCompositeOperation` to `lighter` if you'd prefer to lighten the overlapping areas as shown in Figure 7-39.

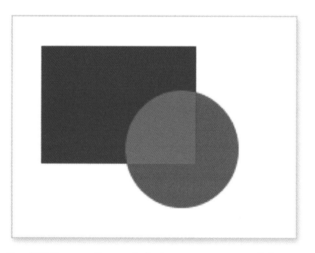

Figure 7-39: The composition operation has been set to `lighter`, which combines the overlapping lightness values of both shapes.

CLIPPING PATHS

While certain composite operations clip shapes in canvas, you can get much more fine-grained control using clipping paths.

To establish a clipping path, draw a shape, and then use `clip()` much as you use `fill()` and `stroke()`:

```
ctx.beginPath();
ctx.arc(80, 90, 40, 0, 2 * Math.PI);
ctx.clip();
```

Instead of drawing the circle with a fill or a stroke, this script sets the circle as a clipping path. Any elements that are drawn subsequently will be rendered only within this path, as shown in Figure 7-40.

Figure 7-40: Two rectangles are clipped within a circle.

You can accomplish similar results using composite operations, but those only work in basic situations. For instance, to clip more than one shape within a given path, composite operations cause problems because each new shape becomes the new path that clips the next shape.

> *Clipping paths can be saved and restored along with the canvas state, which is important when trying to draw new elements after applying a clipping path.*

THE INTERACTIVE CANVAS

Because you're scripting all the elements you've drawn to the canvas, building interactive components should be relatively easy. However, canvas was originally intended for static drawings, so you'll need to jump through some extra hoops to make it interactive.

BASIC ANIMATION

While canvas is often used as an alternative to Flash, it isn't set up as well for building animations. Any element you draw to the canvas remains static, and you cannot interact with it. To create animations you need to draw individual frames and clear the previously drawn frames at each step. This isn't as hard as it may sound because you will be using JavaScript.

Drawing Frames

To animate a rectangle, first draw the rectangle for the initial frame:

```
ctx.fillRect(10, 10, 60, 40);
```

In the next frame, you clear the entire canvas and draw the rectangle in its next position:

```
ctx.clearRect(0, 0, 200, 150);
ctx.fillRect(11, 11, 60, 40);
```

In this frame you start by creating a clear rectangle to remove everything in the canvas, and then draw the rectangle in its next position. The clear rectangle should match up with the size of your canvas element, 200 × 150 pixels in this example.

While using `clearRect` is probably the easiest, there are a number of other ways you can hide the pre-existing canvas content. For instance, you can take advantage of `clip()` or content clipping composite operations such as `copy`, or just redefine the canvas dimensions:

```
var myCanvas = document.getElementById('my-canvas');
myCanvas.style.width = myCanvas.style.width;
```

Redefining the dimensions of the canvas essentially resets it, removing any drawings you have added.

Scripting Animation

Of course it doesn't make sense to redraw every single frame by hand. Instead, you can script the animation using JavaScript.

Beyond the need to clear and redraw the canvas, scripting animations in canvas is similar to scripting the animation of any object in JavaScript. Although you may be more familiar with DOM animations in JavaScript libraries such as jQuery, it is pretty easy to write these animations yourself.

The easiest way to create animations in JavaScript is to take advantage of `setInterval()`, which triggers a given function every time a certain amount of time passes. Then on each iteration of that function, redraw your canvas element one frame further in the animation:

```
var posX = 0,
posY = 0;

function draw() {
    posX++;
    posY++;

    ctx.clearRect(0, 0, 200, 150);
    ctx.fillRect(posX, posY, 50, 50);
}

ctx.fillStyle = 'blue';

setInterval(draw, 100);
```

Here you first set up some global variables for the x and y position of your rectangle, which need to be defined outside of your function so that they can be constantly referenced.

The `draw()` function then adds one to `posX` and `posY`, clears the canvas, and draws the rectangle using the new coordinates.

Finally, you set the `fillStyle` (which does not need to be set every frame), and then call the `draw()` function within `setInterval()`, which calls this function every 100 milliseconds (or .1 second).

This script draws a blue rectangle that slowly moves diagonally down and to the right.

A More Robust Function

While this script is animating the canvas, it is not overly useful unless you want this one particular animation. Fortunately you can easily fold this script into a more reusable function:

```
function animateRect(speed, width, height, color) {
    var posX = 0,
    posY = 0;

    function draw() {
        posX++;
        posY++;

        ctx.clearRect(0, 0, 200, 150);
        ctx.fillRect(posX, posY, width, height);
    }

    ctx.fillStyle = color;
```

173

```
        setInterval(draw, speed);
}


animateRect(100, 50, 50, 'blue');
```

Here a function `animateRect()` accepts values for the speed of the animation as well as the dimensions and `fillStyle` of the rectangle.

You can take this one step further and build in variables to control the start position of the rectangle, as well as the number of pixels it moves in each frame:

```
function animateRect(speed, width, height, color, startX, startY, changeX, changeY)
  {
    var posX = startX,
    posY = startY;

    function draw() {
        posX += changeX;
        posY += changeY;

        ctx.clearRect(0, 0, 200, 150);
        ctx.fillRect(posX, posY, width, height);
    }

    ctx.fillStyle = color;

    setInterval(draw, speed);
}


animateRect(100, 50, 50, 'blue', 0, 0, 1, 1);
```

It's a good idea to build in boundaries for the animation, to stop the motion when the rectangle reaches a certain position:

```
function animateRect(speed, width, height, color, startX, startY, changeX, changeY,
  endX, endY) {
    var posX = startX,
    posY = startY;

    function draw() {
        posX += changeX;
        posY += changeY;

        // clear the interval if it exceeds the bounds
        if ( posX > endX || posY > endY ) {
            clearInterval(rectInterval);
        }
        // otherwise draw the next frame
```

174

```
        else {
            ctx.clearRect(0, 0, 200, 150);
            ctx.fillRect(posX, posY, width, height);
        }
    }

    ctx.fillStyle = color;

    var rectInterval = setInterval(draw, speed);
}

animateRect(100, 50, 50, 'blue', 0, 0, 1, 1, 100, 100);
```

This snippet adds values to control the end positions of the animation. First it adds a boundary check to see if the new position has reached the edge. If so, the interval is cleared; if not, the next frame is drawn.

> To clear the interval, you have to define a variable when you initially call set Interval(), and then pass it to clearInterval().

The boundary check stops the animation, but not at exactly the right point. This is due to the rectangle's dimensions. The coordinates you pass to fillRect() refer to the top-left corner, so the animation will stop when the top-left corner of the rectangle passes the boundaries, as opposed to when any part of the rectangle travels too far.

Thus you should account for those dimensions in your script:

```
function animateRect(speed, width, height, color, startX, startY, changeX, changeY,
  endX, endY) {
    var posX = startX,
    posY = startY;

    // adjust the bounds based on the rectangle dimensions
    if ( changeX > 0 ) endX -= width;
    if ( changeY > 0 ) endY -= height;

    function draw() {
        posX += changeX;
        posY += changeY;

        // clear the interval if it exceeds the bounds
        if ( posX > endX || posY > endY ) {
            clearInterval(rectInterval);
        }
        // otherwise draw the next frame
        else {
            ctx.clearRect(0, 0, 200, 150);
```

```
        ctx.fillRect(posX, posY, width, height);
      }
    }

  ctx.fillStyle = color;

  var rectInterval = setInterval(draw, speed);
}

animateRect(100, 50, 50, 'blue', 0, 0, 1, 1, 100, 100);
```

Now your script takes the end points you defined and adjusts them for the dimensions of the rectangle. If either the x or y has a positive change in value, the script subtracts the corresponding dimension from the end point because that is when the edge will have crossed that line. If the value change is negative, there is no need to adjust for the dimensions of the rectangle because it's already using the correct edge (the top or left edge).

> *If you plan to use this function in canvases with different sizes, you may want to build in a variable for the canvas size. Use it to adjust the width and height of the* clearRect().

MOUSE INTERACTION

Although adding something as simple as a click event handler to a DOM element is easy; mouse interactions are much more complicated when you're trying to interface with canvas elements. Much like the difficulties you encountered when animating the canvas, this has to do with the static rendering of elements. The basic problem is that when you draw a rectangle to your canvas, you can't select the rectangle and attach a click event.

This isn't to say that you can't attach click event handlers to the elements you draw to the canvas. Adding these interactions is not impossible; it is just considerably more difficult.

Basically, you attach a click handler to the entire canvas element, and then determine the mouse position relative to that element on each click. After comparing this position against the position of your canvas shapes, you can determine if the user has clicked on them.

Determining the Boundaries of a Click Event

For instance, let's say you draw a rectangle:

```
ctx.fillRect(20, 15, 100, 80);
```

Taking into account the dimensions of this rectangle and its starting point, you can determine which coordinates in the canvas are contained within the rectangle. Because it starts at an x coordinate of 20 pixels and is 100 pixels wide, the x value of the mouse click has to be between 20 and 120. The rectangle's y coordinate of 15 pixels and height of 80 pixels mean that the y value of the mouse click has to be between 15 and 95. If both the *x* and *y* coordinates of the mouse click fall between these bounds, you can deduce that the click has occurred on your rectangle.

Determining the Mouse Position

Before you can determine whether the mouse click has occurred within your shape, you must first establish the mouse position relative to the canvas element. To do so, start by setting up a click event on your canvas element:

```
var canvas = document.getElementById('mycanvas');

if ( canvas.getContext) {
    var ctx = canvas.getContext('2d');

    ctx.fillRect(20, 15, 100, 80);

    canvas.onclick = function(ev) {
        var pos = getCanvasPosition(ev, canvas);
    };
}
```

For simplicity's sake, set up this click handler using the basic `onclick` syntax (and the DOM identifier for your canvas element). Feel free to use a more robust click handling syntax if you prefer.

The click handler calls the custom function `getCanvasPosition()`, passing in the event object and the canvas DOM reference. Next, create this function to determine the relative mouse position within your canvas element:

```
function getCanvasPosition(ev, canvasElement) {
    var x, y;

    if (ev.pageX || ev.pageY) {
        x = ev.pageX;
        y = ev.pageY;
    }
    else {
        x = ev.clientX + document.body.scrollLeft + document.documentElement.
    scrollLeft;
        y = ev.clientY + document.body.scrollTop + document.documentElement.
    scrollTop;
    }

    x -= canvasElement.offsetLeft;
    y -= canvasElement.offsetTop;

    return [x, y];
}
```

This function may look complex because it incorporates a variety of methods to determine the mouse position across different browsers. Basically, it establishes the mouse position in the overall page, and then subtracts the position of the canvas element to ascertain the relative mouse position within the canvas.

Tying It All Together

You can use the mouse position, and compare it against the position of the rectangle you drew:

```
function getCanvasPosition(ev, canvasElement) {
    var x, y;

    if (ev.pageX || ev.pageY) {
        x = ev.pageX;
        y = ev.pageY;
    }
    else {
        x = ev.clientX + document.body.scrollLeft + document.documentElement.
    scrollLeft;
        y = ev.clientY + document.body.scrollTop + document.documentElement.
    scrollTop;
    }

    x -= canvasElement.offsetLeft;
    y -= canvasElement.offsetTop;

    return [x, y];
}

var canvas = document.getElementById('mycanvas');

if ( canvas.getContext) {
    var ctx = canvas.getContext('2d');

    ctx.fillRect(20, 15, 100, 80);

    canvas.onclick = function(ev) {
        var pos = getCanvasPosition(ev, canvas),
        posX = pos[0],
        posY = pos[1];

        // determine if it's in the bounds
        if ( posX > 20 && posX < 120 && posY > 15 && posY < 95) {
            // what to do if it has been clicked
            alert('Rectangle clicked');
        }
    };
}
```

The click event on the canvas determines the mouse position using the `getCanvas Position()` function. The script compares these values against the dimensions and position of your rectangle. If the click falls within the rectangle bounds, it triggers an `alert()` to indicate that it has been clicked.

Determining Click Events on More Complex Shapes

While this method is effective, it can be difficult, especially when you are dealing with complex shapes, transformations, or animations. Determining whether a set of coordinates is within the boundaries of a static rectangle is relatively easy; you just have to keep track of where it has been drawn. But this becomes much more difficult when you are dealing with a rotating, shape-changing blob.

To calculate click events on more complex shapes, you will have to use advanced geometrical math to determine whether a click location is within the boundaries of the shape.

USING PHYSICS LIBRARIES

You can certainly create your own physics functions to control interactions in your canvas applications, but you should know that there are a number of excellent physics libraries that can save you a lot of time when compared to building these functions from scratch.

One such physics library is Box2DJS, which is a JavaScript port of the library Box2D. Box2DJS handles a variety of functionality, from gravity to collision detection and movable joints.

You can download Box2DJS here: `http://box2d-js.sourceforge.net/`.

179

3D CANVAS

At the beginning of this chapter, you created your canvas by setting the context to 2D with `getContext('2d')`. Until recently, `2d` was the only context available in canvas, and there was no way to create truly 3D canvas drawings. While there were a number of techniques that you could use to create mock 3D effects, these ultimately relied on hacks to simulate 3D using the native 2D canvas context.

WEBGL AND OPENGL

Fortunately, robust 3D capabilities have now been added in a number of WebKit browsers, using Web-based Graphics Library (WebGL), which is essentially a mechanism to access OpenGL via web elements such as canvas.

Setting the WebGL Context

To use WebGL with canvas, set the context to `'experimental-webgl'`:

```
var ctx = canvas.getContext('experimental-webgl');
```

Because the WebGL specification is still being developed, the context must use the `experimental` prefix, similar to the `-webkit` prefix you used for many experimental CSS3 attributes. Eventually the context will be simplified to `webgl`.

While this technique will set the WebGL context in supportive browsers, a number of browsers are left out. WebGL is supported in recent versions of Chrome (10+), as well as Safari for Mac on Snow Leopard (Mac OSX v.1.0.6 or higher). However, Safari in older versions of Mac OS, as well as older versions of Chrome cannot use this context. Additionally, at the time of this writing WebGL isn't built into iOS or Android.

So it is important to provide a failsafe for non-supportive browsers, and for this you can use the basic JavaScript `try-catch` method:

```
var ctx = null;

try {
    ctx = canvas.getContext('experimental-webgl');
}
catch(e) {
    // what to do if WebGL isn't supported
    alert('Sorry your browser does not support WebGL');
}
```

Working With WebGL

Working with the WebGL context in canvas is completely different from working with the 2D context because WebGL uses OpenGL methods and syntax.

OpenGL is very robust, providing a wide variety of graphics support. You can use it to create everything from three-dimensional shapes, to animated textures, to lighting and effects.

Learning OpenGL can provide you with a lot of useful tools, but the learning curve to using it may be very steep if you are unfamiliar with the principles of 3D programming and physics.

3D CANVAS LIBRARIES

There are also a variety of JavaScript libraries that interface with OpenGL. These tools handle a lot of the heavy lifting with OpenGL, and provide a more intuitive set of functions you can use to create many of the same effects.

Three.js

Three.js is a JavaScript library that is essentially a very easy-to-use 3D engine. It handles a wide variety of tasks, from building three-dimensional objects, to animation, lighting, and particle physics. It even provides controls for camera position and incorporating audio.

Best of all, three.js provides a number of different rendering options. In newer browsers it can use the hardware accelerated WebGL, but it also can support rendering in canvas using the 2D context for less supportive browsers. It can even render in SVG (which will be discussed in Chapter 9).

Download and learn more about three.js here: `https://github.com/mrdoob/three.js/`.

Processing.js

Processing.js is another JavaScript library that aims to make 3D interfacing much easier. It supports many of the same features as three.js with a couple of key differences.

- 3D rendering in processing.js requires WebGL, so it cannot be used to make three-dimensional objects within the 2D canvas context.
- Processing.js provides a 2D graphics engine, which does work with the 2D canvas context.

Download and learn more about processing.js here: `http://processingjs.org/`.

CANVAS INSPIRATION

Now that you have the tools you need to create canvas applications, you should take a look at what has been already created by other developers. As you will see, canvas is a very versatile element that can be used to create remarkable web apps.

GAMES

One of the more obvious uses of canvas is for the creation of video games. With the considerable amount of functionality available in the native canvas, as well as a variety of useful graphics and physics libraries that have been created, developers have been able to create some very impressive video games using JavaScript and the browser alone.

- **FastKat:** In FastKat, shown in Figure 7-41,you accelerate in a 3D space, avoiding objects as you gain points for travelling faster and faster. Because it's built with three.js, and doesn't rely on WebGL for 3D support, it can also be played across a wide variety of canvas-supportive browsers.

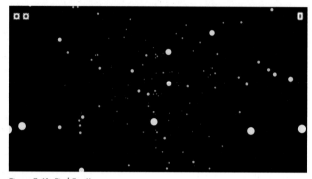

Figure 7-41: Find FastKat at `http://www.omiod.com/games/fastkat.php`.

Figure credit: FastKat by Andrea Doimo

- **Canvas rider:** Canvas rider, shown in Figure 7-42, is an off-road bike simulator with really impressive physics support.

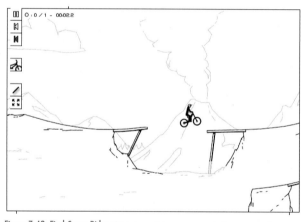

Figure 7-42: Find Canas Rider at `http://canvasrider.com/`.

Figure credit: Canvas Rider

- **Arena 5:** Arena 5, shown in Figure 7-43, is a classic-style arcade game in which you fly around shooting three-dimensional shapes.
- **Sinuous:** Sinuous, shown in Figure 7-44, is a 2D mouse control game where you avoid objects and gain a variety of power-ups.

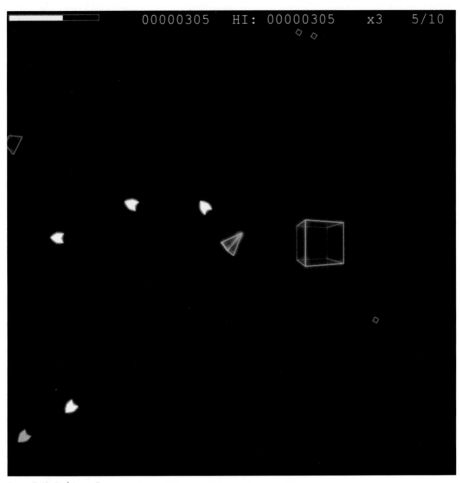

Figure 7-43: Find Arena 5 at `www.kevs3d.co.uk/dev/arena5/`.

Figure credit: Kevin Roast

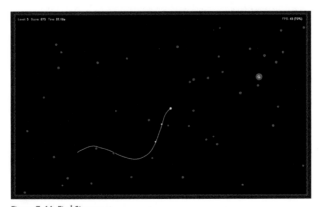

Figure 7-44: Find Sinuous at `www.sinuousgame.com`.

Figure credit: Hakim El Hattab, all rights reserved

- **Z-Type**: Z-Type, shown in Figure 7-45, is a typing game in which you type strings of letters to blow up ships.

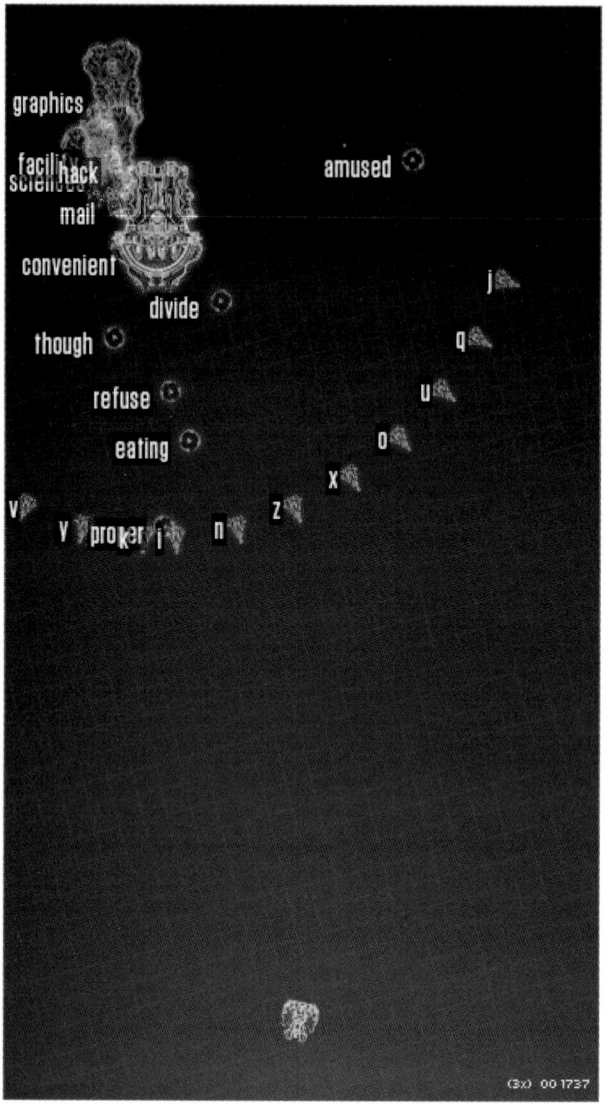

Figure 7-45: Find Z-Type at `http://www.phoboslab.org/ztype/`.

Figure credit: Dominic Szablewski

AUDIO / VIDEO

With the audio and video support implicit in HTML5 capable browsers, applications that incorporate rich media are a very sensible use of the canvas element.

- **Rome - 3 Dreams of Black:** As shown in Figure 7-46, this is an interactive 3D music video experience created for Danger Mouse and Daniele Luppi. It uses WebGL to create a variety of immersive 3D graphics and provides the user limited control over the viewpoint.

Figure 7-46: Find Rome —3 Dreams of Black at www.ro.me.

Figure credit: @radical.media LLC

■ **9elements Audio Visualization:** This interactive audio visualization, shown in Figure 7-47, not only renders based on audio data, but can also be manipulated by mouse interactions.

Figure 7-47: Find 9elements Audio Visualization at http://9elements.com/io/projects/html5/canvas/.

Figure credit: 9elements

■ **Arcade Fire – The Wilderness Downtown:** This canvas application, shown in Figure 7-48, connects with Google Maps Streetview, to create a unique music video set in the user's hometown (via an address that is provided at the start of the video).

Figure 7-48: Find Arcade Fire - The Wilderness Downtown at www.chromeexperiments.com/arcadefire/.

Figure credit: @radical.media LLC

DRAWING AND CREATION TOOLS

Canvas was originally built as a drawing tool, so it makes sense that a number of drawing and rendering tools have been created using canvas.

- **Voxels:** This 3D editing tool allows you to build shapes out of cubic building blocks, and ultimately create your own three-dimensional scene. (See Figure 7-49.)

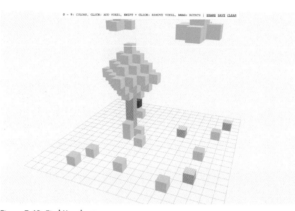

Figure 7-49: Find Voxels at `http://mrdoob.com/129/Voxels`.

Figure credit: Mr.doob

- **Sketch:** This drawing tool, shown in Figure 7-50, animates drawings by rendering the lines as you draw them, and then vibrating them after completion.

Figure 7-50: To play around with Sketch go to `http://hakim.se/experiments/html5/sketch/`.

Figure credit: Hakim El Hattab, all rights reserved

- **Bomomo:** This new take on a standard drawing application is shown in Figure 7-51. Instead of using conventional tools such as a pen and paintbrush, you render graphics on the canvas using a variety of interesting effects.

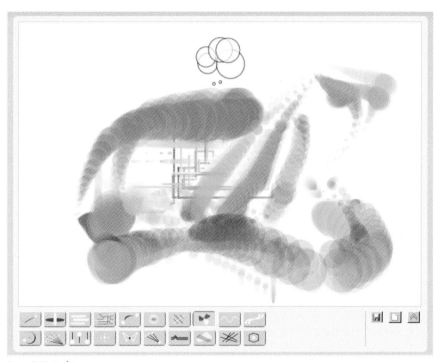

Figure 7-51: Find Bomono at `http://bomomo.com/`.

Figure credit: Phillipp Lenssen

MATH / PHYSICS

The rendering capabilities of canvas are ultimately based in geometry, and there are a number of math and physics applications built in canvas.

- **Touch Trigonometry:** This tool, shown in Figure 7-52, provides an interactive and intuitive way to learn the various functions of trigonometry as they relate to the unit circle.

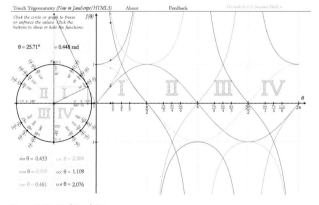

Figure 7-52: Find Touch Trigonometry at `www.touchtrigonometry.org`.

Figure credit: Matthew Trost

- **Physics Sketch:** Shown in Figure 7-53, this tool allows you to draw shapes, which are then affected by gravity and physics. So once you draw a shape, it falls to the ground, rolling around and displacing other shapes as it would in the real world.

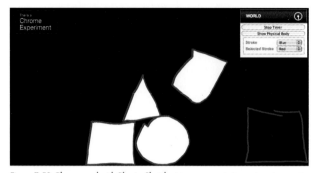

Figure 7-53: Play around with Physics Sketch at `http://physicsketch.appspot.com/`.

Figure credit: Ando Yasuchi

- **Ball Pool:** This is an interactive physics experiment that not only allows users to create new balls, but to shake their browser window to move the balls around. (See Figure 7-54.)

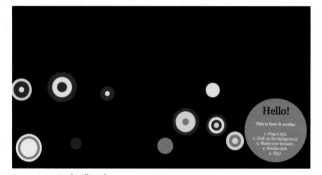

Figure 7-54: Find Ball Pool at `www.chromeexperiments.com/detail/ball-pool/`.

Figure credit: Mr.doob

VISUAL EFFECTS

There are also a number of miscellaneous visual effects that have been created using the canvas element.

- **Cloth Simulation:** This impressive cloth simulation incorporates both gravity and mouse interaction for a realistic cloth effect. (See Figure 7-55.)
- **Parcycle:** Shown in Figure 7-56, Parcycle provides particle effects that follow the mouse cursor and are controlled by a variety of settings.

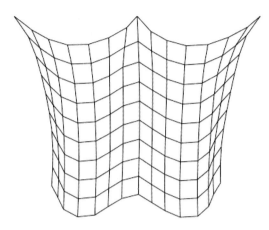

Figure 7-55: Find Cloth Simulation at `http://andrew-hoyer.com/experiments/cloth/`.

Figure credit: Andrew Hoyer

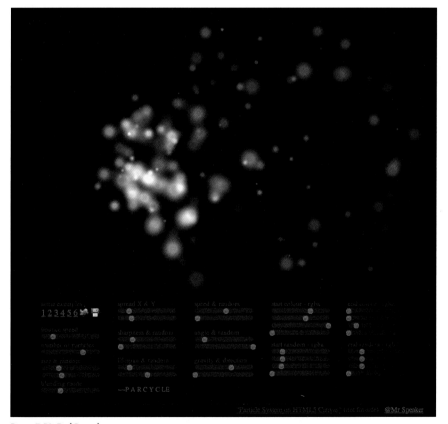

Figure 7-56: Find Parcycle at `www.mrspeaker.net/dev/parcycle/`.

Figure credit: Earle Castledine

- **Starfield:** This is an interactive star-scape, where the viewpoint flies through space and is controlled by mouse movement. (See Figure 7-57.)

Figure 7-57: Find Starfield at www.chiptune.com/starfield/starfield.html.

Figure credit: Christophe Résigné

- **Textify.it:** This program, shown in Figure 7-58, allows users to upload an image, which it then renders using text characters in a canvas element.

Figure 7-58: Find Textify it at http://textify.it/.

Figure credit: Hakim El Hattab, all rights reserved

- **Canvas Cycle:** This program, shown in Figure 7-59, creates organic 8-bit animation in canvas, and may be a pre-cursor to other animation effects.

Figure 7-59: Find Canvas Cylcle at www.effectgames.com/demos/canvascycle/.

Figure credit: Greg Walberg

MORE CANVAS INSPIRATION

If the demos listed have left you wanting more, you can find more stunning canvas experiments and creations throughout the web. Some great sources for canvas inspiration are http://mrdoob.com/, www.chromeexperiments.com, and http://hakim.se/experiments.

SUMMARY

The canvas element provides remarkable capabilities for creating visually stunning graphics in web browsers. Instead of relying on hacking visualizations together using DOM styling, you can draw directly on the screen, rendering any shapes you need.

In addition to drawing shapes, canvas also provides a variety of controls for styling these objects. You can leverage everything from gradients to shadows to blend modes.

As the trend towards the open-web moves forward, the canvas element has gained an unprecedented amount of attention as an alternative to Flash. This is because it can be used to create rich applications such as video games with complex animations and even 3D support.

However, building these types of applications in canvas can be more cumbersome than building similar apps in Flash. Among other reasons, this is due in part to the fact that richer media elements such as audio and video need to be bootstrapped together alongside the canvas.

That said, the fact that canvas runs directly in the browser without any third-party plugins provides a variety of advantages. Not only does it avoid reliance on black-box closed-source applications, but it allows browsers to optimize directly for canvas. This means performance boosts both from software optimizations as well as hardware acceleration.

8 HTML5 FORMS

HTML5 INTRODUCES A variety of exciting form features, from new UI elements to advanced functionality, all available at the browser level.

Prior to HTML5, web forms were fairly simple. Developers could use a handful of form elements: text inputs, file inputs, multi-line text areas, drop downs, check boxes, and radio buttons. These elements were sufficient for basic forms, but as the web evolved, so did its forms. Web forms became more interactive, including a variety of richer elements such as date pickers, number sliders, and validation.

However, implementing these richer forms meant JavaScript plugins and UI libraries such as jQuery UI, YUI, and Dojo. While these third-party scripts made forms more interactive and easier to use, they came at the price of added complexity, longer download time, and performance loss.

Fortunately, HTML5 brought a number of powerful UI elements directly into the browser. Now, with a line of simple markup you can include rich form elements that previously required JavaScript.

In this chapter you learn how to use HTML5 number spinboxes and sliders, as well as features still being developed. You also learn how certain HTML5 input types improve mobile experiences with special contextual keyboards as well as how to make your forms more interactive using placeholder text, autofocus, and validation. Finally, you learn techniques you can use to recreate all these features in non-supportive browsers.

SPECIAL INPUT TYPES

HTML5 introduces a number of new input types that you can begin using in your projects right away. In HTML5-compliant browsers, the user will see a rich form element, such as a number slider or date picker. In older, non-supportive browsers, the user will see a plain text input. Thus there is no loss in using the fancier HTML5 input types because they degrade naturally to basic text inputs.

NUMBER

HTML5's number spinbox provides an intuitive set of controls for setting a number value, as shown in Figure 8-1.

Figure 8-1: A number spinbox created using a native HTML5 input type

To use this special number input, simply set the input type to number:

```
<input type="number" />
```

Set the default value of the field with the value attribute used in other form elements:

```
<input type="number" value="10" />
```

> *Set the value attribute whenever using a number input because valueless numbers cause problems in older versions of WebKit.*

The number input provides a variety of options you can control with markup alone.

Controlling the Increment

To control how much the number changes which each adjustment, simply set the step attribute:

```
<input type="number" value="10" step="5" />
```

In this example, every time the user clicks the spinbox's up or down arrow, the number adjusts by 5 instead of the default value of 1. You can set the step value to any number, even a decimal:

```
<input type="number" value="10" step="0.5" />
```

Be careful with the syntax of a decimal step value: a value of .5 will not be recognized; a number must precede the period, like the 0.5 value used in this example.

Controlling the Range

You can control the minimum and maximum values of the number input by setting the min and max attributes:

```
<input type="number" value="10" step="5" min="0" max="50" />
```

The min and max values control the boundaries of the number input, stopping the up and down controls before the number exceeds the range.

The min value also affects the start point of the step attribute. For instance, if the min is set to 3 and the step is set to 5, the number spinbox cycles through 3, 8, 13, 18, and so on.

This may be a bit counterintuitive because the increment is not dependent on the initial value of the field. For instance, if the min is set to 3, the step is set to 5, and the value is set to 10, clicking the up arrow changes the number to 13, not 15.

Issues with Direct User Input

One advantage of the number input type is that it retains the text input field, allowing users to directly input a number if they would prefer to avoid the spinbox controls. While this provides a better user experience, it can cause problems if a user enters an invalid number.

For instance, if users set values outside of the min and max range, the browser will not notify them until they try to submit the form (you'll learn more about form validation later in this chapter).

Furthermore, if a directly inputted value is outside of the spinbox range, it causes additional problems in older versions of WebKit because the spinbox controls become disabled. Newer versions handle this better, bumping the value into the range after the controls are clicked, but it will not automatically fix a value outside of the range until the controls are used.

Additionally, in older versions of WebKit users can enter text values into the number input.

> *Newer WebKit versions format the numbers a little more nicely, because they add a comma to numbers like 1,000.*

SLIDER

HTML5's number slider produces essentially the same result as the number spinbox, but with a different UI, as shown in Figure 8-2.

Figure 8-2: The range slider is a different way to set number values in HTML5.

To use the slider input, simply set the input type to `range`:

```
<input type="range" />
```

Setting Other Attributes

The `range` input type supports all the attributes you used with number spinboxes: `value`, `step`, `min`, and `max`:

```
<input type="range" value="10" step="5" min="0" max="50" />
```

When using this input type, make sure to set the starting point (`value`) as well as the range (`min` and `max`). If you don't set these attributes, the `min` and `max` are set to 0 and 100, and the `value` is set to 50, halfway between the `min` and `max`.

Styling the Slider

While most browsers do not allow you to style the HTML5 range slider, WebKit-based browsers like Chrome and Safari are the exception. To do so, first override the default styling using `-webkit-appearance`:

```
input[type="range"] {
    -webkit-appearance: none;
}
```

```
input[type="range"]::-webkit-slider-thumb {
    -webkit-appearance: none;
}
```

This example removes the default styling from both the slider bar (`input[type="range"]`) and the control ball (`input[type="range"]::-webkit-slider-thumb`). Next you can define some of your own custom styles:

```
input[type="range"] {
    -webkit-appearance: none;
    background-color: blue;
    height: 2px;
}
```

```
input[type="range"]::-webkit-slider-thumb {
    -webkit-appearance: none;
    height: 10px;
```

```
   width: 10px;
   background-color: red;
   border-radius: 5px;
}
```

When styling the slider, you need to set a `width` and `height`, as well as a `background-color` for the `::webkit-slider-thumb`, or it will not be visible. You should also set a `background-color` for the `input[type="range"]` as well as a `height`.

In Figure 8-3 a blue slider bar has a red control ball.

Be careful when applying custom styles to an HTML5 input type because they will also be visible in non-supportive browsers. For instance, the range input is not supported in iOS Safari on iPhone, so these styles affect the basic text input field that is rendered instead. Thus it is a good idea to skip special styling or apply iPhone-specific CSS to overwrite these styles.

Figure 8-3: Custom styling has been applied to this HTML5 input slider.

COLOR AND DATE PICKERS

Color and date pickers are included in the HTML5 spec for web forms, but unfortunately neither is supported in WebKit at the time of this writing.

The color picker is completely unsupported, and will fall back to a normal text input in WebKit, so feel free to start using it now by setting the type attribute to `color`. However, the date picker produces a very inadequate and problematic fallback in WebKit and should most likely be avoided altogether.

Usability Problems in the Date Picker

The date picker is semi-supported, meaning that WebKit renders it as a number spinbox. This can be a usability nightmare because each click of the controls adjusts the date by one day. That means your users have to click 30 times to get to the next month. Strangely, you can actually set the `step` attribute here to make this a little more usable, for instance set it to 30 to increment by 30 days per click:

```
<input type="date" step="30" />
```

The user still has to adjust the date manually for more fine-grained control, and you can only increment by a number of days, rather than a more intuitive step such as one month.

To make matters worse, the format of the date renders in *Y-m-d*, so September 30, 2011 renders as `2011-09-30`, as shown in Figure 8-4.

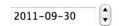

Figure 8-4: The date format in the date input type leaves a lot to be desired.

197

October 15, 1582

If you don't set the `value` attribute, newer versions of Chrome and Safari start from the current date, but older versions do something much worse. You might think it would start with the beginning of Unix time, December 31, 1979. But the date picker actually starts with October 15, 1582, as shown in Figure 8-5.

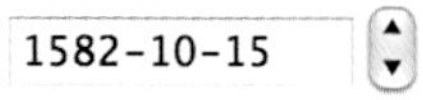

Figure 8-5: In older versions of WebKit the date picker starts on October 15, 1582.

That's not a typo; the date input actually starts in 1582. This might be useful if your form concerns the fall of the Spanish Armada, but for most forms this is terrible for usability.

> Why 1582? The answer lies in the history of the Gregorian calendar, which was adopted in 1582, with a ten-day season correction on October 15. This left a gap between October 4 and 15, 1582.

Other Date Inputs

There are a few additional input types that concern date and time: `month`, `year`, `week`, `datetime`, and `datetime-local`. `month` and `year` can actually be pretty useful even in the semi-supported state because users will be clicking only through larger increments (beware: the format of `month` is still year-month, like `2011-09`).

While the `week` input type is an interesting option, its display format is very confusing, as shown in Figure 8-6.

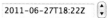

Figure 8-6: The `week` input type has a strange format.

`datetime` and `datetime-local` are even more unusable than the standard `date` picker because the spinbox adjusts individual minutes, which is not to mention the strange display format, shown in Figure 8-7.

Figure 8-7: The `datetime` input type has a strange format and is extremely unusable.

CONTEXTUAL KEYBOARDS

HTML5 also introduces a number of input types that have special implications for certain mobile devices. At first glance, these types look exactly like standard text inputs, and indeed they are nothing more for desktop browsers and mobile devices with hardware keyboards.

However, on many mobile devices these input types alter the keyboard that is displayed. Instead of the standard QWERTY keyboard, these special input types display a contextual keyboard that makes it significantly easier to enter the given information.

> *These input types also have implications for HTML5 validation which is discussed later this chapter.*

Email Addresses

One contextual keyboard is for entering email addresses:

```
<input type="email" />
```

By setting the input type to email, you flag mobile browsers such as iOS Safari to use the standard QWERTY keyboard, except with special buttons for the at symbol (@) and the dot (.), as shown in Figure 8-8.

Phone Numbers

Another contextual keyboard is available for entering phone numbers:

```
<input type="tel" />
```

If you set the input type to tel, it causes browsers such as iOS Safari to display the numeric keypad instead of the standard keyboard, as shown in Figure 8-9.

Figure 8-8: The email input type keyboard on iPhone

199

Figure 8-9: The tel input type keypad on iPhone

URLs

Additionally, there is a contextual keyboard for entering web addresses:

```
<input type="url" />
```

The `url` input type causes some mobile browsers to display special buttons to make URL entry easier. For instance, iOS Safari includes a dot (.), slash (/) and a dot-com (.com), as shown in Figure 8-10.

Numbers

Mobile browsers also provide a special keyboard for numeric input, which can be called using the `number` input type you used earlier for number spinboxes:

```
<input type="number" />
```

Although iOS Safari doesn't render the spinboxes, it does use a special numeric keyboard as shown in Figure 8-11.

This special keyboard is almost a better UI than the spinboxes, but it is unfortunately used only with the `number` input type. For some reason the `range` input type does not use the numeric keyboard in iOS Safari (or even the slider UI).

Figure 8-10: The `url` input type keyboard on iPhone

Figure 8-11: The `number` input type keyboard on iPhone

SEARCH BOX

The last special input type offered in HTML5 is the search box:

```
<input type="search" />
```

The `search` input mimics the in-browser web search input both in appearance and functionality. Before any text is entered, it just looks like a rounded rectangle text input as shown in Figure 8-12:

But when the user starts typing in the field, a cancel button appears as shown in Figure 8-13.

This cancel button can be used to clear the text the user has typed into the search box.

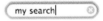

Figure 8-12: The `search` input type without any text added

Figure 8-13: The `search` input type includes a cancel button.

Styling the Search Box

Although one reason to use the search box is to mimic the in-browser styling, you can also style this input manually if you only want the functionality. To do so you again need to use the `-webkit-appearance` property:

First style the input field itself:

```
input[type="search"] {
    -webkit-appearance: none;
    border: 1px solid black;
}
```

Then style the cancel button using the `::-webkit-search-cancel-button` pseudo-element:

```
input[type="search"]::-webkit-search-cancel-button {
    -webkit-appearance: none;
    width: 10px;
    height: 10px;
    background-color: red;
    border-radius: 5px;
}
```

That creates a custom search box styling as shown in Figure 8-14.

Figure 8-14: Custom styling has been applied to this search input.

INTERACTIVE FUNCTIONALITY

Besides the additional input types, the HTML5 spec also includes a variety of interactive functionality such as placeholder text, autofocus, and form validation. Previously, developers had to rely on tools such as JavaScript to include these interactive elements, but with HTML5 you can add them to your forms using markup alone.

PLACEHOLDER TEXT

Placeholder text is displayed in a form element before a user types text. To add placeholders to your form elements, simply include the `placeholder` attribute:

```
<input type="text" placeholder="Placeholder text" />
```

This displays the placeholder text in your form element as shown in Figure 8-15.

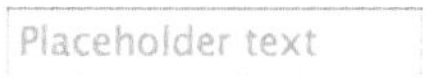

When users focus into the field, the placeholder text disappears, and is replaced with whatever text they enter. Additionally, if they remove their input, the field displays the placeholder.

> Placeholder text

Figure 8-15: Placeholder text has been added to this field.

Styling Placeholder Text

You can style the placeholder text using the `::-webkit-input-placeholder` pseudo-element:

```
input::-webkit-input-placeholder {
    font-style: italic;
    color: green;
}
```

This adjusts the styling of the placeholder text as shown in Figure 8-16.

> Placeholder text

Figure 8-16: Placeholder text with custom styling.

AUTOFOCUS

Another useful form feature is autofocus, which brings the focus into a certain field when the page loads, so the user doesn't have to click into the element.

To autofocus on a field using HTML5, attach the `autofocus` attribute:

```
<input type="text" autofocus />
```

Advantages of HTML5 Autofocus

Native HTML5 `autofocus` is better than JavaScript alternatives for a couple reasons. First, it doesn't require extra scripts and can easily be handled on the markup level. But more importantly, the autofocus occurs faster than it does using a JavaScript `focus()` script because JavaScript cannot be called until the field is loaded (at the earliest).

Furthermore, if the user starts typing into a different field while the page is loading, a JavaScript focus script can hijack the focused field and lead to a bad user experience.

Autofocus Support

Autofocus is supported in Chrome and newer versions of Safari (starting with Safari 5.1).

Autofocus is not completely supported in iOS Safari, which may be a deliberate UX decision. When encountering a field with autofocus, iOS Safari scrolls down to the field in question, but will not focus into the field (which would trigger the keyboard interface).

FORM VALIDATION

Basic form validation is enabled by default in modern WebKit browsers. The validation is related to the `type` attribute of the input field. For instance if the `type` is set to `email`, the browser determines whether a valid email address has been entered. If the user tries to submit a form without a valid email address, the browser displays an error message and moves the focus into the invalid input as shown in Figure 8-17.

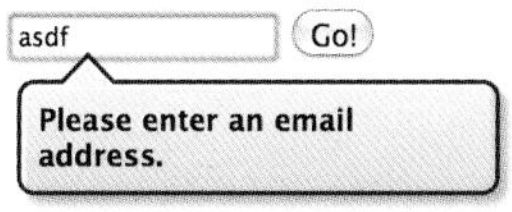

Figure 8-17: An error message occurs if the text does not correctly match the input type.

HTML5 form validation is also available for the `url` input type, where the browser determines whether the user has included a valid URL.

Form validation also works with the `number` input type. In this case, the browser not only ensures that it is a valid numeric input, but also that the number falls within the range set by the `min` and `max` attributes.

Custom Validation Rules

You can supply your own custom validation rules using the `pattern` attribute and regex:

```
<input type="text" pattern="[a-zA-Z]+" />
```

In this example, the field is matched against the regular expression `[a-zA-Z]+`, which accepts only letter values (no numbers, spaces, or special characters).

If the supplied input does not match the pattern, a generic error message is displayed as shown in Figure 8-18.

Required Fields

HTML5 also includes an easy way to mark specific form fields as required. You just add the `required` attribute to any form element:

```
<input type="text" required />
```

If the user tries to submit the form with this field left empty, the browser shows an error notification as shown in Figure 8-19.

Keep in mind that it is important to include the `required` attribute on any elements you want to require, even if they are subject to other validation rules. For instance, the validation of an `email` input is not enough to make it required; the form submits an empty field successfully unless the `required` attribute has been added.

Disabling Validation

Form validation is enabled by default in HTML5-compliant browsers. If you want to skip validation, add the `novalidate` attribute to your form element:

```
<form novalidate>
    <input type="email" />
    <input type="submit" value="Go!" />
</form>
```

This disables all form validation: type checks, pattern checks, and required fields.

Unfortunately there is no way to disable validation on a single field; `novalidate` can only be applied to the entire form.

Advantages of HTML5 Validation

Besides reducing the need for external JavaScripts, HTML5 validation has a number of other benefits:

- It removes any possibility for error when validating the special input types, which is useful for trickier validation such as email addresses.

Figure 8-18: This error message is displayed because the string '123' doesn't match the regex in the `pattern` attribute.

Figure 8-19: This form has been submitted with a required field left blank.

- Validation occurs even if the user does not have JavaScript available. For crucial forms, it is still important to have a backend validation fail-safe, in case the user posts directly (or is using a non-supportive browser).
- The native error messages are localized to the default language of the browser.

Styling Validation

WebKit allows you to style the validation message using four different pseudo-elements:

```
::-webkit-validation-bubble {}
::-webkit-validation-bubble-top-outer-arrow {}
::-webkit-validation-bubble-top-inner-arrow {}
::-webkit-validation-bubble-message {}
```

These four elements make up the validation error message. To get a better idea of the structure of the validation message, take a look at this markup:

```
<div> <!-- ::-webkit-validation-bubble -->
    <div> <!-- ::-webkit-validation-bubble-top-outer-arrow -->
        <div></div> <!-- ::-webkit-validation-bubble-top-inner-arrow -->
    </div>

    <div> <!-- ::-webkit-validation-bubble-message {} -->
        <b>Please match the requested format</b>
    </div>
</div>
```

Now you can apply any custom styling you want using these pseudo-elements. When building your CSS, remember that you can disable the default styling by setting `-webkit-appearance: none;`.

Changing the Validation Message

While most of the error messages explain the validation problem well, the generic message associated with the `pattern` attribute leaves a lot to be desired.

Mozilla offers an easy way to customize the text of the error message, but it is unfortunately not available in WebKit. However, there is a hack that you can use to set your own text for any error message:

```
<input type="text" pattern="[a-zA-Z]+" oninvalid="setCustomValidity('You may only
  enter letters.')" />
```

This technique relies on two methods: the `oninvalid` event listener, which triggers a function when the field fails validation, and the `setCustomValidity()` method, which is called to trigger the validation error with the supplied message (and overwrite the default message).

While this hack displays the custom message, it does come with a few downsides. First, native validation messages are localized to the user's browser language, whereas this hardcoded message only displays in whichever language you write it in. Additionally, the error message displays regardless of the validation problem. For instance, if you use a `pattern` and a `required` attribute, this message shows for both errors.

For these reasons, it is a good idea to avoid overwriting the default error messages for `email`, `url`, and `number` unless you are extremely unhappy with the default text. And, if you have multiple validation rules on a single field, you may want to build in a check to determine which issue triggered the error.

CROSS-BROWSER SUPPORT

While these HTML5 features add more advanced UI elements and functionality to your forms, sadly they do not work in all browsers. However, with the assistance of JavaScript, you can get decent support for these features across non-supportive browsers.

CROSS-BROWSER SUPPORT FOR SPECIAL INPUT TYPES

Browser support for the special HTML5 input types is spotty, even in modern browsers like Chrome and Safari.

However, for non-supportive browsers it is relatively simple to create a JavaScript fallback for all the fancy form elements.

Detecting Support

The first step to creating a JavaScript fallback is detecting whether it is necessary. After all, if the native HTML5 form elements are available, it is usually better to use them.

To discover whether the HTML5 input types are supported, create an input element, set its `type` to a special input type, and then determine whether the `type` has reverted to the standard text input:

```
var i = document.createElement('input');
i.setAttribute('type', 'range');
if (i.type == 'text') {
    // what to do if the input type is unsupported
}
```

Building a jQuery UI Backup for the Range Input

If the type is unsupported, create a backup using a JavaScript UI library.

For instance, to build a jQuery UI backup for the range input you include the necessary jQuery UI scripts and stylesheets. Then, after detecting support, create a jQuery script to hide any range inputs, and replace them with a jQuery slider:

```
var i = document.createElement('input');
i.setAttribute('type', 'range');
if (i.type == 'text') {
    // what to do if the input type is unsupported

    $('input[type="range"]').each(function() {
        var $thisSlider = $(this);

        // hide the range input
        $thisSlider.hide();

        // add div after the input, to become a jQuery UI slider
        $('<div />').insertAfter($thisSlider).slider();
    });
}
```

This creates the slider graphics, but this slider is still not hooked into the values of the original range input. Luckily you can leverage these attributes to set various options in the `slider()` API:

```
var i = document.createElement('input');
i.setAttribute('type', 'range');
if (i.type == 'text') {
    // what to do if the input type is unsupported

    $('input[type="range"]').each(function() {
        var $thisSlider = $(this);

        // hide the range input
        $thisSlider.hide();

        // add div after the input, to become a jQuery UI slider
        $('<div />').insertAfter($thisSlider).slider({
            value : $thisSlider.attr('value') || 50,
            min : $thisSlider.attr('min') || 0,
            max : $thisSlider.attr('max') || 100,
            step : $thisSlider.attr('step') || 1
        });
    });
}
```

Here you set each of the appropriate options based on the attributes of the range input. Notice that there are default values for each of these options; this makes sure that a useful value is set if the attribute is not defined (in fact, these particular defaults line up with the default values of the HTML5 range input).

Finally, tie the jQuery UI slider to the range input, to make sure any changes in the slider are saved to the form element:

```
var i = document.createElement('input');
i.setAttribute('type', 'range');
if (i.type == 'text') {
    // what to do if the input type is unsupported

    $('input[type="range"]').each(function() {
        var $thisSlider = $(this);

        // hide the range input
        $thisSlider.hide();

        // add div after the input, to become a jQuery UI slider
        $('<div />').insertAfter($thisSlider).slider({
            value : $thisSlider.attr('value') || 50,
            min : $thisSlider.attr('min') || 0,
            max : $thisSlider.attr('max') || 100,
            step : $thisSlider.attr('step') || 1,
            // call this when the slider changes
            change : function(ev, ui) {
                // change the value of the range input
                $thisSlider.val(ui.value);
            }
        });
    });
}
```

Creating Other Backups

Following this model, you can create backups for any other form elements you need.

jQuery UI provides a nice date picker that you can use to back up any date input types. If you need a color picker, consider using the Color Picker jQuery plugin, which you can download from www.eyecon.ro/colorpicker/. For a number spinbox, look into the Numeric Form Widget jQuery plugin at http://plugins.jquery.com/project/numericpicker.

Shortcomings of This Backup Technique

These backups work reasonably well, although there are a couple of shortcomings with this approach.

First and foremost, these UI libraries are very large and will be downloaded by all browsers, regardless of native HTML5 form support. There are two ways to get around this issue: first you can use browser-sniffing to include these files only for particular browsers. Alternatively, you can use an asynchronous approach, such as including jQuery UI via a Google Libraries API call after the feature detection fails. For more information on the Google Libraries API, visit http://code.google.com/apis/libraries/devguide.html#jqueryUI.

There are additional problems concerning the detection script. While the script works for completely unsupportive browsers, it is insufficient for browsers that support HTML5 but do not support the particular form element (or only support it partially like the WebKit date picker). Unfortunately, to provide backups for these browsers, you have to resort to browser-sniffing.

CROSS-BROWSER SUPPORT FOR INTERACTIVE FUNCTIONALITY

A single jQuery plugin can be used to get reasonable support for the majority of the advanced interactive functionality options provided in HTML5. Where this fails, there are other techniques you can use to fill in the rest of the functionality in HTML5 forms.

209

HTML5 Form Plugin

First, download the HTML5 Form plugin from www.matiasmancini.com.ar/ajax-jquery-validation-html5-form.html.

After your form has loaded, select the form element and enable the HTML5 form support:

```
$('#myForm').html5form();
```

This automatically builds in support for a number of HTML5 features in any browsers that do not support them. Best of all, the features do not require any additional markup—the form pulls the needed values directly from the attributes used to control the form in HTML5.

The HTML5 Form plugin supports a variety of HTML5 features: placeholder text, maxlength support, a number of form validation attributes, and it can validate required fields as well as the email and url input types.

Shortcomings of the HTML5 Form Plugin

The HTML5 Form plugin is useful, yet it does have some shortcomings when compared with full HTML5 support. One advantage of HTML5 form features is that they don't require the user to download any extra JavaScript; with this plugin, users download the JavaScript even if they don't end up using it. To get around this, you could include this script for only non-supportive browsers.

Browser-sniffing is an issue with this plugin because it doesn't use feature detection to determine when to use the jQuery backup.

Then, there are a number of holes in the functionality of the HTML5 Form plugin: the `autofocus` attribute is completely unsupported, and there are gaps in validation.

In the validation, the `number` input type is not validated against, and you cannot use a custom validation regex with the `pattern` attribute. For more robust validation, try the h5Validate plugin (`http://plugins.jquery.com/project/h5Validate`), although the functionality is a bit different from what you may expect.

Supporting Autofocus

While `autofocus` is unsupported by the HTML5 Form plugin, building in custom support is relatively easy using jQuery. After the page loads, detect autofocus support by creating an input element and detecting whether the `autofocus` attribute is available:

```
$(function() {
    if ( !('autofocus' in document.createElement('input')) )
});
```

If autofocus is unavailable, select any `input` with the `autofocus` attribute, and trigger the `focus()` event:

```
$(function() {
    if ( !('autofocus' in document.createElement('input')) ) {
        $('input[autofocus]').focus();
    }
});
```

While this works in most non-supportive browsers, there are issues in some browsers that support HTML5 but not the `autofocus` attribute (such as Safari 5). These browsers recognize that `autofocus` is a possibility for input elements, so the feature detection script fails, even though the attribute is not actually supported.

If you need more robust detection, you may have to resort to browser sniffing, or otherwise write a hacky script to determine if the field you want is focused, and if not, focus it.

SUMMARY

HTML5 makes forms more interactive and easier to use without relying on JavaScript form plugins. JavaScript alternatives require additional downloads, initiate slower and introduce potential error points when compared to HTML5 implementations.

With HTML5, you can take advantage of engaging interface elements such as sliders and spinboxes, as well as contextual keyboards in many mobile devices. You can also introduce usability improvements such as placeholder text, autofocus and validation.

Although some browsers do not support HTML5 form functionality, it is fairly easy to provide fallback solutions using JavaScript. These scripts can leverage the markup used in HTML5 forms, to make cross-browser integration seamless. However, fallback solutions should only be loaded in non-supportive browsers to avoid the pitfalls of JavaScript wherever possible.

9

SCALABLE VECTOR GRAPHICS

SCALABLE VECTOR GRAPHICS (SVG) is a unique image format that saves visual data based on vectors rather than pixels. Unlike most image formats on the web, vector-based images scale perfectly to any dimensions because SVGs record the actual shapes and lines used to create the image, as opposed to raster image formats which record the pixels of the shapes at a specific resolution.

The shapes that build an SVG can be accessed at runtime, which means that the shapes in SVGs not only can be altered dynamically, but also can be attached to interactive mouse events in the browser.

Prior to HTML5, SVGs could be included like any other image: with an img tag, back-ground-image, and so on (however only in browsers that support this format).

The HTML5 spec includes a new svg element, which you can use to create complex SVG images directly through markup. These SVGs are com-pletely accessible via JavaScript, which means that they can be used to create rich applications. The apps are similar to those built with the canvas element, with one key difference: the shapes drawn to SVGs are not rendered statically as pixels, and can thus be freely manipulated and animated.

In this chapter you look at some of the advan-tages of using SVG. Then you discover some automated techniques for generating SVG, both on your computer using Adobe Illustrator, and directly in the browser using a variety of JavaScript libraries. The JavaScript libraries range from general toolkits for creating SVG apps, to specific tools you can use to create charts and even 3D graphics support. Finally, you learn how to handcode SVG shapes, complete with advanced ·styling options and total interactivity.

ADVANTAGES OF USING SVG

Although some older browsers do not support SVG images, the numerous advantages of SVG make it an attractive option for site development.

VECTORED IMAGE FORMAT

The main advantage of SVG is that it is based on vectors, not pixels. Pixel-based image formats such as JPEG and PNG look great if you display them at the same size they were saved, but become pixelated if you resize them. Pixelization is especially pronounced when the graphics are enlarged, as shown in Figure 9-1.

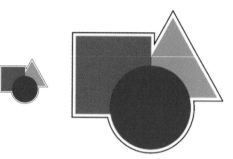

Figure 9-1: Pixel-based image formats create problems for resizing.

On the other hand, vector-based images retain their appearance perfectly at any resolution, as shown in Figure 9-2.

Even at their native resolution, SVGs look better because they are completely lossless and display better on screens with a higher pixel density, such as iPhone.

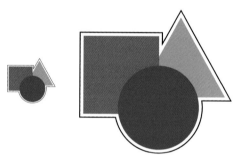

TOTAL INTERACTIVITY

While drawings built with HTML5 canvas are mostly static, SVG elements can be freely accessed with JavaScript. This means that you can manipulate SVGs at runtime, changing properties such as color, size, and position, as well as attaching event listeners such as click handlers to the individual shapes in the SVG.

Figure 9-2: Formats like SVG resize smoothly to any dimensions.

SEARCH ENGINE OPTIMIZATION (SEO)

Any text in an SVG will be indexed by search engines such as Google. While this has important implications for all images with text, it is especially useful for graphical charts and other data visualizations. Best of all, the text is indexed whether you encode the SVG as an `svg` element in HTML5, or save it as an `.svg` file.

Conversely, the text in other image formats is completely lost in the encoding, making it too difficult for search engines to parse. Developers can get around this issue by using techniques such as replacement text and the image `alt` attribute. However, that adds development time and markup, and these conventional techniques have problems when accommodating a large amount of text. The `alt` attribute can't have more than 255 characters, and replacement text may cause hidden content issues if it used too heavy-handedly.

FILE SIZE

Finally, depending on the image, SVG images may have a smaller file size. Although photographic images should usually be saved as JPEGs, certain shape-based images may be smallest when saved as an SVG. On the other hand, PNG and GIF formats index colors, so they can be smallest depending on the complexity of the shapes.

In general, vector image formats like SVG are best for graphics such as charts, graphs and basic logos. This is because SVG tends to be smallest when made up of simple shapes, or images that incorporate gradients or large amounts of text. That's because SVG encodes these elements directly, as opposed to their result in pixels.

Additionally, SVG's file size does not depend on resolution, so SVGs are often smaller than a very large PNG or GIF image.

AUTOMATICALLY GENERATING SVG

There are a number of options for automatically building SVG images, allowing you to avoid handcoding SVG and create more complex images.

GENERATING SVG FILES

Although HTML5 introduced the `svg` element, SVG has been around much longer as the file extension `.svg`. SVG files have almost all the same advantages as the `svg` element.

Most vector graphics programs such as Adobe Illustrator can easily export SVG files. Once exported, including the SVG in your page is as simple as an `img` element or `background-image` property.

These exported SVGs are typically static. Fortunately there is an add-on for Adobe Illustrator that you can use to create parameterized SVGs as well as export SVG styles as CSS, which can later be altered programmatically. This add-on is the CS5 HTML5 Pack, which can be downloaded here: `http://labs.adobe.com/technologies/illustrator_html5/`.

> To learn more about parameterized SVGs, go here: `www.w3.org/TR/2009/WD-SVGParamPrimer-20090616/`.

SVG LIBRARIES

There are a number of JavaScript libraries available for creating remarkable SVG components. These libraries provide a lot of advanced functionality and make creating rich SVG elements practically effortless.

Standard SVG Libraries

Raphaël is an SVG library that makes creating SVG elements much easier. It features an intuitive API for building SVG images, as well as a number of hooks for manipulating the images and making them more interactive. Raphaël also provides Vector Markup Language (VML) support for browsers that do not support SVG. Learn more about Raphaël here: `http://raphaeljs.com/`.

Another useful SVG library is SVG Web. It supports a wide variety of browsers; using native SVG support where available, and a Flash backup for non-supportive browsers. Learn more about SVG Web here: `http://code.google.com/p/svgweb/`.

SVG Charts

There are also a number of SVG charting libraries available. One free and excellent option is the Google Charts API: `http://code.google.com/apis/chart/`.

amCharts also provides a lot of advanced functionality if you are willing to pay for a license. Visit this link for more information: `www.amcharts.com/javascript`.

3D Support with SVG

There is also a variety of 3D graphics libraries that use SVG, including:

- Three.js, which you learned about in Chapter 7. It uses Canvas and WebGL in supportive browsers, and reverts to SVG wherever WebGL is unsupported. You can learn more about Three.js here: `https://github.com/mrdoob/three.js`.
- SVG-VML-3D, which can be used to create 3D graphics in SVG with a VML backup for older versions of IE. Learn more about SVG-VML-3D here: `www.lutanho.net/svgvml3d/`.

HANDCODING SVG IMAGES

While SVGs have been available for some time as `.svg` files, HTML5 introduces a system for building SVGs directly in the markup. Similar to the canvas element, this allows you to draw elements directly in the browser, but it has a couple of notable advantages.

Unlike canvas elements, SVG drawings do not require JavaScript, so not only can you build them directly in the markup, but they will also still render for users with JavaScript disabled. But more importantly, once drawn, canvas drawings are completely static, whereas SVGs can be manipulated with JavaScript to create rich applications (if JavaScript is available).

The canvas element is still more versatile when it comes to complex drawings and advanced styling, but the simplicity and interactivity of the SVG element makes it an attractive alternative in many situations.

INCLUDING SVG MARKUP

To include SVGs, you first create an `svg` element in your markup:

```
<svg xmlns="http://www.w3.org/2000/svg">
...
</svg>
```

This is the container of your SVG image—you add the shapes you want to draw within this element later.

By default, the `svg` element expands to fill the browser window, making it a good idea to set at least a height value so your other content doesn't get pushed too far below your SVG:

```
<svg height="200" xmlns="http://www.w3.org/2000/svg">
...
</svg>
```

>   *The* `xmlns` *attribute defines the XML structure of the SVG element.*

DRAWING SHAPES AND LINES

You can easily add basic shapes such as rectangles, circles, and ellipses to your `svg` element.

Rectangles

Adding a rectangle to your `svg` element is simple using the `rect` element:

```
<svg height="200" xmlns="http://www.w3.org/2000/svg">
    <rect width="150" height="100" fill="blue" />
</svg>
```

This example sets the rectangle's basic attributes, defining the dimensions of the rectangle as well as the fill color. Figure 9-3 shows the blue rectangle created by this code.

The `fill` attribute accepts a variety of formats: color keywords such as `blue` and `red`, as well as hex and RGB values. It even accepts RGBa values to create semi-transparent elements.

Figure 9-3: A rectangle drawn with SVG

You can also set the x and y attributes to position the rectangle within your svg element:

```
<rect width="150" height="100" x="20" y="30" fill="blue" />
```

This example moves the rectangle 20 pixels to the left and 30 pixels down.

Circles

Use the `circle` element to draw circles in your SVG:

```
<circle r="50" cx="50" cy="50" fill="red" />
```

The basic attributes of the `circle` element are a bit different. First, you set the radius of the circle (50 pixels in this example) using the r attribute. Then you define the coordinates of the center of your circle, using the cx and cy attributes. Finally, you set the fill color (red in this example) using the `fill` attribute. Figure 9-4 shows the example circle.

Triangles and Polygons

You can draw triangles and polygons with any number of sides using the `polygon` element:

Figure 9-4: A circle drawn with SVG

```
<polygon points="0,0 50,50 100,0"
  fill="orange" />
```

With the `polygon` element, you define the coordinates of each corner, so in this case an orange triangle is drawn from (0,0) to (50,50) to (100,0), as shown in Figure 9-5.

You can add as many coordinates as you want to the `points` attribute, to create a polygon with any number of corners.

Figure 9-5: A triangle drawn with SVG

Lines

Use the `line` element to add straight lines to your SVG:

```
<line x1="0" y1="0" x2="100" y2="50" stroke="green" />
```

This defines the start `(0,0)` and end `(100,50)` points of your line. Notice that the `stroke` attribute is used here to draw the green line shown in Figure 9-6.

By default the line is 1 pixel wide, but you can also adjust this width by setting the `stroke-width` attribute:

Figure 9-6: A line drawn with SVG

```
<line x1="0" y1="0" x2="100" y2="50"
  stroke="green" stroke-width="5" />
```

> *Strokes can be applied to any element. A rectangle, for instance, can be drawn with both a fill and stroke.*

Polylines

The `line` element draws a line between two points, but you can also create a line with any number of vertices using the `polyline` element:

```
<polyline points="0,0 100,50 75,75 75,0" fill="transparent" stroke="green" />
```

The `polyline` element uses the same syntax as `polygon`; the only difference is that it doesn't connect the endpoints, as shown in Figure 9-7.

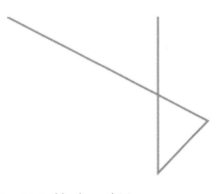

Figure 9-7: A polyline drawn with SVG

If you want to draw only lines, it is important to set the `fill` to `transparent` as well as define the `stroke` attribute. If you do not set the `fill` attribute, it automatically fills the polyline with the default black shown in Figure 9-8.

Ellipses

You can add ellipses to your SVG using the `ellipse` element:

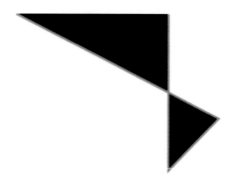

Figure 9-8: A polyline without a transparent `fill` attribute

```
<ellipse cx="80" cy="50" rx="80" ry="50"
  fill="purple" />
```

The `ellipse` element syntax is similar to the `circle` element: you set the coordinates of the center using `cx` and `cy`, and then define the radius. The only difference is that you can define two radii: the horizontal radius (`rx`) and the vertical (`ry`). This example draws a purple ellipse as shown in Figure 9-9.

Layering Multiple Shapes

Figure 9-9: An ellipse drawn with SVG

Unlike the canvas element, there are no options to control the stacking order of SVG elements. This means that each new shape you draw is added on top of those drawn previously. For instance, if you draw a rectangle and then a circle, the circle is rendered on top of the rectangle as shown in Figure 9-10:

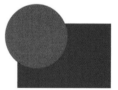

```
<svg height="200" xmlns="http://www.w3.org/2000/svg">
    <rect width="150" height="100" x="20" y="30" fill="blue"
  />
    <circle r="50" cx="50" cy="50" fill="red"></circle>
</svg>
```

Figure 9-10: The circle is drawn on top of the rectangle because it occurs last in the markup.

> With SVG shapes you cannot adjust the layering with CSS `z-index`. You must instead rely on the order in the DOM.

ADDING TEXT, LINKS AND IMAGES

In addition to drawing basic shapes, you can also add text, links, and external images to your SVG.

Adding Text

Add text to your SVG with the `text` element:

```
<svg height="200" xmlns="http://www.w3.org/2000/svg">
    <text x="20" y="50">Smashing WebKit</text>
</svg>
```

When using the `text` element, you can set the x and y coordinates of the text, but remember that x and y define the SVG's bottom-left corner by default. However, you can adjust this point horizontally by setting the `text-anchor` attribute:

```
<text x="20" y="50" text-anchor="middle">Smashing WebKit</text>
```

The `text-anchor` can be set to `middle`, `right`, or the default `left`.

You can also adjust the font size, weight, or family of your text using CSS:

```
<text x="20" y="50" style="font-size: 24px; font-weight: normal; font-family:
Arial;">Smashing WebKit</text>
```

You cannot use the CSS `color` property to adjust the font color because the color of the text is set with the SVG `fill` attribute:

```
<text x="20" y="50" fill="red" style="font-size: 24px; font-weight: normal;
font-family: Arial;">Smashing WebKit</text>
```

In addition to setting the `fill` color, you can add a stroke to your text using the `stroke` attribute, as shown in Figure 9-11.

Smashing WebKit

Figure 9-11: A purple stroke has been added to this text.

Adding Links

You can also add a link to any element you draw in SVG. Simply wrap it in an `a` element:

```
<a xlink:href="http://www.smashingwebkit.com/">
    <circle cx="50" cy="50" r="50" fill="red" />
</a>
```

221

In this example, the red circle links to the URL www.smashingwebkit.com. You can also attach a target to the link if you'd like it to open in a new window:

```
<a xlink:href="http://www.smashingwebkit.com/" target="_blank">
```

You can nest any number of elements within a single a element, and they all link to the given URL.

> Notice that the links here use the xlink:href attribute as opposed to the standard href. This syntax must be used for any links in your SVG.

Adding Images

To incorporate raster images into your SVG, take advantage of the image element:

```
<image xlink:href="myimage.jpg" width="100" height="100" />
```

In addition to the xlink:href attribute, it is also necessary to set the width and height of the image element. The linked image stretches to fit the dimensions you define. The aspect ratio of the original image is unaltered—if one dimension is too large, the image is simply centered.

Incorporating raster images into your SVG can be a great technique for reducing file size. For instance, you can combine vector shapes with a raster photograph to avoid having to rasterize the entire image. Furthermore, if you scale the image, the vector portion will scale smoothly, which is useful since rasterized shapes scale especially poorly, whereas rasterized photos tend to scale a bit better.

ADDING GRADIENTS

In addition to using plain block colors, you can also apply gradients to the shapes you draw in SVG.

Linear Gradients

To apply a linear gradient, you must first define the gradient in a defs element:

```
<svg height="200" xmlns="http://www.w3.org/2000/svg">
    <defs>
      <lineargradient id="mygradient">
        <stop offset="0%" stop-color="white" />
        <stop offset="100%" stop-color="blue" />
      </lineargradient>
    </defs>
</svg>
```

Here you created a linear gradient and added two color stops: white at 0% and blue at 100%. You can add as many color stops as you need.

> Color stops in SVG gradients work the same as CSS3 color stops, which you learned about in Chapter 3. Color stops define points at which the color of the gradient changes, with smooth color transitions between different stops.

Apply the gradient to a shape's `fill` attribute by referencing its `id`:

```
<rect width="150" height="100" fill="url(#mygradient)" />
```

This applies a linear gradient from left to right as shown in Figure 9-12.

To adjust the angle of the linear gradient, use coordinates similar to those of the `line` element:

```
<lineargradient id="mygradient" x1="0%"
  y1="0%" x2="0%" y2="100%">
  <stop offset="0%" stop-color="white" />
  <stop offset="100%" stop-color="blue" />
</lineargradient>
```

Figure 9-12: This rectangle has a linear gradient applied to it.

`x1` and `y1` define the start point of the gradient, and `x2` and `y2` define its end point. In this example the gradient goes from top to bottom. (See Figure 9-13.)

Radial Gradients

Similarly, you can apply radial gradients:

```
<defs>
  <radialgradient id="mygradient">
    <stop offset="0%" stop-color="white" />
    <stop offset="100%" stop-color="blue" />
  </radialgradient>
</defs>
```

Figure 9-13: The angle of this linear gradient has been adjusted so it renders vertically.

If you apply this gradient to the same rectangle, it stretches nicely to the rectangle's edges, as shown in Figure 9-14.

To adjust the center point of the gradient, use the `cx` and `cy` attributes:

```
<radialgradient id="mygradient" cx="10%"
  cy="10%">
  <stop offset="0%" stop-color="white" />
  <stop offset="100%" stop-color="blue" />
</radialgradient>
```

Figure 9-14: The radial gradient stretches all the way to the edges of the rectangle, as opposed to creating a circular gradient in the center.

This example centers the gradient closer to the top-left corner, as shown in Figure 9-15.

To alter the radius of the gradient, use the `r` attribute:

```
<radialgradient id="mygradient" cx="10%"
  cy="10%" r="30%">
  <stop offset="0%" stop-color="white" />
  <stop offset="100%" stop-color="blue" />
</radialgradient>
```

Figure 9-15: The center point of this radial gradient has been adjusted.

This sets the radius to 30% as opposed to the default 50%, as shown in Figure 9-16.

Adjusting Gradient Opacity

Normally you adjust opacity using RGBa colors, but the color stops in SVG gradients must be adjusted differently. You must define a `stop-opacity` attribute:

```
<stop offset="100%" stop-color="blue"
  stop-opacity="50%"/>
```

Figure 9-16: The radius of this radial gradient has been reduced.

This renders the blue color stop at 50% opacity instead of the default 100%.

USING CSS INSTEAD OF HTML ATTRIBUTES

Some of the SVG element attributes can also be applied using CSS. For instance, you can apply a fill color to all the circles on your page using the `fill` property:

```
svg circle {
    fill: blue;
}
```

Similarly, you can set `stroke` and `stroke-width` via CSS:

```
svg circle {
    fill: blue;
    stroke: green;
    stroke-width: 5px;
}
```

This technique can make styling a number of elements much easier, and can be combined with CSS `class` and `id` hooks in the markup.

> *Unfortunately many CSS properties will not work with SVG elements. For instance, you cannot apply drop shadows with* –webkit-box-shadow, *or skew and rotate shapes with* –webkit-transform.

JAVASCRIPT INTERACTION

Unlike canvas drawings, any shapes you add to your SVG element remain part of the DOM, and can be accessed via JavaScript. Simply add an `id` to the shape, and select it with JavaScript:

```
<svg height="200" xmlns="http://www.w3.org/2000/svg">
    <rect id="myrect" width="100" height="30" />
</svg>

<script type="text/javascript">
var $rect = document.getElementById('myrect');
</script>
```

> *You can also select SVG shapes using a jQuery selector—*$('rect') *or* $('#myrect'), *for instance.*

Adding Mouse Events

Because you can access SVG shapes using JavaScript, you can easily attach mouse events. For instance, you can attach a click event using jQuery:

```
$('#myrect').click(function() {
    alert('Rectangle clicked!');
});
```

While you may not be overly impressed with applying this event to a rectangle, remember that it can be applied to any shape you want. You can create a circle, along with a click event that is triggered only if the user clicks within the actual circle.

Conversely, if you apply a click event to a `div` with a circle background, the event fires if a user clicks the circle or anywhere within the square corners surrounding it.

Adjusting Attributes

Some attributes can be easily adjusted using jQuery's `attr()` method. For example, you can change the fill and stroke color of an SVG element:

```
$('#myrect').attr('fill', 'blue').attr('stroke', 'green');
```

However, other attributes, such as the rectangle dimensions, or positioning cannot be adjusted in this manner. Instead you have to drill into the DOM, and set specific properties. For instance, you can adjust the x position of your rectangle using `x.baseVal.value`:

```
$('#myrect')[0].x.baseVal.value = 100;
```

Or you can set the width using `width.baseVal.value`:

```
$('#myrect')[0].width.baseVal.value = 150;
```

> `$('#myrect')[0]` refers to the DOM reference of this element, not the jQuery object.

Animating

Because you can adjust these attributes directly, animation is also much easier with SVGs than it is with the canvas element. Simply change the values within a basic animation using `setInterval()`:

```
// cache a var for the x position and DOM reference
var xPos = 0,
$rect = $('#myrect')[0];

// set an interval to move the rectangle every 50 milliseconds
setInterval(function() {
    // adjust the rectangle's position
    $rect.x.baseVal.value = xPos;

    // adjust the x position var
    xPos++;
}, 50);
```

SUMMARY

SVG is unique among web-based image formats since it is the only format that is based on vectors. It is particularly useful for creating graphics for charts, graphs, logos and other simple shapes, since the SVG version is typically smaller in size when compared with other raster formats.

Additionally, since SVG is based on vectors, the image quality is completely independent from the dimensions. This means that SVG images scale well both large and small.

HTML5 introduces the SVG element, which allows you to build these graphics directly through markup. When compared with similar drawing techniques in HTML5 canvas, the SVG element has certain advantages. First, it will render even when JavaScript is not enabled. Furthermore, if JavaScript is enabled, it is much easier to interface with SVG drawings than it is with canvas, since SVG elements remain accessible to JavaScript.

Handcoding SVG elements can be time-consuming, but there are fortunately a variety of JavaScript libraries that can help generate these drawings. In addition to streamlining basic SVG creation, these libraries can help you to create complex applications such as 3D animations and SVG charts.

IV MOBILE WEBKIT

10 DEVELOPING FOR iOS AND ANDROID

ACROSS THE GLOBE, users are moving away from desktop and laptop computers, and opting to browse the web on mobile devices. In developed countries, users want an easier, more portable way to access the Internet. However, in many developing countries, these devices are the only practical way to get online. Indeed, many users are skipping over the desktop and laptop entirely, and accessing the web for the first time with a mobile device.

Although Symbian has historically had a dominant grip on the smartphone market, two comparatively new groups of mobile devices have been gaining a substantial foothold, and trending toward taking over the entire smartphone market in the years to come. These two groups are Apple devices built on iOS (iPhone, iPad, and iTouch), and devices built with Android (a wide variety of phones and tablets from a number of manufacturers).

There are a variety of concerns that come up when developing for iOS and Android devices. First, screen sizes in desktop browsers have increased to a point that developers have been able to shift focus away from issues such as which content appears "above the fold." But with mobile devices, especially phones and smaller tablets, these screen real estate issues have again presented a driving force in site design.

But the advantages of mobile devices far outweigh the screen issues. When building for mobile, you can use a variety of features that are only available on these advanced devices. This means that you can leverage support for dialing phone numbers, geolocation, and motion detection, to name a few. Furthermore, the relative newness of these devices and operating systems ensures a great deal of support for modern CSS3 and HTML5 features.

In this chapter you learn how to adjust your CSS based on the viewport and orientation of the device, as well as best practices for detecting mobile devices. You also explore some design patterns that should be followed when creating mobile stylesheets.

You explore how to leverage some uniquely mobile features in your web pages, and how to use multi-touch events, geolocation, and the accelerometer. You figure out how to interface with the cellular features of smartphones, to send voice calls, and text messages, and learn how to use the camera, video, and microphone capabilities in your web forms.

You also look at some of the shortcomings of iOS, and discover techniques you can use to get around issues such as lack of Flash support.

VIEWPORT AND ORIENTATION

Screen adjustments in desktop browsers are relatively simple: the only thing that can change is the pixel dimensions of the display.

Mobile browsers introduce a couple new issues:

- The viewport does not display all sites at their native resolution. Instead, it zooms the content based on the page dimensions, or viewport controls specified in the markup.
- In many mobile devices the user can alter the screen orientation, viewing the same website either horizontally or vertically.

Both zoom level and device orientation make styling responsive pages for mobile devices significantly more complicated. Conventional methods such as server-side device detection prove useless in these efforts because the user can adjust these variables without refreshing the page.

CONTROLLING THE VIEWPORT

The viewport controls how much mobile browsers zoom into a web page, as shown in Figure 10-1.

By default, Mobile WebKit attempts to set the viewport to a useful zoom level. If a width is defined for the page, it typically scales to fill that width. In more fluid layouts, it scales to 980 pixels wide because that is a sensible width for desktop browsers.

However, the default width is often unsatisfactory for many mobile sites. Although users can resize the content as needed, it is always best to offer an optimal zoom level from the initial page load.

Figure 10-1: The same website viewed with different zoom levels

Setting the Default Zoom Level

You can adjust the initial zoom level using the viewport meta tag:

```
<meta name="viewport" content="width=500" />
```

This example sets the viewport width to 500, meaning that 500 pixels of the website is shown across 100% of the screen. You can also set the width to `device-width` if you want to resize the viewport to match the width of the device:

```
<meta name="viewport" content="width=device-width" />
```

Although you could set this manually, for instance to a width of 320 pixels to match the width of iPhone 4, that isn't very foolproof. The 320 pixels measurement matches iPhone only in portrait mode, and will be off if the user rotates his device into landscape. Furthermore, other devices do not match this measurement; 320 pixels would be far too narrow in tablets like iPad, for instance.

Thus, setting the width to `device-width` ensures that there is a one-to-one relationship between the pixels in the site and on the device, regardless of the device dimensions.

> *You can also set the height of the viewport, either using a pixel measurement or* `device-height`*.*

Adjusting the Zoom Constraints

You also can set the minimum and maximum amount that the viewport can be resized. That constrains the level to which a user can adjust the viewport size after the initial zoom level has loaded. You set those values using `minimum-scale` and `maximum-scale:`

```
<meta name="viewport" content="width=device-width, minimum-scale=0.5, maximum-
  scale=4.0" />
```

This example allows the user to zoom out until the content is half the initial size, or zoom in to four times the default size. Thus if the `device-width` is 320 pixels, the user can zoom out to 640 pixels (content at half-size), or zoom in to a viewport width of 80 pixels (content four times as large).

By default, iOS Safari sets the `minimum-scale` to 0.25 and the `maximum-scale` to 1.6. It is usually a good idea to stick close to those defaults in all mobile browsers, but you can set the values to anything between 0.0 and 10.0.

> *It may be tempting to set the minimum zoom level to 0 and the maximum to 10, to allow the user to resize the viewport as much as he wants. However, it is usually best to offer smarter constraints that better match the needs of your page.*

Adjusting the Initial Scale

By default the `initial-scale` is set to 1.0, and you should leave this value alone in most cases. However, you can adjust it if necessary:

```
<meta name="viewport" content="width=device-width, initial-scale=2.0,
minimum-scale=0.5, maximum-scale=4.0" />
```

In this example, the `initial-scale` is set to 2.0, which zooms in to twice the initial size. So, if the `device-width` is 320 pixels, the page initially loads at 160 pixels (which doubles the size of the content). Afterward, the same minimum and maximum scale values apply as when you don't use `initial-scale`.

Disabling Zooming

To disable zooming altogether, set `user-scalable=no`:

```
<meta name="viewport" content="width=device-width, user-scalable=no" />
```

This prevents the user from resizing the viewport at all and should be applied only if you have a very good reason. In almost all scenarios, disabling zooming creates a frustrating user experience, and should be used with extreme caution.

> *Disabled zooming is ignored by many devices since it takes control away from the user.*

Adjusting the Scale Based on DPI

Android browser offers another option for the viewport meta tag, which allows you to adjust the viewport dimensions to accommodate the DPI (or dots per inch) of the screen. This provides more fine-grained control based on the pixel density of the screen. By appropriately targeting the screen DPI, you can ensure that images look as crisp as possible:

```
<meta name="viewport" content="target-densitydpi=device-dpi" />
```

Here, the pixel density of the viewport will match the pixel density of the screen, ensuring that the page displays clearly. Alternatively, you can set your own value for the target DPI, from 70 to 400, but in most cases it's best to stick to `device-dpi`.

ADJUSTING CSS USING MEDIA QUERIES

You learned about media queries and creating responsive web pages in Chapter 4. Mobile browsers include a number of new parameters that you can leverage with media queries to provide CSS adjustments.

Device Width and Height

You already may have used the `min-width` and `max-height` media query parameters to adjust styling based on the window size. That makes sense for desktop browsers because the browser window is not always the same size as the screen.

However, in mobile browsers the window size is always the size of the screen, so it makes more sense to use the device-based media queries `min-device-width` and `max-device-width`.

For instance, here's how you can target all devices that are up to 320 pixels wide:

```
@media (max-device-width: 320px) {
    /* styles go here */
}
```

This will not target desktop browsers with smaller windows because the media query is based on the device instead of the window size. However, you may want to apply the same styles to desktop browsers with tiny windows. If you are simply optimizing the screen for small window sizes, it is probably better to apply it across the board using the `max-width` parameter.

Device Orientation

The previous `max-device-width` media query targets iPhones 3 and 4 that are being held in portrait mode because their screen is 320 pixels wide. If the user rotates his screen into landscape mode, the `max-device-width` changes to 480 pixels, as shown in Figure 10-2.

Figure 10-2: The difference between portrait and landscape mode for iPhone 4

There is also a media query you can use to adjust styling based on the orientation of the device. To take advantage of orientation media queries, use the `orientation` parameter:

```
@media (orientation: portrait) {
    /* portrait styles here */
}
```

This targets devices in portrait mode. You can also apply special styles for landscape mode:

```
@media (orientation: landscape) {
    /* landscape styles here */
}
```

Device Resolution

You can adjust styling based on the resolution of the device, which means that you can style pages differently based on the pixel-density of the screen. WebKit offers a special media query for pixel density, `-webkit-device-pixel-ratio`:

```
@media (-webkit-min-device-pixel-ratio: 2) {
    /* high resolution styles here */
}
```

This targets higher density screens, such as iPhone 4, while ignoring lower density screens such as older iPhones.

To apply the same high-resolution styles across more browsers, there are a few additional media queries you can add. First, there is a similar media query for Mozilla, `-moz-device-pixel-ratio`. Additionally, there is a cross-browser version that is based on DPI, but the premise is the same:

```
@media (-webkit-min-device-pixel-ratio: 2),
    (min--moz-device-pixel-ratio: 2),
    (min-resolution: 300dpi) {
    /* high resolution styles here */
}
```

This applies the high-resolution styles for more browsers. 300dpi is equivalent to a `device-pixel-ratio` of 2. Also, pay attention to the Mozilla media query; the syntax is slightly different.

ACCESSING VIEWPORT, ORIENTATION AND RESOLUTION VIA JAVASCRIPT

Besides meta tags and media queries, you can also hook into the device viewport, orientation, and resolution using JavaScript.

Viewport

Although the viewport is not readily accessible from JavaScript, you can access some viewport properties using a hack involving the viewport meta tag. Here's how:

1. Select the meta tag, using jQuery:

   ```
   $('meta[name="viewport"]');
   ```

   If you are not using `jQuery`, *you can alternatively apply an ID to the meta tag and use* `document.getElementByID()`.

2. Retrieve the viewport info using the `attr()` method:

   ```
   $('meta[name="viewport"]').attr('content');
   ```

   Unfortunately, this will be a string of the viewport data, so you will need to write a script to parse out the data you need.

3. Set the viewport info using the same `attr()` method:

   ```
   $('meta[name="viewport"]').attr('content', 'minimum-scale=0.25');
   ```

Be aware that this will overwrite all the viewport settings, not just the particular values you set. You can use this technique to alter the scale at will, thereby zooming into the page:

```
$('meta[name="viewport"]').attr('content', 'initial-scale=4');
```

This technique works only if the user has not zoomed into the page manually.

Orientation

You can access the screen orientation in JavaScript with `window.orientation`:

```
console.log( window.orientation );
```

This outputs the orientation in degrees—0 for portrait mode, and 90 or –90 for landscape (depending on which way the device has been rotated). The `onorientationchange` event fires when the orientation changes:

```
window.onorientationchange = function() {
    alert('orientation changed');
};
```

You cannot get information about the new orientation from the event itself, so you have to tap into `window.orientation` within your event handler to make any orientation-based adjustments.

> *Later in this chapter you'll learn how to get more fine-grained details about the device's position in all three dimensions.*

Resolution

You can access the screen resolution in JavaScript by using `window.devicePixelRatio`:

```
console.log( window.devicePixelRatio );
```

In pixel-dense devices such as iPhone 4, this returns a value of 2, and in older, less dense devices, it returns 1.5.

DETECTING MOBILE

Frequently you will want to serve different versions of your website to mobile and desktop visitors. Whether you simply want to restyle the layout or add a great deal of mobile-specific functionality, the techniques for doing so rely on accurately detecting which users are on which devices.

There are several approaches to detecting mobile, from backend user agent detection to CSS media queries. Other alternatives include testing user agents and media queries with JavaScript, or relying on the user to manually click a link to view the mobile version of the site.

USER AGENT DETECTION

The most foolproof way to detect mobile devices is user agent (UA) detection performed on the backend. With this technique, you retrieve the user agent string, and compare it against a list of mobile browsers.

Advantages of User Agent Detection

The main advantage of UA detection is that it is the most accurate method of mobile detection. You can use it to successfully target all mobile devices, or even to provide different support for different groups of devices, such as phones and tablets.

A backend technique like this is the only way to gain control over the markup. Other methods allow you to hide only unwanted content from mobile users, but backend UA detection allows you to avoid ever serving extra markup to your mobile users. This enables you to reduce the file size for mobile devices, which often have problems with bandwidth. Furthermore, you can make additional changes as needed directly in the markup, instead of relying entirely on a mobile stylesheet.

Drawbacks of User Agent Detection

The UA detection approach does have some drawbacks because it's often difficult to perform it completely accurately. The list of mobile user agent strings is constantly growing, which means that you have to revisit your detection script as new devices hit the market. Additionally, you have to rely on the device to accurately convey its true user agent. While you might think that most devices relay this information correctly, historically that has not always been the case. In fact, many browsers and devices spoof different user agents explicitly to pass this type of detection. For instance, most user agents start with Mozilla to get around the Netscape checks of the '90s, and for several years Opera pretended to be IE.

A backend method like this allows you to detect devices, but it cannot provide any information about the device orientation. Depending on the backend language, it may be difficult to retrieve the connection type. You will need to include additional front-end functionality to accommodate any changes based on these characteristics.

UA String Services

There are a number of services that can help you get around the difficulties surrounding mobile device detection. These services not only take all the guesswork out of mobile detection, but also provide ongoing support as new devices are released. One such service is called Mobile-ESP, an open source project that provides PHP and JavaScript APIs for fine-grained mobile device detection. Learn more about MobileESP here: `http://blog.mobileesp.com/`.

Another open source mobile detection service is called Detect Mobile Browser. This project provides scripts in a number of languages that you can use to detect mobile devices. For more information, go here: `http://detectmobilebrowser.com/`.

For more fine-grained mobile detection, consider using WURFL: `http://wurfl.source forge.net/`. WURFL is a frequently updated XML file that provides information about which devices are mobile and the capabilities available in each device. WURFL offers a completely free solution for targeting the specific features of each mobile device, to ensure that you only offer functionality where it's applicable. Many APIs leverage WURFL, for instance Tera-WURFL for PHP (`http://dbapi.scientiamobile.com/wiki/index.php/Main_Page`).

MEDIA QUERIES

Besides altering styling based on screen dimensions and orientation, you can also use media queries to detect mobile devices. Although less accurate, this approach does provide a reasonable amount of mobile detection with very little effort. The main drawback is that this approach allows you to change only CSS styling.

Handheld Media Type

The W3C specifies the handheld media type for mobile devices to simplify mobile media queries. You can use this media type to provide mobile CSS for supportive browsers:

```
@media handheld {
    /* handheld styles here */
}
```

However, the handheld media type is not supported by many mobile browsers, including most based on WebKit. Don't expect this to change in the future because device manufacturers have no interest in supporting this media type.

Mobile websites are typically a stripped-down version of the original site. In an effort to set themselves apart from their competitors, modern device manufacturers have opted to trick websites into serving the fuller, more feature-rich version. Theoretically, this provides users with a more enjoyable experience, but it makes mobile development more difficult.

Device Size and Orientation Detection

The only way to detect Mobile WebKit with media queries is to approximate which visitors are using mobile devices by leveraging other properties. You explored this type of detection earlier this chapter. The main idea is to use a combination of `device-width` and `orientation` to target the devices you need. For instance, to target iPhone (and similar devices), you can use this media query:

```
@media (max-device-width: 320px and orientation: portrait),
    (max-device-width: 480px and orientation: landscape) {
    /* iPhone styles here */
}
```

iPhones 3 and 4 have a `device-width` of 320 pixels in portrait mode and 480 pixels in landscape mode, so this media query handles both situations. If you need finer grained control, you can also incorporate `-webkit-min-device-pixel-ratio`. iPhone 4 has a pixel-ratio of 2, whereas earlier iPhones have 1.5.

Hybrid Approach

If you are concerned with mobile browsers other than iOS Safari and Android browser, you can use a hybrid approach that combines the preceding media query with the `handheld` media type. For more information about this approach, go here: `www.alistapart.com/articles/return-of-the-mobile-stylesheet`.

Disadvantages of Media Queries

The media queries technique has a couple of disadvantages in addition to affecting only CSS styling:

- It doesn't catch all mobile devices—for instance, most tablets are larger than smartphones.
- It catches any devices of this size, not only WebKit devices.

If you are only restyling content for smaller screens, these issues are probably not a problem; the mobile styles work well on any small screens, and the desktop styles work well on larger tablets. However if you are using these styles to provide crucial, mobile-only styling, this method may not be the best choice.

Furthermore, media queries can be used only to alter styling and cannot adjust the markup on the page. You can usually find workarounds to get mobile pages to display the way you want, but you still end up serving mobile users a lot of markup that they may not necessarily need.

241

DETECTION WITH JAVASCRIPT

Using JavaScript to detect mobile devices can provide the same accuracy level as backend user agent detection, and can also include detection for additional properties such as connection speed.

User Agent Detection

To access the user agent string in JavaScript, simply call `navigator.userAgent`. You can also get the browser version using `navigator.appVersion`:

```
var uaString = navigator.userAgent,
version = navigator.appVersion;
```

Compare this user agent against a list of mobile devices, and you can have the same level of accuracy as backend device detection. Unfortunately, it also suffers the same difficulties.

Match Media

Although not specific to mobile, media queries are particularly useful for including mobile-specific stylesheets. You can use a similar feature in JavaScript, `matchMedia()`:

```
if (window.matchMedia('(max-device-width: 480px)').matches) {
    // the device width is 480px or smaller
}
```

`matchMedia()` enables you to use any of the media queries you used in CSS, with the same syntax. At the time of this writing, `matchMedia()` is available only in iOS 5+, but you can provide backward compatibility using the Respond.js polyfill, which is available here: `https://github.com/scottjehl/Respond`.

Detecting Connection Speed

Besides screen size, the other major difference in mobile browsing is reduced bandwidth. Cell networks are typically slower than WiFi connections, and it is a good idea to serve these users smaller pages.

Unfortunately it is not as simple as detecting whether a user is on a mobile device. For instance if a user is on a tablet device, it is most likely connected to WiFi. But even tablet users may be connected to a mobile network, either through a connection in the tablet, or by tethering it to their phone. Phone users may be connected to WiFi, and even if they are not, there are large bandwidth differences between different cell networks. For example, a 2G connection is significantly slower than a 4G connection.

You cannot reliably detect the connection type in iOS, but Android 2.2+ does offer a technique you can use to get an idea of the user's bandwidth. To use this, tap into `navigator.connection`:

```
if ( navigator.connection.type == navigator.connection.WIFI ) {
    // user is on WIFI
}
```

> Because `navigator.connection` is available only in Android, make sure to use a `typeof` check so it doesn't throw an error in other devices.

For more insight into the `navigator.connection` object, take a look at its contents:

```
{
    "type": "2",
    "UNKNOWN": "0",
    "ETHERNET": "1",
```

```
    "WIFI": "2",
    "CELL_2G": "3",
    "CELL_3G": "4",
    "CELL_4G": "5"
}
```

To hook into the detection object, you can either compare individual properties as in the preceding example, or set up a `switch()` statement to handle all the cases:

```
switch(navigator.connection.type) {
    case "1":
    case "2":
        // wifi and ethernet connections
    break;

    case "3":
        // slow 2G networks
    break;

    case "4":
        // somewhat faster 3G networks
    break;

    case "5":
        // fast 4G networks
    break;

    default:
        // unknown connections
    break;
}
```

This separates out actions for each connection type. You may consider lumping 4G in with the Ethernet and WiFi connections.

> *This type of detection is not always foolproof. For instance, if the user has a tablet tethered to a phone, it registers as a WiFi connection.*

NO DETECTION

Some sites opt to avoid mobile detection all together, and instead allow the users to choose which version of the site they visit. With this technique, a link is provided to the mobile site, as shown in Figure 10-3.

Figure 10-3: IKEA has a link to its mobile site in the header.

© Inter IKEA Systems B.V. 1990-2010

It's a good idea to place the link somewhere noticeable at the top of your document, such as in the main navigation. The link then points to a special mobile subdomain—for instance, `http://m.smashingwebkit.com/`.

This has the advantage of providing the users total control of their experience. However, the link clutters the interface for non-mobile users. Additionally, if mobile users do not notice the link, they will never visit the mobile version of the site (and at a minimum will have to download the full version of the site the first time they visit).

> It's usually best to detect mobile rather than rely on users to manually visit the mobile site.

STYLING FOR MOBILE

There are a number of patterns you should follow when designing the stylesheet for the mobile version of your website.

MAXIMIZE SCREEN REAL ESTATE

The main issue with mobile stylesheets is the reduced screen size in many mobile devices. Most tablets do not have problems displaying similar amounts of content as desktop browsers, but smartphones are another story.

> When resolving screen size issues, it is best to use media queries to adjust the layout based on the screen dimensions. If you adjust the layout for all mobile browsers, you will run into problems with tablets. For instance, if you detect only iOS, you will serve the same stylesheet for iPad as you do for iPhone.

Use Single Columns

The most important rule to follow when creating a smartphone stylesheet is to simplify your layout into a single column. Most sites supply multiple columns of content to desktop browsers, but there is simply not enough space for that content on mobile phones.

Try to eliminate any supplemental columns that are not absolutely vital to the user experience. Do you have a list of featured posts in a sidebar next to a main blog entry? These should probably be removed for mobile phones. If any side columns are mission critical, add them below the main content column. Simply use CSS to remove the floats (or whatever else positions the side column).

You may consider using two columns in horizontal layouts.

Resize Content

It's also a good idea to resize any large content on your page. Shrink the logo, as well as any oversized images, headlines, and so on.

REDUCE FILE SIZE

Mobile network speeds are significantly slower than most landline broadband services so you should also take whatever measures you can to reduce the file size of the pages you serve to mobile devices. Remember, even if a user has a 4G phone, he might not be in a 4G service area, or the connection might be spotty.

Bandwidth concerns affect tablets as well.

245

Remove Extraneous Content

You already made a number of bandwidth reducing changes when adjusting for smaller screen sizes. Removing extraneous content and resizing large elements are the best ways to cut down on the amount of data the user has to download. So make sure to remove any nonessential elements that were not removed earlier. However, don't go overboard removing content for mobile. Mobile users still need a useful experience, and are expecting more and more out of mobile websites as time goes on.

If an element is nonessential for mobile, it may be extraneous for desktop as well.

Responsive Images

You can take this one step further by making sure that the images you serve are as small as possible. It is not enough to resize images visually if you are still serving mobile users the original full-size image data.

When it comes to background images, you can easily serve a new, lower-resolution image for mobile browsers within your stylesheets. However images included via the `img` element can prove more difficult.

For these images, you can take advantage of an open source responsive images script released by Filament Group. This script serves mobile content first, to ensure that mobile browsers receive the smallest image possible. Then larger images are served to desktop browsers, so the resolution of the image is not compromised for users who have the available bandwidth. For more information, go to `https://github.com/filamentgroup/Responsive-Images`.

MISCELLANEOUS CHANGES

In addition to layout and bandwidth issues, there are a variety of other concerns when creating mobile stylesheets.

Other Size Issues

A couple additional issues for you to consider stem from smaller screens on mobile phones. First, increase the font-size of any smaller fonts because these tend to be illegible on mobile devices. Second, increase the clickable area on any links, by adding extra padding, for instance. Clicking on most mobile devices is performed with the user's finger, and is much less precise than using a mouse. Thus, a larger clickable area is a very good idea.

When styling clickable areas, consider using real physical measurements such as 10mm instead of the pixel or em measurements typically used in CSS. A good standard for click targets is 10mm (or larger).

Positioning Issues

Floated elements often present problems in mobile browsers, so consider removing any floats that aren't absolutely necessary (and thoroughly testing those that are). Fixed positioning does not work in older versions of Mobile WebKit, so you should consider alternative techniques for these elements, such as `position: absolute`.

Mouseover States

As mentioned earlier, most smartphones and tablets do not use a mouse. That means any mouseover events are irrelevant, and that you cannot rely on `:hover` to provide UI cues that a link is clickable. If you have applied any essential functionality through a `:hover` state or a JavaScript `mouseover` event, you need to provide a different solution. Consider using the `:active` state or a click event instead.

ACCESSING DEVICE FUNCTIONALITY

There are a variety of unique interface options provided by mobile devices. Using this advanced functionality, you can create rich mobile experiences that respond to touch events, the motion of the device, as well as the user's physical location. You also can interface with the cellular capabilities on smartphones, triggering voice calls as well as text messages.

TOUCH EVENTS

iOS and Android provide a number of custom touch events you can leverage with JavaScript to create a uniquely mobile experience. Although similar to click events, touch events offer more complexity, incorporating multi-finger touches, dragging, and even gestures such as rotation.

Basic Touch Event

There are a variety of touch events that you can use to track touch interactions with mobile devices. They work similarly to other events in JavaScript; simply set up a function with an event listener:

```
var el = document.getElementById('my-element');

el.addEventListener('touchstart', function(e) {
    // what to do with the event
});
```

This event is triggered when the user's finger first touches the device screen. You can return the coordinates of this touch event using pageX and pageY within the e.touch object:

```
el.addEventListener('touchstart', function(e) {
    var x = e.touch.pageX;
    var y = e.touch.pageY;
});
```

pageX and pageY return the position of the touch event relative to the entire page. You can also use screenX and screenY to return position relative to the screen, or clientX and clientY to return position relative to the viewport.

> *The basic touch event is similar to the click event, except that it fires immediately, whereas the click event has a 300ms delay in iOS Safari.*

Other Touch Events

There are a couple additional touch events that compliment touchstart. The touchend function tracks the point at which the user lifts his finger off the screen. When compared to mouse events, touchstart is like mousedown and touchend is like mouseup. In Android, touchend works practically the same as touchstart:

```
el.addEventListener('touchend', function(e) {
    var x = e.touch.pageX;
    var y = e.touch.pageY;
});
```

247

However this code will not work in iOS because that operating system removes the event from the e.touch object on touchend. Instead, you have to use e.changedTouch:

```
el.addEventListener('touchend', function(e) {
    var x = e.changedTouch.pageX;
    var y = e.changedTouch.pageY;
});
```

e.changedTouch tracks the position of any touch event that has changed. This event also works in Android, so it's a good idea to stick to this event for touchend.

> *When detecting basic click events it is usually preferable to use* touchend *instead of* touchstart, *since it gives the user a chance to make their click more precise or drag away if they click the wrong item.*

touchmove is a touch event you can use to track whenever the position of the touch changes. Because it fires while the user is still touching the screen, it is useful for detecting drag events:

```
el.addEventListener('touchmove', function(e) {
    var x = e.touch.pageX;
    var y = e.touch.pageY;
});
```

> *When compared with mouse events,* touchmove *is similar to* mousemove.

touchstart, touchmove, and touchend are available in both iOS and Android 2.2+.

Multi-Touch Events

You can also use the standard touch events to track multi-touch events. Multi-touch events occur when the user places another finger (or more) on the screen during a touch event.

Earlier, you used e.touch to get the x and y coordinates of a single touch event. With multi-touch events, there is an additional array of touch events, e.touches, which provides the coordinates of each finger press. For instance, you can use the e.touches array to track both locations in a two-finger press:

```
el.addEventListener('touchstart', function(e) {
    var x1 = e.touches[0].pageX;
    var y1 = e.touches[0].pageY;
    var x2 = e.touches[1].pageX;
    var y2 = e.touches[1].pageY;
});
```

The e.touches array registers all touches, even those outside of the target element. If you want to confine the event to only the touches that occur within the target, you can use the e.targetTouches array. To register only those touches that have changed, you can use e.changedTouches.

> Multi-touch tracking can be used with all the different touch events: touchstart, touchmove, and touchend.

Gesture Events

Gesture events are available only in iOS. They are pre-established touch events that you can use to create more interactive touch interfaces. While touch events map the precise location of finger presses, gesture events track predefined actions such as rotation and pinching. You could recreate gestures using complex multi-touch events, but gesture events provide a shortcut for handling touch actions that iOS users are already comfortable using.

Similar to touch events, there are three gesture events: gesturestart, gesturechange, and gestureend. Within gesture events there are a couple additional features you can leverage: e.rotation and e.scale.

```
el.addEventListener('gesturechange', function(e) {
    var rotation = e.rotation;
    var scale = e.scale;
});
```

e.rotation returns the degrees of rotation from the start of the gesture. For instance, if the user rotates 90 degrees clockwise, it returns 90. Rotation events occur when the user presses two fingers to the screen and rotates them.

e.scale is used to track pinch events. It returns a ratio based on the original distance between the user's fingers. At the start position, the user's fingers return an e.scale value of 1, If the space doubles, e.scale returns a 2; if the space is halved, it returns 0.5.

Gesture Event Example

In iOS the rotate gesture rotates an element and the pinch gesture scales it. You can link gesture event listeners up with -webkit-transform to perform these changes visually in the browser:

```
el.addEventListener('gesturechange', function(e) {
    el.style.webkitTransform = 'rotate(' + e.rotation + 'deg)' +
        ' scale(' + e.scale + ')';
});
```

Here you set the element's -webkit-transform attribute in JavaScript to reflect the rotation and scale of the gesture, as shown in Figure 10-4.

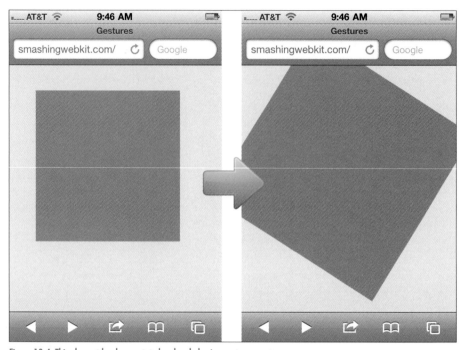

Figure 10-4: This element has been rotated and scaled using gesture events.

The next time the user performs a gesture on the element, the transformation starts from scratch, with the rotation at 0 and the scale at 1. Thus, you should cache any previously performed gestures with JavaScript variables:

```
var rotation = 0;
var scale = 1;

el.addEventListener('gesturechange', function(e) {
    el.style.webkitTransform = 'rotate(' + e.rotation + rotation
        + 'deg)' + ' scale(' + e.scale * scale + ')';
});

// cache the new rotation and scale starting point gestureend
el.addEventListener('gestureend', function(e) {
    rotation += e.rotation;
    scale *= e.scale;
});
```

This script incorporates any previous gestures on the element when calculating the -web-kit-transform values, and saves the new starting point when the gesture ends.

> When adding gesture events to your page, it is a good idea to set user-scalable=no in the viewport meta tag, so that pinch gestures do not affect the browser window.

GEOLOCATION

Geolocation can be leveraged by applications that want to know the user's physical location. Although not strictly confined to mobile devices, geolocation plays an important part in mobile development because the devices often include Global Positioning System (GPS), which can provide precise information about the user's latitude and longitude.

Basic Geolocation

You can access geolocation via JavaScript using the `navigator.geolocation` API. First determine if geolocation is available, and then use `getCurrentPosition()` to return the coordinates:

```
if ( navigator.geolocation ) {
    navigator.geolocation.getCurrentPosition(function(position) {
        alert('Location: ' + position.coords.latitude + ' ' + position.coords.
    longitude);
    });
}
```

`getCurrentPosition()` accepts a success callback function, which defines a position object. You can tap into the latitude and longitude of this position using `coords.latitude` and `coords.longitude`.

This type of geolocation is not limited to mobile devices; it's actually available in all modern browsers. However in desktop browsers the positioning is calculated based on efficient lookups such as the user's IP address, and is therefore not overly accurate.

More Precise Geolocation

Many mobile devices such as smartphones can provide more accurate geolocation information using GPS. To tap into more precise positions, use the `watchPosition()` method, which works similarly to `getCurrentPosition()`:

```
if ( navigator.geolocation ) {
    navigator.geolocation.watchPosition(function(position) {
        alert('Location: ' + position.coords.latitude + ' ' + position.coords.
    longitude);
    });
}
```

As you can see, `watchPosition()` also accepts a callback function that returns an object containing the user's latitude and longitude.

Geolocation Tracking

`watchPosition()` also sets up an interval to return position changes over time. This is similar to combining a `setInterval()` with `getCurrentPosition()`, but the `watchPosition()` is better for device power consumption since it only fires when relevant changes are made.

`getCurrentPosition()` fires only once, but `watchPosition()` may fire additional times. The callback executes whenever the user's location has changed significantly, or more precise geolocation information becomes available (if the first location is based on IP, for instance, and the next location is based on GPS).

To stop the position interval, you can use `clearWatch()`, which works similarly to `clearInterval()`:

```
var positionTimer = navigator.geolocation.watchPosition( function(position) {
    navigator.geolocation.clearWatch(positionTimer);
});
```

This function clears the position interval after the first time it is executed.

> *The first callback* `watchPosition()` *fires is typically a fairly rough estimate of the user's location. For more precise positioning, it is best to call* `clearWatch()` *later using* `setTimeout()`, *or by setting a counter to clear the interval after the second or third time it executes.*

Geolocation Security

It stands to reason that browsers would not enable geolocation information by default because it presents a privacy issue to users. That's why, when geolocation is invoked, the user typically has to accept a prompt to allow this functionality, as shown in Figure 10-5.

The website "http://smashingwebkit.com" would like to use your current location.

☐ Remember my decision for one day

Don't Allow   Allow

Figure 10-5: A prompt to accept geolocation in Safari

Although most modern browsers support geolocation, it is always important to check if geolocation exists before working with it because the user may not accept that functionality.

GYROSCOPE AND ACCELEROMETER

The gyroscope and accelerometer in mobile devices provide a unique opportunity to access data regarding the precise orientation and motion of the device in three dimensions. Both are accessible via JavaScript in iOS devices, but are not available in Android Browser at the time of this writing.

Gyroscope Support

Earlier you learned how to use `window.orientation` and the `window.orientation change` event to access the approximate orientation of the device. However, that returns only information describing whether the device has been rotated into portrait or landscape mode.

The gyroscope provides precise information regarding the orientation of the device in all three dimensions. By leveraging this data, you can access the exact number of degrees the device has rotated across three axes. To retrieve the gyroscope data, bind an `ondevice orientation` event to the `window` object:

```
window.ondeviceorientation = function(e) {
    var xRotation = e.alpha;
    var yRotation = e.beta;
    var zRotation = e.gamma;
}
```

This technique works well in modern iOS devices such as iPhone 4 and iPad 2, but it does not work in older iOS devices.

Accelerometer Support

With older iOS devices, you can access the accelerometer to return information about the device's three-dimensional motion. To access this data using JavaScript, simply bind an `ondevicemotion` event to the `window` object:

```
window.ondevicemotion = function(e) {
    var xMotion = e.accelerationIncludingGravity.x;
    var yMotion = e.accelerationIncludingGravity.y;
    var zMotion = e.accelerationIncludingGravity.z;
}
```

In devices such as iPhone 4 that have a gyroscope, you can also access more accurate accelerometer information using the `acceleration` object instead of `accelerationIncludingGravity`:

```
window.ondevicemotion = function(e) {
    var xMotion = e.acceleration.x;
    var yMotion = e.acceleration.y;
    var zMotion = e.acceleration.z;
}
```

Accelerometer and Gyroscope in Android

Many Android devices include gyroscopes and accelerometers, but these attributes are only available in native apps at the time of this writing. However PhoneGap, an open source mobile framework, creates a bridge between these complex features and JavaScript, allowing you to build native apps using JavaScript, HTML, and CSS. PhoneGap apps cannot run in the browser, but they do allow you to build complex RIAs using the web development techniques with which you are already comfortable.

> *PhoneGap is discussed in greater detail in the next chapter.*

DIALING PHONE NUMBERS

One advantage of browsing the web on a phone is that the browsing experience can be integrated seamlessly with the cellular network. This means that you can call phone numbers directly from the browser, simply by clicking on them.

iOS and Android automatically detect phone numbers, but they do not always parse the number perfectly, so it is sometimes better to flag the number explicitly. Setting up a phone number for dialing is as easy as defining it in the markup:

```
<a href="tel:+12125551234">(212) 555-1234</a>
```

Simply use a basic link with the `tel:` prefix, and the link trigger a prompt to dial the number, as shown in Figure 10-6.

> *It is a good idea to add the +1 to the beginning of your number so it works internationally. .*

Hiding Clickable Numbers in Non-Mobile Devices

Be careful when using link dialing because these numbers are clickable in all browsers. Fortunately, a couple of techniques let you avoid potential conflicts. First, you can use media queries to hide the styling in non-mobile devices. Although this approach is easiest, the numbers are still clickable, even if that isn't readily apparent to the user.

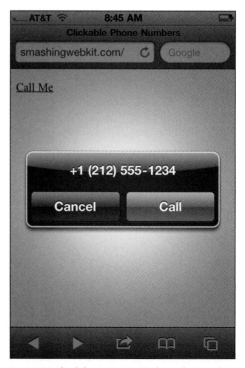

Figure 10-6: This dialog pops up in iOS when a phone number is clicked.

Second, you can use backend browser-sniffing to add the phone number links only for phones. While this approach is mostly foolproof, it can be the most challenging to develop because you not only have to build in hooks wherever you want a phone number, but you also have to accurately detect the device based on the UA string.

> *Be careful when detecting mobile devices for phone numbers because not all Mobile WebKit devices are phones. For instance, the iTouch is similar in a lot of ways to the iPhone, but only the iPhone can be used for voice calls.*

Using JavaScript to Apply Clickable Numbers

Arguably the best approach is to combine markup with JavaScript to progressively enhance web pages with clickable phone numbers. You first wrap the number in an unstyled span:

```
<span class="phone-number">(212) 555-1234</span>
```

In mobile browsers use a JavaScript library such as jQuery to pull in all these phone number links, and convert them into clickable numbers:

```
$(function() {
    $('span.phone-number').each(function() {
        var $this = $(this),
        theNumber = $this.text();

        $this.replaceWith('<a href="tel:' + theNumber + '" class="phone-number">' +
theNumber + '</a>');
    });
});
```

This script finds each of these phone number spans, and replaces it with a clickable phone link. It pulls the number from the text of the span, but if you would rather use different text, you can simply include the number in the `href` attribute of the span:

```
<span href="(212) 555-1234" class="phone-number">Call Me</span>
```

Be sure to pull the phone number as well as the text from the call to action:

```
$(function() {
    $('span.phone-number').each(function() {
        var $this = $(this),
        theNumber = $this.attr('href'),
        theText = $this.text();

        $this.replaceWith('<a href="tel:' + theNumber + '" class="phone-number">' +
theText + '</a>');
    });
});
```

For simplicity, the +1 prefix has been omitted from these examples, but you can add it to your script.

Disabling Automatic Telephone Number Linking

To ensure that the phone numbers on your page are *not* clickable, you can disable the automatic linking using a meta tag:

```
<meta name="format-detection" content="telephone=no" />
```

This causes iOS Safari and Android's browser to refrain from parsing your page for clickable phone numbers. This does not affect any numbers that you flag yourself using the `tel:` link syntax.

Dialing Phone Numbers with JavaScript

You can also dial phone numbers in iOS and Android using JavaScript. The easiest way uses a hack to redirect the browser to the phone number link. Simply use `window.location` to point to a phone number using the same syntax from a standard link:

```
window.location = 'tel:+12125551234';
```

Because the URL is not an actual web page, it dials the number, while keeping the current page in the browser.

TEXT MESSAGING

You can also trigger text messages from the browser. Simply attach links with an `sms:` prefix:

```
<a href="sms:+12125551234">Text Me</a>
```

When this link is clicked, it triggers the text message dialog using this number. See Figure 10-7.

Remember, the same issues concerning non-mobile devices exist with SMS, so make sure to take measures to hide or remove these links in non-mobile browsers.

Figure 10-7: This SMS message was triggered using a HTML link.

Multiple Recipients

To send text messages to multiple recipients, simply separate these by a comma:

```
<a href="sms:+12125551234,+12125556789">Text Us</a>
```

When the user clicks this link, both of these numbers are loaded into the SMS text message dialog.

Text Messaging with JavaScript

You can trigger text messages with JavaScript, using the same technique you used for dialing phone numbers. Simply use `window.location` to point the window to a link with the SMS scheme:

```
window.location = 'sms:+12125551234';
```

You can also use this technique with multiple recipients, using the same syntax you used earlier.

CONTEXTUAL KEYBOARDS

In Chapter 8 you learned how to leverage HTML5 form elements to trigger contextual keyboards. These keyboards make it easier for users to enter particular data, such as phone numbers and URLs. To take advantage of this interface, just use special input types in your markup:

```
<input type="tel" />
<input type="email" />
<input type="url" />
<input type="number" />
```

When focused, these inputs trigger a contextual keyboard that provides easier data entry for phone numbers, email addresses, URLs, and numbers respectively, as shown in Figure 10-8.

> Some devices provide hardware keyboards, and will simply ignore the contextual information from these fields (except for validation purposes).

Figure 10-8: Special keyboards for entering phone numbers and email addresses in iPhone

DISABLING AUTOCORRECT

Autocorrect is notorious for annoying mobile users because it often "corrects" words that the user meant to type, thereby changing the meaning, as shown in Figure 10-9.

Figure 10-9: Autocorrect often corrects words that are not misspelled.

Despite its shortcomings, autocorrect is a useful feature because the keyboards on mobile devices are often small and lead to a number of miss-clicks.

That said, there are certain situations where autocorrect does not make sense. For instance, autocorrect causes problems in any situation where the user is entering data that is not necessarily made of real words, such as usernames or email addresses.

The email input type automatically disables autocorrect, but you can also disable autocorrect manually on any form field:

```
<input autocorrect="off" />
```

To enable autocorrect on a field from which it is automatically removed, set it to on:

```
<input type="email" autocorrect="on" />
```

You can also disable autocomplete and autocapitalize on any form field:

```
<input autocorrect="off" autocomplete="off" autocapitalize="off" />
```

MEDIA CAPTURE

Newer versions of Android offer a number of media capture techniques you can leverage in your web pages. This allows integrated support of the camera and microphone on Android devices. You can allow users to capture a photo for a file input:

```
<input type="file" accept="image/*;capture=camera" />
```

This triggers the camera, and allows the user to take a photo, which will be integrated into the file input.

Alternatively, you can capture video:

```
<input type="file" accept="video/*;capture=camcorder" />
```

And you can capture audio with the microphone:

```
<input type="file" accept="audio/*;capture=microphone" />
```

> *These capture options are available only in Android 3.0+ and are not available at all in iOS.*

SPECIAL CONCERNS FOR IOS

iOS provides advanced functionality, but there are a number of issues that make developing for iOS Safari more challenging. While Android is open source, iOS is decidedly closed, and the majority of iOS-specific issues relate to these devices being locked down.

For instance, you probably know that iOS devices cannot play Flash. While decisions like these move open web standards forward and improve performance on iOS devices, the fact remains that these issues can prove difficult for developers to circumvent.

USING HTML5 INSTEAD OF FLASH

The most difficult issue that pertains specifically to iOS is the lack of Flash support. Although users can freely install the Flash plugin in almost every other browser, it cannot be installed in iOS Safari unless the user "jailbreaks" the device.

Jailbreaking iOS is a fringe activity for technically savvy users, which also comes with a number of problems, such as voiding the warranty. Thus you can expect that the vast majority of iOS devices cannot play Flash.

Flash Versus HTML5

Flash is a relatively old standard for web development, and the days of websites built entirely in Flash are all but gone. However, there are still a number of more complex and interactive components that lend themselves nicely to Flash approaches. Fortunately new standards in modern browsers such as HTML5 provide a viable alternative for many of these Flash solutions.

The only problem is that this can often segment development. HTML5 is still somewhat new, and older browsers such as IE versions 8 and lower do not support a number of the features necessary for avoiding Flash. However iOS does not support Flash, so the only way to support a reasonable market share is to provide two versions: an HTML5 version for iOS and other modern browsers, and a Flash fallback for any browsers that fall short.

Supporting Flash Video

Providing cross-browser support for video is relatively straightforward using a combination of differently encoded formats. As you learned in Chapter 6, you'll need a couple different formats for HTML5 video, as well as a Flash fallback for older browsers.

Although this approach can be tedious, it is still relatively simple because you can encode different video formats automatically.

Supporting Flash Applications and Games

Porting Flash applications and games to HTML5 can be much more time-intensive because in many cases you have to refactor the Flash code into HTML5 and JavaScript. Fortunately, Google released Swiffy, a free tool that converts Flash apps into HTML5 automatically, using a combination of SVG and JavaScript.

Although SVG is somewhat unsupported, it is available in WebKit, and most importantly in iOS Safari. This means that you can use Swiffy to convert your Flash apps for iOS, and use the original Flash version for any browsers that do not support SVG.

As Figure 10-10 shows, using Swiffy (`http://swiffy.googlelabs.com/`) is easy.

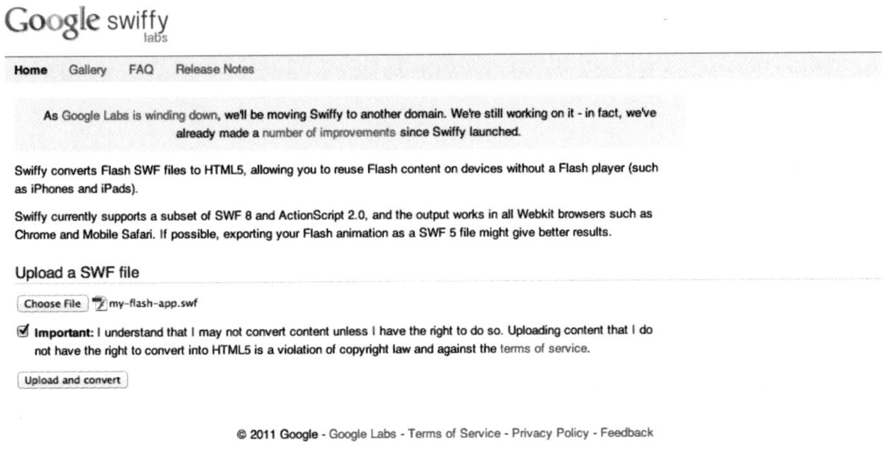

Figure 10-10: Converting SWFs with Swiffy is a piece of cake.

If there are any problems with the conversion, Swiffy notifies you (see Figure 10-11).

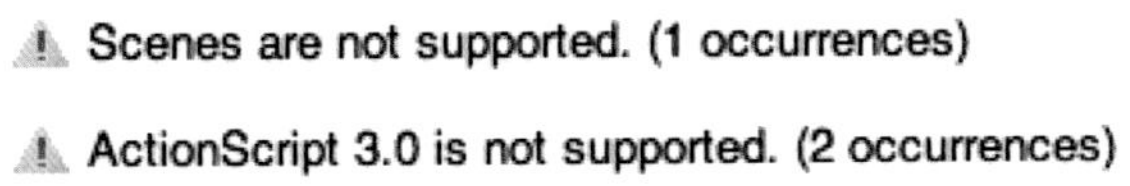

⚠ Scenes are not supported. (1 occurrences)

⚠ ActionScript 3.0 is not supported. (2 occurrences)

Figure 10-11: Swiffy provides notifications of any problems encountered with the conversion.

It's important to thoroughly test any applications you convert with Swiffy. Swiffy makes this easy by providing both a standard test link for desktop browsers as well as a QR code you can scan to test the app on mobile devices, as shown in Figure 10-12.

If the automatic conversion fails in one way or another, you have to decide whether it is worth converting the SWF manually. The choice depends on a number of factors: the simplicity of the code, the importance of the feature, and the number of iOS users that visit your site.

Swiffy output

You can download or preview the Swiffy conversion at the following URL. Just right click and "Save link as..." to download. The URL will expire after 15 minutes.

- my-flash-app.html

You can also scan the following QR code to preview the Swiffy conversion on your mobile device.

Figure 10-12: Swiffy provides a QR code for easy testing on mobile devices.

OTHER CONCERNS

Besides the lack of Flash support, there are a number of other issues with iOS that you may encounter when building your mobile website.

@font-face Issues

Although iOS supports custom font embedding using `@font-face`, it cannot support most of the file formats used in other browsers. To use custom fonts in iOS, you need to use the SVG format. While this format scales well due to its vectored representation, it is typically larger than other formats such as TTF. Thus it is a good idea to use the smaller formats wherever they are available, with an SVG fallback for iOS (as you learned in Chapter 5).

As Figure 10-13 shows, this technique is easy using Font Squirrel's `@font-face` generator: `www.fontsquirrel.com/fontface/generator`.

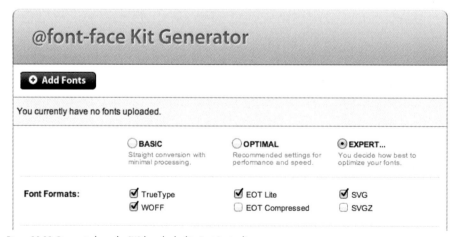

Figure 10-13: Be sure to keep the SVG box checked in Font Squirrel's generator.

File Input Types

Another issue you should consider when developing for iOS is that the file input type is completely unsupported. iOS devices do not expose their file structure, so users cannot browse the device for a document, song, or video, as they would on a desktop computer or other mobile device.

SUMMARY

The advanced interface options available in mobile devices provide a unique opportunity to create stunning experiences for mobile users. However, when building mobile websites, it is important to be aware of both the features and shortcomings of these devices.

The screen size is probably the largest drawback to these devices, but the variety of extra viewport and orientation options allow you to better accommodate these smaller screens. The other major shortcoming of mobile is reduced bandwidth, so take measures to reduce the file size of your mobile pages. Additionally certain compromises also need to be made for iOS devices, such as avoiding Flash components.

Mobile devices present certain development challenges, but the additional features they provide more than make up for the headaches. Mobile devices, and especially iOS and Android devices, provide a wide variety of advanced features you can leverage to improve your pages.

You can take advantage of multi-touch events as well as a number of predefined touch gestures. You can leverage geolocation, the gyroscope and accelerometer, and you can interface with the cellular capabilities of the devices, to fire off voice calls and text messages.

All things considered, mobile development is more exciting than it is cumbersome, and you should be thrilled any time you are able to create a unique mobile experience.

11

BUILDING A WEB APP THAT FEELS LIKE A NATIVE IOS OR ANDROID APP

TECHNOLOGIES SUCH AS HTML5, CSS3, and JavaScript have progressed to a point that web apps can rival native apps. Widespread adoption of these standards and substantial advancements in features have provided developers with an entire toolkit of new functionality. This blurs the line between native and web apps, allowing you to create full-featured applications directly in the browser.

In this chapter you explore the pros and cons of building a web app rather than a native app for iOS and Android, and you learn a variety of techniques to make your web app feel more like a seamless native app.

You discover how to create attractive bookmark icons so users can launch your web app directly from their device home screen. You learn how to run web apps in full screen mode, to take advantage of as much of the device display as possible, as well as techniques to maximize the screen size when full screen mode isn't an option.

You look at several JavaScript libraries that are especially geared toward mobile devices. These libraries streamline mobile development, allowing you to leverage touch gestures, mobile theming and more.

You learn how to mirror the native look and feel of iOS and Android apps, copying native styling and interface elements. These techniques make web apps feel more like native apps and less like mobile websites.

The chapter also shows you how to take apps offline, using the HTML5 cache manifest, local storage, and offline SQL databases. This allows users to access your app even if they do not have Internet connectivity.

Finally you discover how to use the PhoneGap framework to build native apps using the HTML, CSS, and JavaScript skills you already have. Because PhoneGap apps run natively on the device, you can also access a variety of native app functionality via easy-to-use JavaScript APIs.

WEB APPS VERSUS NATIVE APPS

When building a rich Internet application (RIA), there is one crucial decision to make. Unless your time and budget is unlimited, you need to decide if it is better to build a native app that runs on the device itself, or to build a web app that users access through the device's web browser.

Building a web app comes with a number of advantages. You can leverage basic web development skills and cross-develop applications for a variety of mobile devices (as well as desktop browsers). Additionally, you avoid the margin-destroying fees associated with the iOS App Store and Android Market.

There are also a number of benefits to building native apps. Native apps can take advantage of the entire display of the device screen, as well as a number of more advanced features that are not available to browser-based applications. Furthermore, the iOS App Store and Android Market provide effective distribution methods for your app that can often be worth their fees (if your app is a paid app in the first place).

ADVANTAGES OF WEB APPS

When building an RIA for mobile, there are a variety of reasons to build a web app instead of an app that runs natively on the device.

Mobile web apps are designed to run in the browser of mobile devices. They are built using standard web development technologies such as HTML, CSS, and JavaScript.

Parallel Development

Although certain technologies can be reused, native app development typically means fragmenting development efforts for different platforms.

Building web apps ensures that the app can be used on a number of devices with a single development path. In fact, depending on the technologies you use, web apps can even work on most desktop browsers. This means reduced development time when building for multiple platforms.

Because web apps run within the browser, you can use the same web development skills you use for desktop browsers. HTML, CSS, and JavaScript all can be used to create your app, meaning that you will not have to learn several native application languages like Objective-C for iOS, Java for Android, and any other languages you need for other device platforms.

There are certain things you should keep in mind when building a cross-platform web app. If you are planning a desktop component to your app, you need to understand which technologies will not be available in the desktop version. Hardware-specific features such as touch events, precise geolocation, and accelerometer support will be absent in the desktop version.

Additionally, older desktop browsers will not support some of the more modern web development techniques used in mobile apps, such as HTML5, CSS3, and local storage.

Avoiding the App Store and Android Market

From a business perspective, one key reason app developers opt for web apps instead of native apps is to avoid the fees associated with selling native apps. Both the iOS App Store and the Android Market charge margin-destroying fees of 30%.

Recent revisions to the App Store terms of service prevent publishers from increasing their rates to recoup this percentage: apps sold in the App Store cannot exceed the price of the same app on the web or on other devices.

Additionally, both the App Store and Android Market have enigmatic acceptance policies. There is nothing worse than spending countless hours developing a native iOS or Android app, only to have it rejected from the App Store or Android Market.

No Downloads

Web apps have the advantage of not requiring the user to download and install an application. Users are sometimes wary of installing new apps on their device, and are generally more willing to visit a web page. This willingness often depends on your app's niche: if it serves a temporary or periodic need, users will be much less willing to install than if it is something they use daily.

ADVANTAGES OF NATIVE APPS

Although web apps are typically more valuable from a business perspective, native apps also provide a number of advantages. Mainly, native apps are more powerful—both from a performance perspective and in the functionality they are able to leverage.

Display Size

A main disadvantage of web apps is that they have a reduced screen size when compared to their native counterparts. That's because the app runs within a web browser instead of as a standalone application. Because a certain amount of the device display is devoted to the web browser, there's less space for the application interface.

To get an idea of this problem, take a look at the difference between a physical calculator and the native calculator app on an iPhone in Figure 11-1.

Although both of these tools accomplish the same tasks, the physical calculator's interface is entirely devoted to the single use case, whereas the iPhone's calculator also contains the iPhone interface.

Figure 11-1: A physical calculator next to a calculator app on iPhone

Thanks to Crispin Semmens for the calculator photo (www.flickr.com/photos/conskeptical/361554984/)

Now look at the native iPhone calculator compared to a web-based calculator viewed on an iPhone, as shown in Figure 11-2.

The web-based calculator has even less of the device devoted to the calculator interface because it is contained within the iPhone interface and the iOS Safari interface.

Figure 11-2: iPhone's native calculator next to a web-based calculator

Calculator.com by Athera Corporation

> *Later in this chapter you learn some techniques to mitigate this issue in web apps and free up more of the display for your application.*

More Functionality

Besides more screen real estate, native apps also have a number of more advanced device features. Although certain hardware features such as geolocation and accelerometer support (in iOS 4.2+) are exposed to the web browser, other features can be used only by native apps.

Device manufacturers do not allow complete functionality in the web browser for a variety of reasons, including the following:

- **Security:** Native apps have to be installed by the user, but web apps can run simply by the user visiting a URL. Native apps not only have to be explicitly allowed by the user, but also are subject to malicious software checks in the App Store and Android Market. This means that manufacturers are more comfortable allowing native apps more access to the device.
- **Revenue:** It is not in the device manufacturers' best interest to allow all of the device features in web apps. Web apps provide no revenue to the device manufacturer, whereas native apps go through the App Store and Android Market.

Later in this chapter you learn how to use PhoneGap to build fully functional native apps using web app technologies.

Performance

Native apps can often outperform their web-based counterparts. The advantage to this is two-fold:

- Native apps are standalone and do not need to run inside a web browser.
- Native apps leverage device-specific technologies, such as Objective-C, which can be used to manage memory-usage and in general build higher performance applications.

That said, a poorly built native app still runs slowly, and there are many measures you can take to make your web-based application run faster.

CREATING A BOOKMARK ICON

The home screens in iOS and Android supply a menu of application icons, as shown in Figure 11-3.

Figure 11-3: The home screen menu on iPhone

These icons are typically associated with native apps, but you can also create a home screen icon as a launch point for your web app.

BOOKMARKS VERSUS DOWNLOADS

When a user bookmarks a web page that contains a web app, the app's icon appears on the user's home screen. Instead of downloading the app from the App Store or Android Market, the user has access to the app via the icon.

In iOS the user must select Add to Home Screen when bookmarking the page.

In fact, there is nothing you need to do to allow users to save your web app to their home screen. The only problem is that the default icon leaves a lot to be desired. In iOS, the icon contains a shrunken screenshot of the page that is bookmarked, as shown in Figure 11-4.

Figure 11-4:
The default bookmark icon in iOS uses a screenshot of the page.

Android uses a default bookmark icon.

CREATING A CUSTOM ICON

You can use a process similar to building favicons for desktop browsers to create your own custom icon.

Create a square pixel icon, save it as a PNG, and add the bookmark to your page. If you are concerned only with iOS, you can save the image as `apple-touch-icon.png` and upload it to the root folder of your website (similar to how you can upload `favicon.ico` without including any markup).

To provide the icon for Android users (as well as iOS), specify the location using a special link tag in your HTML head:

```
<link rel="apple-touch-icon" href="/images/my-bookmark-icon.png" />
```

Even though the link includes the word "apple," Android and iOS both pick up on this bookmark icon syntax.

Android 2.1 and higher can read this icon link. Prior versions can only read in the `apple-touch-icon-precomposed`, *which you learn about later in this section.*

Different Sized Icons

You might be wondering what dimensions to use when creating your icon imagery. Different devices use different sizes for their bookmark icons, so the optimal solution involves including a couple different bookmark icons for your app.

For instance, older iPhones (3GS and earlier) use a 57×57-pixel icon, whereas iPhone 4 uses 114×114 and iPad uses 72×72.

Fortunately, you can flag all of these sizes in your link using the `sizes` attribute:

```
<link rel="apple-touch-icon" href="bookmark-icon.png" />
<link rel="apple-touch-icon" sizes="72x72" href="ipad-icon.png" />
<link rel="apple-touch-icon" sizes="114x114" href="iphone4-icon.png" />
```

Here, you start with the 57×57-pixel icon for older iPhones. This link does not include the `sizes` attribute because these older devices do not support it. Then you include the 72×72 icon for iPad, followed by the 114×114 icon for iPhone 4.

> *The 72×72 icon works for both iPad and iPad2.*

Glossy Effect

Don't bother adding the rounded corners or glossy effect you see on other iOS and Android icons—both of these visual effects are added automatically as shown in Figure 11-5.

Figure 11-5: iOS automatically adds rounded corners and a glossy effect.

If you want to add the glossy effect yourself, or to avoid the glossiness altogether, you can include your bookmark links with the `-precomposed` suffix:

```
<link rel="apple-touch-icon-precomposed" href="bookmark-icon.png"/>
```

You can also use this with all the icon sizes you used earlier:

```
<link rel="apple-touch-icon-precomposed" sizes="72x72" href="ipad-icon.png" />
<link rel="apple-touch-icon-precomposed" sizes="114x114" href="iphone4-icon.png" />
```

Precomposed icons still include the rounded corners, as Figure 11-6 shows.

Figure 11-6: The icon on the right uses the `-precomposed` suffix.

BOOKMARK SCRIPT

Many web app developers expect their users to be savvy enough to know that they can add an app to their home screen. However, you may be tempted to create a Bookmark This Page link and trigger the bookmarking via JavaScript. While this technique works in some browsers, it unfortunately does not work in iOS Safari or Android Browser.

> *JavaScript bookmarking is not allowed in Mobile WebKit because it can be abused by websites to create an invasive user experience.*

Although you cannot trigger the bookmarking automatically, you can still suggest that users bookmark your web app. While you could simply ask them, it is better to interact with the device interface and show users exactly where they can create the bookmark.

The Mobile Bookmark Bubble (`http://code.google.com/p/mobile-bookmark-bubble/`) is an open-source script that is geared toward iOS devices. This script provides a bookmark popup in the mobile app that points at the bookmark button, as shown in Figure 11-7.

The Mobile Bookmark Bubble provides a number of nice features, such as using local storage to cache whether the promo has been displayed already, so as to not annoy users.

> *The icon used in the Mobile Bookmark Bubble is pulled from your page. By default, it looks for a link with* `apple-touch-icon-precomposed`, *so make sure to change this line in the script if you aren't using a precomposed icon (on line 229 of the source).*

Figure 11-7: The Mobile Bookmark Bubble is a quick way to add a bookmark callout to your web app.

273

FULL SCREEN MODE

One of the main disadvantages of web apps is a reduced screen size compared to native apps. In addition to taking up valuable screen real estate, the browser UI can be a distracting and often irrelevant visual element that detracts from the app experience. Fortunately, iOS provides full screen mode, which allows web apps to use more of the device display.

Full screen mode can be triggered only if the user launches the web page from a bookmark icon. That means that you cannot use full screen mode if the user navigates to the web app manually through his browser.

> *Enabling full screen mode is another reason to encourage users to add your web app to their home screen.*

ENABLING FULL SCREEN MODE

Enabling full screen mode is as easy as including a meta tag in your HTML head:

```
<meta name="apple-mobile-web-app-capable" content="yes" />
```

This tag triggers full screen mode, which hides the browser interface. Full screen mode removes the top browser bar and bottom navigation bar, as shown in Figure 11-8.

Full Screen Mode Splash Pages

Another way to make your web app feel more like a native app is by displaying a splash page while loading in full screen mode.

Build the splash page graphic, creating a 320×460 pixel image. Upload the image to your website, and reference it using the following link tag in your HTML head:

```
<link rel="apple-touch-startup-image" href="my-splash-page.png" />
```

> *Splash pages only work in iOS 3.0+.*

These splash dimensions work for iPhone; for iPad your graphic needs to be 768×1004 pixels.

> *Be careful when using splash pages, since they can be perceived as slowing down access to the app.*

Figure 11-8: Comparing a web app in the default browser shell to one in full screen mode

Styling the Status Bar in Full Screen Mode

You can also style the color of the status bar that is used in full screen mode. By default, apps in full screen mode use the same gray status bar used in iOS Safari, but you can change that to a black bar by using a metatag in your HTML head:

```
<meta name="apple-mobile-web-app-status-bar-
  style"content="black" />
```

The black bar mirrors the status bar used in most native apps, as shown in Figure 11-9.

You can also set the status bar style to `black-translucent` to create a translucent status bar, which displays over the web content. This allows you to maximize even more of the display for your app.

> You cannot set the status bar style to any color you want; the only options are `default`, `black`, and `black-translucent`.

Figure 11-9: A black status bar in full screen mode

Determining if in Full Screen Mode

Because your web app uses full screen mode only if it is opened from the user's home screen, you cannot guarantee that it will be viewed in this mode. Fortunately you can ascertain whether the app is in full screen mode using JavaScript:

```
if (window.navigator.standalone) {
    // full screen mode
}
else {
    // regular browser mode
}
```

Determining whether the app is in full screen mode allows you to tailor the site to how it is being experienced. For instance, adding a back button in full screen mode since the browser back button is unavailable.

HIDING THE BROWSER BAR

While you can't always use full-screen mode, there is a trick you can use to clean up the phone interface and provide more real estate for your mobile app for all visitors.

The technique is to trigger a scroll event on the initial page load:

```
window.addEventListener('load', function() {
    setTimeout(function(){
        window.scrollTo(0, 1);
    }, 0);
});
```

This script uses a load event as well as a timeout to trigger the scrolling (both are necessary to avoid errors). It hides the top browser bar, thereby freeing up a lot more of the screen for your web app as shown in Figure 11-10.

This technique works for both iOS and Android.

CHOOSING A JAVASCRIPT LIBRARY

A variety of JavaScript libraries are designed to help you develop better apps for mobile devices. These libraries

Figure 11-10: The scroll technique hides the browser bar and frees up more room for your web app

bridge the gaps in different devices and provide useful features such as touch gestures and mobile theming.

While there are several good options, it is important to pick the best library for your particular situation. Feature-rich libraries like Sencha Touch work well for complex sites and web apps, but might be overkill for simpler websites. Simpler libraries like jQTouch are easy to implement on basic websites, but may not include all the features you need in a more complicated situation. Lghtweight libraries like Zepto.js are ideal for creating high-powered apps that only need basic functionality.

SENCHA TOUCH

Ideal for advanced mobile applications, Sencha Touch is a feature-rich framework that offers a variety of functionality for iOS, Android, and Blackberry touch devices, as shown in Figure 11-11.

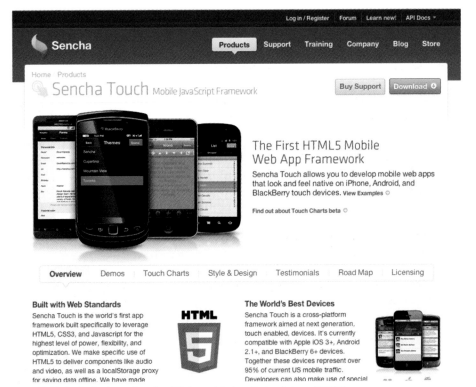

Figure 11-11: Sencha Touch provides rich mobile interactivity based in JavaScript and HTML5.

© 2011 Sencha Inc.

Sencha Touch is perfect if you are creating a complex mobile application because it provides a wide variety of features. It offers a number of touch event listeners, interface options, and geolocation support to name a few.

But Sencha Touch is more than a mobile library; it is a framework with a data model and model-view-controller (MVC). While this is great for large mobile applications, it may be overkill for your particular situation. Of all the mobile frameworks, the learning curve on Sencha Touch is by far the steepest.

> *Sencha Touch is especially useful if you are building a standalone app using PhoneGap, which you learn more about later this chapter.*

Touch Gestures

Sencha Touch offers a series of touch gestures that you can use across these devices.

Besides saving time, these are very useful when you are building cross-platform mobile applications because touch events differ depending on the device. Instead of fragmenting development efforts, and potentially offering reduced functionality on certain devices, Sencha Touch allows you to cross-develop for all these devices at once.

Data Integration

Sencha Touch incorporates some features that you can use to handle data on the front end. Essentially an MVC, these features integrate into the backend with AJAX (asynchronous JavaScript and XML), JSONP—JavaScript Object Notation with padding—or YQL (Yahoo! Query Language), and then bind the data to specific components or themes. The data can additionally be taken offline using local storage.

> *Local storage is covered later this chapter.*

Touch Charts

Sencha Touch also offers a data visualization library called Touch Charts, as shown in Figure 11-12.

Touch Charts is a lightweight yet powerful charting library that is specifically designed for mobile. It offers bar graphs, line graphs, and pie charts, with a variety of customization options.

Licensing

Depending on your project, licensing of Sencha Touch is most likely free. The basic commercial license is free, and there is also an open-source license if you are working on an OS project.

However, you need to purchase a license if you want to distribute the code with a commercial product. Additionally, Touch Charts will have a $99 licensing fee after it is out of beta.

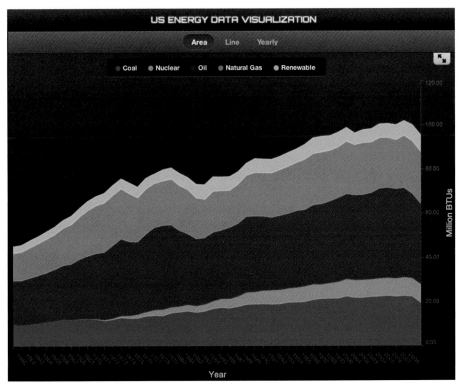

Figure 11-12: A demo visualization of U.S. energy consumption built with Touch Charts

© 2011 Sencha Inc.

JQUERY MOBILE

jQuery Mobile (see Figure 11-13) is an easy-to-use mobile framework built for a wide variety of touch-based platforms, such as iOS, Android, Blackberry, Windows Phone, Palm, and Symbian.

jQuery Mobile is a good library to use if you want to support a lot of platforms. Its main features are a UI library of form controls and a variety of touch gestures. If you are already using jQuery, the mobile core is very lightweight, adding only about 20kb worth of JavaScript.

Furthermore, if you are already comfortable with jQuery development, jQuery Mobile provides an easier access point for mobile-specific libraries.

UI Elements

One of jQuery Mobile's prime advantages is the rich UI library it provides. This library streamlines your UI themes, providing utilities to create toolbars, buttons, and form elements.

Toolbars are an important component to include in most mobile apps because they provide a simple navigational element. iOS and Android users are familiar with this type of interface, so using toolbars helps web apps feel more like native apps.

The form elements in jQuery Mobile provide a very user-friendly interface for entering data. Besides having basic form controls, they provide a variety of additional components, such as sliders, flip switches and button bars, as shown in Figure 11-14.

Figure 11-13: jQuery Mobile supports a wide variety of platforms.
© 2011 jQuery Project

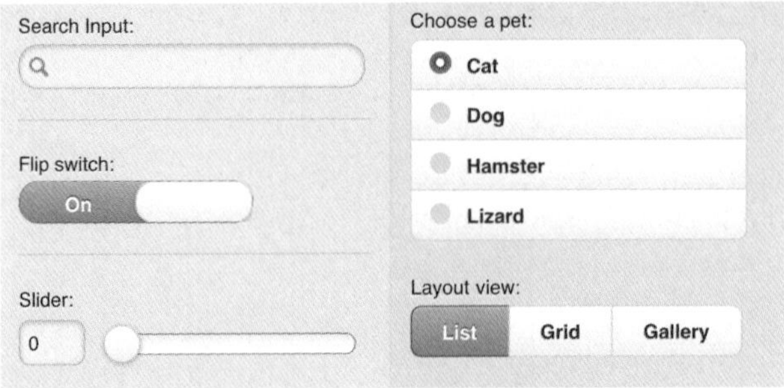

Figure 11-14: jQuery Mobile offers a variety of user-friendly form controls.
© 2011 jQuery Project

Even the basic form controls such as check boxes and radio buttons are useful in jQuery Mobile. This library focuses a lot of attention on usability for touch devices, and even these basic controls lead to a much better user experience on mobile sites.

Touch Gestures

jQuery Mobile presents a couple touch gestures you can leverage to unify interactive events across the vast number of platforms the library supports.

It does not offer as many touch events as Sencha Touch, but you can still take advantage of basic gestures like tapping, holding, and swiping.

jQuery Mobile provides a handful of other events, such as orientation change and scroll events, as well as events you can use to change pages in your app.

JQTOUCH

jQTouch is a jQuery plugin that supports a handful of touch-based devices such as iOS and Android, as shown in Figure 11-15.

Although somewhat limited compared to other libraries, jQTouch is simple to use. Its slight learning curve enables you to create unique mobile apps quickly.

The library provides a number of features, including basic gesture support, with detection for swiping.

It also offers support for page changes, along with several animated page transitions, such as slide, dissolve, fade, and 3D flip. These transitions can be triggered easily in your markup and use WebKit keyframe animations, so they are completely customizable. 3D animations revert to 2D fallbacks in non-supportive browsers.

Additionally, jQTouch provides theme support—with a default Apple theme—and the capability to create your own custom themes. If you are building for iOS, this theme gives you a substantial head start on styling your app, and there are other themes for Android as well.

jQTouch was a precursor to Sencha Touch.

Figure 11-15: jQTouch supports iOS and Android.
© 2009–2010 David Kaneda

ZEPTO.JS

Zepto.js is a very lightweight mobile library, weighing in at just over 6kb. This micro library provides some useful functionality for Mobile WebKit browsers, as shown in Figure 11-16.

Zepto.js does not provide nearly the number of features as other mobile libraries, but its small file size makes it a very attractive option for mobile development, where bandwidth concerns often drive programming decisions.

Zepto.js is standalone, meaning that you do not need any other JavaScript library to use it. It is also compatible with jQuery syntax, so it's useful for lightweight JavaScript apps and as a component in larger jQuery-based apps.

Figure 11-16: Zepto.js provides a variety of functionality in only 6KB.

© 2011 Thomas Fuchs

RENDERING THE IOS UI USING CSS3

When building a web app for an iOS device like iPhone or iPad, it is usually a good idea to copy iOS' basic look and feel. This is a standard employed by most native iOS apps, and is instrumental to making your app feel more like an iOS app and less like a mobile web page.

Mirroring the iOS UI has two parts: using iOS visual styling on elements such as buttons and navigation and recreating various interface elements such as on-off switch toggles and number/date spinning wheels.

> When recreating the iOS styling, make sure to include these features only for iOS devices.

RECREATING IOS STYLING

Many mobile JavaScript libraries provide iOS theme support.

jQTouch's default Apple theme is particularly close to the iOS interface. However, it's probably not wise to include jQTouch just for themes because you can easily recreate a lot of the iOS styling using CSS.

In fact, you can build all the styling you need without images, using a CSS3 technique pioneered by Estelle Weyl (`www.standardista.com/css3-native-iphone-app`).

iOS Background

The first step to your iOS-style theme is to include a similar background, as shown in Figure 11-17.

Figure 11-17: The standard iOS background has gray vertical stripes.

You can create this background effect using CSS3 gradients:

```
body {
    background-color: #C5CCD4;
    background-image: -webkit-gradient(linear,
```

```
        left top, right top,
        color-stop(0.7142, #C5CCD4),
        color-stop(0.7142, #CBD2D8));
    -webkit-background-size: 7px 1px;
    background-size: 7px 1px;
}
```

This technique uses `background-size` to tile a linear gradient.

> *You can accomplish the same effect with* `-webkit-repeating-linear-gradient`, *but browser support is better for the basic linear gradient and* `background-size`.

iOS Title Bar

You can create the title bar for iOS, starting with some markup:

```
<header>
    <h1>Page Title</h1>
</header>
```

> *Feel free to use HTML5 elements such as* `header` *because this app is geared toward modern platforms.*

Then style this title bar like the iOS title bar:

```
header {
    background-color: rgb(109, 132, 162);
    background-image: -webkit-gradient(linear,
        0% 0%, 0% 50%,
        from(rgba(176, 188, 205, 1)),
        to(rgba(129, 149, 175, 1)));
    border-bottom: 1px solid #2C3542;
    border-top: 1px solid #CDD5DF;
    height: 31px;
    line-height: 30px;
    padding: 7px 10px;
}

h1 {
    color: white;
    font-family: Helvetica;
    font-size: 20px;
    font-weight: bold;
    text-shadow: rgba(0, 0, 0, 0.4) 0px -1px 0px;
```

```
    text-align: center;
    text-overflow: ellipsis;
    overflow: hidden;
    white-space: nowrap;
    margin: auto;
    width: 150px;
}
```

This uses CSS3 techniques such as background gradients and text shadow to create a title bar
that is remarkably similar to the iOS title bar, as shown in Figure 11-18.

Figure 11-18: This iOS-style title bar has been created entirely with CSS.

iOS Buttons

You need to add some buttons to the title bar: both the active button and the back button.
These also can be created using CSS3 alone.

Add the buttons to your `header` element markup:

```
<header>
    <a href="#" class="button cancel-button">Cancel</a>
    <a href="#" class="button done-button">Done</a>
```

```
    <h1>Page Title</h1>
</header>
```

Then style the buttons with CSS:

```
.button {
    color: white;
    font-family: Helvetica;
    font-size: 12px;
    font-weight: bold;
    text-decoration: none;
    text-shadow:  0 -1px 0 rgba(0, 0, 0, 0.6);
    background-color: #2463DE;
    background-image: -webkit-gradient(linear, 0 0, 0 100%,
        from(#7B9EEA),
        to(#376FE0));
    background-repeat:no-repeat;
    -webkit-background-size: 100% 50%;
    background-size: 100% 50%;
    border: 1px solid #2F353E;
    -webkit-border-radius: 4px;
    border-radius: 4px;
    -webkit-box-shadow:
        0 1px 0 rgba(255,255,255, 0.4),
        inset 0 1px 0 rgba(255,255,255,0.4);
    box-shadow:
        0 1px 0 rgba(255,255,255, 0.4),
        inset 0 1px 0 rgba(255,255,255,0.4);
    display: block;
    overflow: hidden;
    white-space: nowrap;
    text-overflow: ellipsis;
    max-width: 80px;
    height: 30px;
    padding: 0 10px;
}

.cancel-button {
    float: left;
    background-color: #4A6C9B;
    background-image: -webkit-gradient(linear, 0 0, 0 100%,
        from(#8EA4C1),
        to(#5877A2));
    border-color: #2F353E #375073 #375073;
}

.done-button {
    float: right;
}
```

287

This styling leverages a number of CSS3 techniques, such as background gradients, border radius, and shadows. It sets up a base styling for all buttons, and then overwrites the background colors for the cancel button. It also floats the cancel and done buttons left and right respectively.

This CSS creates buttons that are very close to those in native iOS apps, as shown in Figure 11-19.

Figure 11-19: The title bar and buttons have been styled entirely with CSS3.

The only noticeable difference from the native iOS title bar is that the back button does not contain an arrow. For that you most likely need to use images.

More iOS Styling

You can follow this model to recreate other elements of the iOS interface as needed. CSS3 provides all the tools you need for most situations, and you can use images whenever you get stuck.

RECREATING IOS UI FUNCTIONALITY

Part of the reason iOS has been so successful in creating a loyal user base is that it provides a unique UI that its users love. When building your iOS web app, recreating some of these interface elements can be instrumental in improving your app's user experience.

Switch Toggles

One standout interface element in iOS is its on-off toggle switch, as shown in Figure 11-20.

Figure 11-20: On-off toggle switches are a familiar feature in iOS apps.

These elements, which function essentially like check boxes, allow the user to slide a setting on or off. This feature is readily accessible for native apps, but you cannot implement the native version in web apps.

Fortunately, there is a jQuery script that recreates this functionality. The iPhone Style Checkboxes script (`http://awardwinningfjords.com/2009/06/16/iphone-style-checkboxes.html`) is a progressive enhancement script that takes standard check box elements (`<input type="checkbox" />`) and converts them into toggle switches.

The script works with touch events, allowing the user to slide the switch on and off, or even click to toggle. This functionality mirrors the native switch, and as Figure 11-21 shows, the look of the jQuery-generated check boxes is remarkably similar to the native element.

There are also Prototype and Ext JS versions of iPhone Style Checkboxes script.

Figure 11-21: The toggle switches generated by the jQuery script are almost identical to the native elements.

Spinning Wheels

Another interface feature used in many iOS apps is the spinning wheel. A limited version of the spinning wheel is already available in the browser, by using a standard `select` element, as shown in Figure 11-22.

The select-based spinning wheel can only be used to set a single option at a time, but the Spinning Wheel script (`http://cubiq.org/spinning-wheel-on-webkit-for-iphone-ipod-touch`) allows you to build elements with multiple spinning wheels, as shown in Figure 11-23.

This interface is ideal for entering related information such as date and time pickers.

289

Figure 11-22: The standard select element triggers a spinning wheel.

Figure 11-23: Multiple spinning wheels in the same element, as generated by the Spinning Wheel script.

RENDERING THE ANDROID UI USING CSS3

Although the mobile community pays a lot of attention to recreating the iOS UI, there is comparatively little focus on recreating the Android UI using HTML, CSS, and JavaScript. That's partially due to Apple efforts to brand the iOS experience: iOS users like the interface, and apps cater to these types of users.

Android is more of a transparent toolkit for creating a mobile interface. Thus, device manufacturers and application developers often take their own paths when it comes to interface design.

While you should probably avoid using a look and feel that is distinctly iOS-oriented, a lot of the same interface features you built for iOS can be reused for Android because the Android interface is similar to iOS in a number of ways.

Interface elements such as buttons and navigation can simply be reskinned from the iOS versions you built earlier. For instance, use black and gray instead of blue and white.

Additionally, a number of mobile JavaScript libraries provide theme support that you can use to create these elements.

GOING OFFLINE

One advantage of native apps is that they can often run regardless of Internet connectivity. This feature is very important for devices such as tablets, which are usually only connected where WiFi is available. Smart phones are not always connected to the mobile network, either—for instance when the user is out of range or flying on an airplane.

Fortunately, offline functionality is available for more than native apps. You can take a number of measures such as aggressive caching and offline SQL databases to allow your web apps to run even when the user is offline. This means that depending on the connectivity needs of your application, it may be able to provide full offline functionality for your users.

Keep in mind that the user will have to download your application at some point. After downloading the app for the first time, the offline features ensure that the user can use the app regardless of Internet access.

> *The techniques described in this section are especially useful for mobile apps, but they can also be used in most modern desktop browsers. However don't expect to use these features in many older browsers.*

DETERMINING IF THE APP IS OFFLINE

When offering offline functionality, you often need to determine whether the application is online. You can ascertain that information using JavaScript:

```
if (window.navigator.onLine) {
    // app is online
}
else {
    // app is offline
}
```

This `if` statement allows you to cater your JavaScript to the user's connectivity, enabling and disabling features as needed.

HTML5 CACHE MANIFEST

The HTML5 cache manifest is a key feature for creating offline applications.

The cache manifest is essentially a text file that specifies a number of files the browser should cache. Whenever a user opens a page with a cache manifest, he automatically downloads and caches all of the files in the app, regardless of which files he uses in that session.

HTML5 cache manifest is available in iOS 2.1+ and Android 2.0+.

Specifying the Cache Manifest

To create a cache manifest, first specify the manifest file in your markup. Do so by adding the `manifest` attribute to the `html` element of your page, pointing to the location of your manifest file:

```
<!doctype html>
<html manifest="/my-cache.manifest">
<body>
...
</body>
</html>
```

Make sure you use the HTML5 `doctype`, or your cache manifest will not work.

Specify the cache manifest on all the pages of your app.

Building the Cache Manifest File

The manifest is essentially a text file with a particular syntax. Every cache manifest file starts with the same first line:

```
CACHE MANIFEST
```

After this, add the path to any files that you want to cache:

```
CACHE MANIFEST
/stylesheet.css
/page2.html
/images/logo.png
```

After the user visits a page with this cache manifest, all of these assets will be available offline.

Links in the cache manifest are relative to the directory of the manifest file.

Serving the Proper Content Type

It isn't enough to simply point to the manifest file you created. To work properly, that file must be served with the content type `text/cache-manifest`.

If you are using an Apache web server, you can add this content-type in your `.htaccess` file:

```
AddType text/cache-manifest .manifest
```

This declaration specifies that any file with the extension `.manifest` be recognized as content-type `text/cache-manifest`.

Which Files To Cache

When you are building a cache manifest file, carefully selecting which files enter the manifest is important.

For most apps, you should probably include all the files you need: any HTML pages, stylesheets, JavaScripts, and images that the app may use.

Depending on the size of your app, though, you may not want to include all these files in the manifest because all the manifest files will be downloaded whenever a user accesses a single page. If you have a very large website, for instance, you definitely do not want the user to download the entire site whenever he hits the first page.

Network Sections

Web apps often include certain pages that are dynamic and require Internet access every time they are loaded. You can specify in your manifest to avoid caching these particular files:

```
CACHE MANIFEST
NETWORK:
/dynamic-page.php
CACHE:
/stylesheet.css
/page2.html
/images/logo.png
```

Here, `dynamic-page.php` will not be cached by the manifest, and if the user tries to access that page while offline, an error is triggered.

When specifying a network section, it is important to use both the `NETWORK:` keyword for non-cached files and the `CACHE:` keyword for those files you want the browser to cache.

Fallback Sections

If for some reason the browser has not cached a given page, you can specify fallback content:

```
CACHE MANIFEST
FALLBACK:
/page3.html /fallback.html
```

Here, if the user accesses `page3.html`, and the page is not cached, `fallback.html` will display instead when the user is offline.

> The cache manifest file is versioned by byte, meaning that if anything changes (even a comment), the entire list of cached resources must be downloaded again.

LOCAL STORAGE

Local storage is another tool you can use when taking web apps offline. Local storage allows you to save JavaScript data in the browser, so that the objects are still available the next time the user accesses the page. Instead of disappearing whenever the page is unloaded, these objects persist anytime the user visits the page (or other pages on your site).

How To Use Local Storage

There are two ways to use local storage. The easier way is to simply treat `localStorage` as an object:

```
// save a string
localStorage.myVar = 'My stored string';

// return the string
alert( localStorage.myVar );

// delete the variable
delete localStorage.myVar;
```

Alternatively, you can use the `localStorage` API:

```
// save a string
localStorage.setItem('myVar', 'My stored string');

// return the string
alert( localStorage.getItem('myVar') );

// delete the variable
localStorage.removeItem('myVar');
```

Here `setItem()`, `getItem()`, and `removeItem()` all have the same effect as the preceding object technique.

To clear all of the data in `localStorage`, use the `clear()` method:

```
localStorage.clear();
```

Session Storage

Data saved with `localStorage` persists as the user visits different pages, or whenever the user returns to the page at a later date. But if you only want to save data for the current session, you can use `sessionStorage` instead.

Except for its duration, `sessionStorage` works exactly the same as `localStorage`:

```
// save a string
sessionStorage.setItem('myVar', 'My stored string');

// return the string
alert( sessionStorage.getItem('myVar') );

// delete the variable
sessionStorage.removeItem('myVar');
```

Limits of Local Storage

Most browsers allow up to 5 megabytes of web storage for each document. Because local storage is mostly used to save strings as key-value pairs, it is unlikely that you will come up against this limit.

That said, it is a good practice to use `removeItem()` and `clear()` to remove any `localStorage` objects you no longer need.

OFFLINE SQL DATABASE

For data-heavy apps, local storage is often insufficient. Fortunately, you can take advantage of offline SQL databases.

Web SQL databases are fully functional SQL databases that are created in the browser. These databases are not only available offline, but can also be accessed using simple JavaScript APIs. If your application does not need a remote database, Web SQL databases can provide an attractive alternative that is easy to use and does not tie up server resources.

Web SQL databases are supported by iOS Safari 3.2+ and Android Browser 2.1+ (as well as current versions of Chrome and Safari).

> *Firefox does not support Web SQL databases, and Mozilla has stated that it will never do so because of ideological concerns. Mozilla has introduced an alternative, IndexedDB, which has garnered decent support but is unsupported in iOS Safari and Android browser at the time of this writing.*

Creating Web SQL Databases

To use Web SQL databases, first create the database using JavaScript:

```
var db = openDatabase('mydb', '1.0', 'My Web SQL Database', 4 * 1024 * 1024, function() {
    // callback on database creation
});
```

The `openDatabase()` method accepts five arguments:

- The name of the database (in this case `mydb`)
- The Web SQL database version you want to use
- A text description of the database
- The estimated size of the database (4MB in this example)
- A callback function that is triggered after the database is successfully created

This function opens an existing database or creates the database. Thus, if the user has already visited a page that created the database mydb, the function opens the existing database rather than creating a new one.

Estimating Database Size

It is important to make a reasonable estimate of the database size so the browser allocates an appropriate amount of memory.

You can specify any size you want for the database, but certain browsers such as desktop and iOS Safari prompt the user to accept any database that exceeds 5MB, as shown in Figure 11-24.

Figure 11-24: iOS Safari alerts the user when a database larger than 5MB is being created.

iOS Safari does not let you create a database larger than 50MB.

Executing SQL Queries

After creating your database, you can execute SQL queries by referencing the variable you assigned with openDatabase():

```
db.transaction( function(tx) {
    tx.executeSql('CREATE TABLE IF NOT EXISTS mytable (id
unique, content)');
});
```

The executeSql() method can accept any SQL string.

You can include multiple queries in each transaction:

```
db.transaction( function(tx) {
    tx.executeSql('CREATE TABLE IF NOT EXISTS mytable (id
unique, content)');
    tx.executeSql('INSERT INTO mytable VALUES (1, "my
content")');
});
```

One advantage to combining multiple queries in the same transaction is that if one of them fails, it rolls back all of the queries in the transaction.

You can pass an error handler function as the second argument in transaction().

Handling Returned Data

Certain types of queries return data that you can handle using a callback:

```
tx.executeSql('SELECT * FROM mytable', [], function(tx,results) {
    for( var i = 0, max= results.rows.length; i < max; i++ ){
        console.log( results.rows.item(i).content );
    }
});
```

The third argument in `executeSql()` includes a callback that handles the data returned from the `SELECT` statement.

The returned results differ from what you may be used to in SQL programming. There is a `rows` object, which contains the data for each row. You can use `rows.length` to determine how many rows are returned, and `rows.item(index)` to access the data of a particular row. You can then iterate through the data of that row, or use a key to access a particular column of the row.

> You can also use `readTransaction()` *if you only want to execute read statements on the database. This has performance advantages because it avoids issues related to table conflicts and locking.*

BUILDING NATIVE APPS WITH PHONEGAP

PhoneGap is an open source framework that allows you to build native apps using HTML5, CSS, and JavaScript. PhoneGap is unique because it provides access to a variety of native device features that are not available in the browser. This functionality is exposed because apps built with PhoneGap run as native apps on the device.

PhoneGap essentially wraps your web app with its framework to provide JavaScript access to native APIs. Best of all, once your app has been built with PhoneGap, it can be deployed to a number of device platforms, such as iOS, Android, Windows Phone, Blackberry, Symbian and WebOS.

299

> *PhoneGap is completely free and open-source, released under either a modified BSD or MIT license.*

ADVANTAGES OF PHONEGAP

Converting your web app into a native app using PhoneGap has a number of advantages. PhoneGap not only exposes native APIs, but can also be used to deploy apps on a variety of platforms at once. PhoneGap is readily extensible, and there are a variety of third-party plugins for the framework (not to mention the support of the PhoneGap community).

Multiple Platforms

When you build your app with PhoneGap, you can deploy simultaneously to a number of device platforms. The mobile platforms supported by PhoneGap include:

- iOS
- Android
- Blackberry
- Symbian
- Windows Phone 7
- WebOS
- Bada

Native App Functionality

Because PhoneGap apps run natively on various devices, the framework exposes a variety of native functionality to your web app. These features are provided via easy-to-use JavaScript APIs.

PhoneGap includes support for:

- Accelerometer
- Geolocation and compass
- Media capture (photo, audio and video)
- Media playback
- Notifications (alert popups as well as sound and vibration notifications)
- File structure and storage
- Contact list
- Connection type (WiFi, 2G, 3G, and so on)
- And more (`http://docs.phonegap.com/`)

The PhoneGap framework is constantly expanding, and new features are scheduled for integration in the future. For more information about proposed enhancements, visit the PhoneGap roadmap: `http://wiki.phonegap.com/w/page/28291160/roadmap-planning`.

The features listed here are all available on newer iOS devices (iPhone 3GS+) as well as Android. However, certain devices do not support all of these features. For a complete feature map, see Table 11-1.

Table 11-1: Support for PhoneGap features across different platforms

	iOS iPhone / iPhone 3G	iOS iPhone 3GS and newer	Android	Blackberry OS 4.6-4.7	Blackberry OS 5.x	Blackberry OS 6.0+	WebOS	Symbian	Bada
Accelerometer	*	*	*		*	*	*	*	*
Camera	*	*	*		*	*	*	*	*
Compass		*	*						*
Contacts	*	*	*		*	*		*	*
File	*	*	*		*	*			
Geolocation	*	*	*	*	*	*	*	*	*
Media	*	*	*						
Network	*	*	*	*	*	*	*	*	*
Notification (Alert)	*	*	*	*	*	*	*	*	*
Notification (Sound)	*	*	*	*	*	*	*	*	*
Notification (Vibration)	*	*	*	*	*	*	*	*	*
Storage	*	*	*			*	*	*	

Chart from www.phonegap.com/about/features

Extensible with Plugins

Although PhoneGap's core provides a substantial feature set, you may find yourself needing additional features for your app. PhoneGap encourages developers to extend the platform, and there are a number of plugins available for it.

PhoneGap does not provide a directory of third-party plugins, but you can find plugins for a number of device features through a simple web search. Once you find a potential plugin to use in your project, make sure that it works in all the platforms you want to support. PhoneGap's core features work across most devices, but PhoneGap plugins often support only a single platform.

Test any plugin thoroughly before making serious efforts to integrate it into your codebase.

301

DISADVANTAGES OF PHONEGAP

The main disadvantage of using PhoneGap is that your app no longer exists on the web, and must instead be installed by the user.

This has two implications. First, the user cannot access your app simply by visiting a web page; he must install it directly on his device.

Second, your app must go through the App Store or Android Market. As discussed earlier, these manufacturer marketplaces come with a variety of disadvantages, from high fees (30%) to a prolonged and potentially disastrous review policy.

> However, the distribution channels provided by these marketplaces are often worth the fees.

GETTING STARTED WITH PHONEGAP

PhoneGap can deploy your app to a number of platforms, but each deployment is somewhat different and must be performed separately. While it is certainly easier than fragmenting development for each platform, you will run into a few issues if you are deploying across the board.

For example, you cannot perform all the deployments in the same operating system: iOS deployment requires Mac OS X, and Blackberry deployment requires Windows. And you have to install additional software for each platform, such as each manufacturer's SDK.

PhoneGap provides information for setting up your project on each platform, including step by step instructions as well as video tutorials. Visit this page to get started: www.phonegap.com/start.

> Even though PhoneGap deploys essentially the same app to multiple platforms, thorough testing is still very important. PhoneGap does not support every feature on every platform, so check Table 11-1 to make sure everything you need is supported. Remember, even mobile devices on the same platform can differ greatly from one another: from OS version to screen dimensions to hardware features.

HOW TO USE PHONEGAP

After setting up PhoneGap for different platforms, building your app is fairly straightforward because PhoneGap allows you to use the HTML, CSS, and JavaScript skills you already have.

Simply build your app like any other web app, placing the file structure in the www directory you set up earlier. Because most PhoneGap features work across all platforms, you can simply copy your app into each platform you're supporting.

> *You cannot use a backend language such as PHP, ASP, or Java with PhoneGap. The app markup must be static HTML.*

PhoneGap supports JavaScript, so you can also include a JavaScript library such as jQuery as well as mobile JavaScript libraries like Sencha Touch or jQuery Mobile.

PHONEGAP APIS

PhoneGap exposes a number of device features that you can access through JavaScript APIs. This provides an easy access point for a variety of functionality that is not normally available in JavaScript.

Notifications

There are several types of notifications that you can access using PhoneGap.

To vibrate the device:

```
navigator.notification.vibrate(100);
```

This causes the device to vibrate for 100 milliseconds. You can set the vibration time to whatever you want, but iOS ignores the time, and vibrates for a pre-set amount of time.

To use an audio notification:

```
navigator.notification.beep(2);
```

You can customize how many times the device beeps—twice, in this example.

There are a couple quirks with iOS. It beeps only once no matter what number you set for the beep count. Additionally, iOS does not provide access to audio notifications, so PhoneGap instead plays an audio file that you must provide. Save a file named beep.wav in the www root of your application.

You also can display a notification as a popup, both as basic alerts as well as confirm dialogs. For more information visit http://docs.phonegap.com/phonegap_notification_notification.md.html.

Accelerometer

iOS 4.2+ exposes the accelerometer to the browser, but it is not available in older iOS versions or in any Android version at the time of this writing. However, PhoneGap provides access to the accelerometer, using a syntax that works simultaneously in a number of platforms.

The framework provides a couple methods you can use to access the accelerometer. First, you can get the current acceleration using `navigator.accelerometer.getCurrentAcceleration()`:

```
navigator.accelerometer.getCurrentAcceleration(function(acc) {
    // on success
}, function() {
    // on error
});
```

This function accepts two callback functions: a success and error callback. In the success callback, you can access information about the acceleration:

```
navigator.accelerometer.getCurrentAcceleration(function(acc) {
    var xAcceleration = acc.x,
    yAcceleration = acc.y,
    zAcceleration = acc.z,
    timestamp = acc.timestamp;
}, function() {
    alert('Error occurred');
});
```

PhoneGap also provides a function you can use to check the acceleration at regular intervals, `navigator.accelerometer.watchAcceleration()`:

```
navigator.accelerometer.watchAcceleration(function(acc) {
    // success function
}, function() {
    // error function
}, {
    frequency: 2000
});
```

`watchAcceleration()` accepts three arguments: a success callback, an error callback, and a set of options. The success callback returns the same acceleration object as `getCurrentAcceleration()`. Within the option object, you can define how frequently you want to check the acceleration.

To clear the interval, you can use `navigator.accelerometer.clearWatch()`:

```
var watchID = navigator.accelerometer.watchAcceleration( successCallback,
  errorCallback );
```

```
navigator.accelerometer.clearWatch(watchID);
```

`clearWatch()` accepts the ID returned by `watchAcceleration()`, so make sure to define a variable when setting the initial interval.

Compass

PhoneGap provides access to the device compass for iOS and Android devices with the appropriate hardware. To get the direction in which the device is currently pointing, use `navigator.compass.getCurrentHeading()`:

```
navigator.compass.getCurrentHeading(function(heading) {
    alert('Heading: ' + heading);
}, function() {
    // error callback
});
```

`getCurrentHeading()` accepts two arguments: success and error callbacks. The success callback returns the direction the device is pointing in degrees from 0 to 359.99 (where 0 is magnetic north).

The compass API also includes a function that watches the heading on an interval. For more information about `watchHeading()` visit the compass API docs (`http://docs.phonegap.com/phonegap_compass_compass.md.html#compass.watchHeading`).

Photo Capture

To capture a photo, use `navigator.camera.getPicture()`. This triggers the device's default camera application, which the user can then use to take a picture. The photo is returned as a data URI that you can use in your application.

```
navigator.camera.getPicture(function(imageURI) {
    // what you want to do with the image URI
}, function() {
    // error callback
});
```

`getPicture()` accepts success and error callbacks, with the success callback returning the URI of the captured image. `getPicture()` also accepts a third argument, which you can use to set a number of options. Learn more in the camera API docs (`http://docs.phonegap.com/phonegap_camera_camera.md.html`).

> *You can also capture audio and video using the capture API: `http://docs.phonegap.com/phonegap_media_capture_capture.md.html`.*

Other APIs

PhoneGap provides a number of other APIs that you can use to get cross-platform support for the contact list, media playback, device file structure, geolocation, connection type, and more.

For more information about everything PhoneGap supports, read the API documentation (`http://docs.phonegap.com/`).

SUMMARY

When building for mobile, it often makes more sense to develop a web app rather than a native app. This decision is driven by business reasons such as fees associated with native app licensing, as well as technical reasons such as problems associated with fragmenting development across multiple platforms.

Between robust mobile JavaScript libraries and a variety of richer functionality available directly in the browser, it is often feasible to avoid native app development altogether, and simply build for the mobile web.

If approached correctly, your web app will be practically indistinguishable from a native app. It can launch from the user's home screen, and take advantage of full screen mode to hide the browser interface. You can also mirror the look and feel of the native UI, including similar styling as well as interface elements.

Furthermore, you can make the app available offline, through aggressive caching, local storage, and offline SQL databases.

With all these features available directly in the browser, the only limitation is that some device hardware features are not exposed at the browser level. Fortunately, the PhoneGap framework provides APIs to access a number of these features, allowing you to build a native app leveraging the web development technologies you are already comfortable using.

V ADVANCED WEBKIT

12 WEBKIT PERFORMANCE

ATTENTION SPANS ON the web are notoriously short, with users often passing judgment in less than a second. You can have the best content in the world, and people still will leave your site if it doesn't load fast enough.

The Internet's fast pace is related to the availability of information; if your site doesn't provide what a user wants quickly, he can just as easily find it elsewhere. Considering the speed of search engines and the quantity of spammy websites, users have been trained to jump ship and try another site remarkably quickly.

The importance of speed is intimately related to business goals—poor performance costs you users and that means less ad revenue and fewer sales. For instance, Amazon.com reported a 1% loss in sales for every 100ms of delay. With a mere tenth of a second making such a difference, imagine what a full second of speed improvements might mean: 10% more revenue.

From *"Make Data Useful"* (2009) `http://sites.google.com/site/` `glinden/Home/StanfordDataMining.2006-11-28.ppt.`

This chapter shows you best practices for improving app performance on the web. You learn how to keep perspective, optimizing the portions of your code that provide the largest gains, while avoiding preoptimization. You learn the difference between perceived and actual performance as well as how to analyze performance using a variety of profiling and benchmarking tools.

You find out how to optimize animations by taking advantage of hardware acceleration and minimizing browser reflows, and how to optimize JavaScript by how you load script files on the page and alleviating performance pain points.

You explore CSS optimization (how to use faster selectors and avoid slower properties) and how to optimize images, including techniques to compress images and serve them properly.

You also learn how to use web sockets as an alternative to repeated AJAX calls, to obtain substantial performance gains when communicating with a remote host.

HOW TO OPTIMIZE

There are a variety of best practices to follow while undertaking any optimization efforts. It is important to avoid optimizing your entire codebase; focus on performance bottlenecks instead. These issues can be ascertained through thorough testing.

KEEPING PERSPECTIVE

When it comes to improving performance, it is always important to keep perspective. Optimizing your codebase can be time-intensive and detrimental to the overall readability and maintainability of your code. Thus it is important to focus optimization efforts where they count, and avoid refactoring your entire site.

Optimizing Where It Counts

When optimizing performance, don't get bogged down in specifics about how to speed up a function or use a faster CSS selector. The biggest performance improvements are often the simplest, and those optimizations are basically the same across all browsers.

You can optimize CSS selectors all day and still have terrible performance if you are making too many HTTP requests or serving bloated files. So address the major performance issues first, and then see if you still need to make smaller optimizations.

In general, the largest performance bottlenecks stem from two things: HTTP requests and file size.

To reduce HTTP requests, use image sprites or data URIs whenever possible to avoid referencing unnecessary image requests (data URIs are covered in Chapter 3). Additionally, make sure to concatenate your JavaScript and CSS files, ideally serving a single JavaScript file and stylesheet.

To reduce file size, ensure that you are compressing all your imagery, minifying your JavaScript, and gzipping JavaScript, CSS, and HTML.

Don't Pre-optimize

As a general rule, avoid pre-optimization any time it jeopardizes the quality of your code. While it may be tempting to optimize every single line of JavaScript, this can lead to problems in your codebase. These optimizations often make code more difficult to read and maintain, damaging the line by line integrity as well as the overall organization of your app fabric.

It's better test your code and make performance improvements whenever you notice a problem. This allows you to focus your efforts where they count, and keep code organization changes to a minimum.

That does not mean that you have free license to write sloppy, poorly performing code. Rather, there are a variety of performance improvements that you can make proactively. If it is just as easy to write faster code, and it doesn't take away from readability or organization, by all means do it.

Optimizing images takes no extra time, for example, and these images are referenced exactly the same as poorly saved images, so there is no loss in this sort of pre-optimization (however make sure not to over-optimize images to the point that they look too low-resolution).

PROFILING TOOLS

Profiling tools are instrumental for performance tuning because they provide detailed information about what is slowing down your site. In addition to settling arguments over which approach is fastest, profiling tools can help you track down areas in which you should focus optimization efforts.

> *When performing optimization tests, it is a good idea to disable any plugins or extensions that you are not using for testing.*

WebKit Profiler and Network Monitor

The WebKit developer tools include a profiler you can use directly in the browser. This tool allows you to monitor the JavaScript that is being executed on the page and locate any bottlenecks that may exist. As Figure 12-1 shows, the profiler returns what percentage of the process is being taken up by which functions.

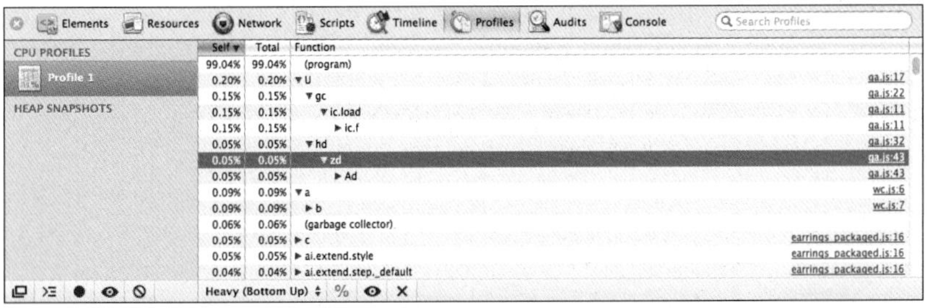

Figure 12-1: The JavaScript profiler in the WebKit developer tools

The developer tools also include a network monitor, which you learned about in Chapter 2. It allows you to see how long external resources are taking to download and instantiate on your page, as shown in Figure 12-2.

Firebug provides similar tools for Firefox.

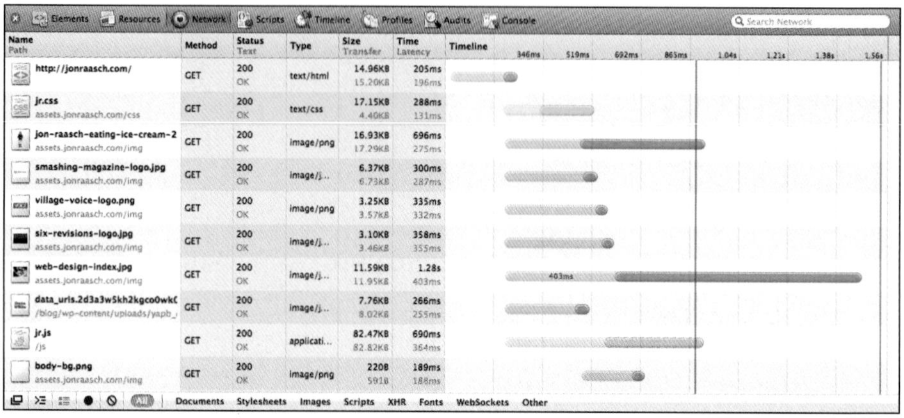

Figure 12-2: The network monitor in the WebKit developer tools

jsPerf

jsPerf (http://jsperf.com/) is also useful for performance testing because it provides a simple way to run JavaScript benchmarks.

With jsPerf, you input two (or more) scripts that you want to compare. These snippets are saved to a page that runs benchmarking tests comparing the scripts. The tests give you insight into which script can be executed faster, as Figure 12-3 shows.

Testing in Chrome 13.0.782.215 on Mac OS X 10.7.1		
Test		**Ops/sec**
parseInt	parseInt(50.5);	49,364,318 ±0.17% 94% slower
Primitive Data Type	~50.5	777,939,224 ±0.14% fastest

Figure 12-3: Two scripts compared with jsPerf

Because jsPerf hosts the scripts, you can easily test a variety of browsers. jsPerf also keeps track of each browser's results, providing a place to compare benchmark tests across environments, as you can see in Figure 12-4.

While jsPerf is useful for comparing different scripts, it is not designed for testing entire apps. If you need that level of assessment, you should consider incorporating a benchmarking script into your code, such as xStats.js (https://github.com/bestiejs/xstats.js).

Browserscope

UserAgent	Primitive Data Type	parseInt	# Tests
Chrome 7.0.517	426,274,677	33,268,325	1
Chrome 9.0.597	546,188,595	42,978,216	2
Chrome 10.0.648	467,082,443	13,055,170	1
Chrome 11.0.696	783,794,379	25,621,723	2
Chrome 12.0.742	525,213,993	20,613,746	1
Chrome 13.0.782	779,066,882	49,282,727	2
Firefox 3.6.11	78,736,109	117,207,784	1
Firefox 3.6.12	4,513,888,889	2,661,404,246	1
Firefox 3.6.15	438,832,208	435,712,223	1
Firefox 3.6.17	268,155,205	315,032,562	2
Opera 10.63	11,111,953	1,403,961	1
Safari 5.1	361,389,580	11,977,696	1

Browserscope thinks you are using **Chrome 13.0.782** No?

Figure 12-4: Benchmarks in different environments are saved and compared.

PERCEIVED VERSUS ACTUAL PERFORMANCE

There are two sides to optimizing performance: perceived performance (how fast the user thinks something is running) and actual performance (how fast it is actually running). This has nothing to do with how savvy the user is; it is related to how quickly key features become available.

For instance, if you have a news article with an image slideshow, the user is probably most interested in reading the article. So you can improve perceived performance by first loading the text of the article, as well as the first image in the slideshow. After these load completely, you can load the slideshow script, and any subsequent images you want to display.

Even though the overall page may take the same amount of time to load, users perceive it as faster because they get what they want sooner. Actual performance is important, but it is much better to focus on perceived performance, which improves user experiences.

The basic approach to optimizing perceived performance involves first getting something on the page as quickly as possible. Even if it's just the site's header and frame, the user thinks the page is loading quickly. Then focus on displaying the main content as soon as you can.

Defer any secondary elements until the end, so they do not get in the way of the primary content. Comments, slideshows, a sidebar of related links, and any other bells and whistles should be offloaded until the very end.

OPTIMIZING ANIMATION

Animation can improve user experiences and make websites feel more interactive, yet it is generally one of the slowest things to accomplish in the browser. Not only does the browser re-render the element for each frame of the animation, but it often has to re-render other elements on the page as well.

When including animation on a page, first consider the performance costs. A slow website leads to a bad user experience, no matter how many animations it includes.

That's not to say that you should avoid animation altogether; you just need to decide whether each animation contributes to a better experience.

There are a number of steps you can take to improve performance as you build the animation. These measures make the page run faster and the animation look smoother.

Optimized animations are easier to render so the browser can display more frames per second and thus provide a smoother looking animation.

USING CSS ANIMATION

CSS animation is generally faster than JavaScript animation. CSS animation works directly in the browser, so it has already been thoroughly optimized. These animations often take advantage of hardware acceleration. Furthermore, CSS animation does not rely on modifying the DOM; the animation is performed directly in the renderer with no middleman.

WebKit-based browsers are capable of two types of CSS animation: transitions and keyframes. The former is somewhat limited, but keyframe animations can be used to build almost any animation that you can build in JavaScript.

Best of all, you can trigger these animations using JavaScript: simply attach the animation to a CSS class and apply that class to an element.

CSS animation is covered in detail in Chapter 3.

AVOIDING REFLOWS

Animations that trigger reflow are considerably slower than those that don't. Fortunately, there are a few easy steps you can take to avoid reflow in your animations.

In WebKit "reflow" is technically called "layout."

What Is Reflow?

Reflow is the process by which the renderer lays out the elements in the DOM so they can be displayed in the browser. For instance, if you alter the `height` of an element, all the elements that follow in the DOM may have to be repositioned. The process of repositioning these elements is known as reflow.

Reflow is triggered by any CSS property that affects layout:

- Box model properties such as `width`, `height`, `margin`, and `padding`
- Positioning properties such as `float` and `position`
- The `display` property
- Other miscellaneous properties such as `text-align`, `line-height`, and `vertical-align`
- Font changes

JavaScript can also trigger reflow either by adjusting one of the styles mentioned earlier, or using one of these tasks:

- Layout based tasks such as `clientHeight`, `offsetLeft`, and `scrollTop`
- DOM adjustments such as `innerHTML`, `innerText`, and `appendChild()`
- Scroll events such as `scrollTo()` and `scrollIntoView()`
- Miscellaneous tasks such as `focus()`

> *You can see a visualization of browser reflow in action in this video:* `www.youtube.com/watch?v=ZTnIxIA5KGw`*. The video features Gecko, but WebKit reflow is essentially the same.*

How To Avoid Reflow

Reflow is the cause of a number of performance issues, but it is of particular importance when it comes to animation because animations can trigger hundreds or even thousands of reflows for the renderer.

There are ways in which you can often avoid triggering reflow even when altering features such as dimensions or positioning. The trick is to avoid using properties that alter the layout of any other elements.

For instance, if you are building an animation that slides an element to the right, don't animate the `margin-left` property. Even if `margin-left` does not move any other elements on the page, the browser isn't smart enough to figure that out and will still trigger reflow.

Instead animate elements with `position: absolute`, or even 2D transformations (which you learned about in Chapter 3).

Another property you can usually avoid is `display: none`. To simply hide an element, you can often use `visibility: hidden` or `opacity: 0` to accomplish the same result. However, if you want other elements to move up and replace the hidden element, there is no way to avoid reflow.

HARDWARE ACCELERATION

Hardware acceleration taps into the device's video card to handle the heavy lifting for processor intensive graphics. The resulting GPU rendering has considerable performance gains compared to standard rendering.

Triggering Hardware Acceleration

When executing animations on elements, there is a hack you can use to trigger hardware acceleration and greatly improve performance. It increases the frame-rate of the animation and makes it appear significantly smoother.

To trigger hardware acceleration, simply apply this CSS to the element:

```
-webkit-transform: translateZ(0);
```

3D transformations use hardware acceleration in many browsers. This hack applies a superficial 3D transformation that does not alter the appearance of the element, but still triggers hardware acceleration.

Once this property is applied to an element, you can animate it more smoothly.

Hardware acceleration improves both CSS and JavaScript animation.

Testing Hardware Acceleration

It can be hard to tell when hardware acceleration has been triggered on the page. Rather than guess based on how quickly an animation seems to be running, there are a few tricks you can use to ascertain when the browser is using hardware acceleration.

In Chrome, navigate to the URL about:flags. On this page, find Composited Render Layer Borders, as shown in Figure 12-5, and click Enable.

With this feature enabled, red borders are added to any element that has hardware acceleration, as shown in Figure 12-6.

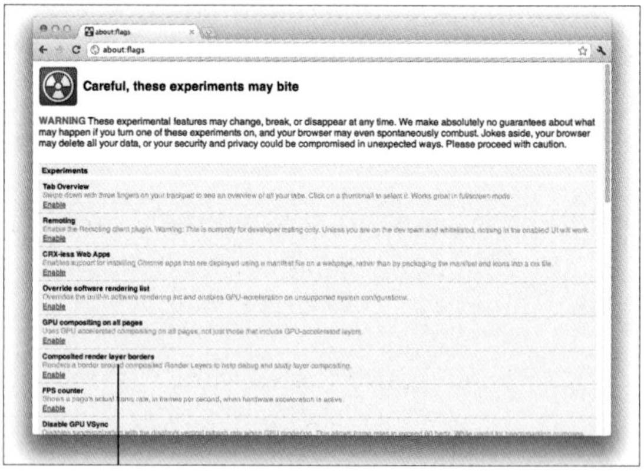

Figure 12-5: Chrome's about:flags page

You can do something similar in Safari and the iOS Simulator. For Safari, open the file `/Applications/Safari.app/Contents/MacOS/Safari`, find the line that contains `CA_COLOR_OPAQUE`, and set it to:

```
$ CA_COLOR_OPAQUE=1
```

You need to change the same setting for the iOS Simulator. Open the file `/Developer/Platforms/iPhoneSimulator.platform/Developer/Applications/iPhone\ Simulator.app/Contents/MacOS/iPhone\ Simulator`, and change the same flag.

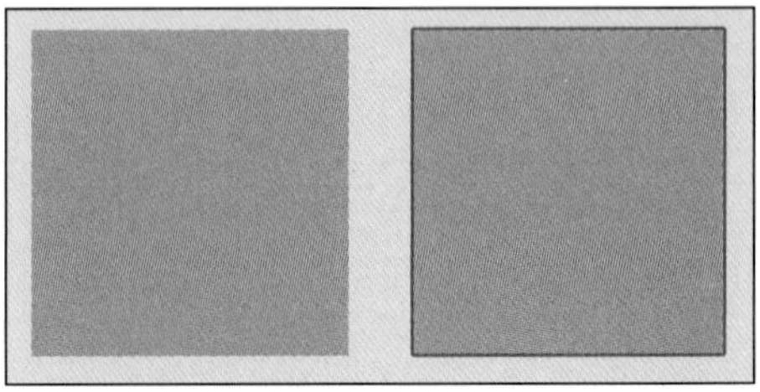

OPTIMIZING JAVASCRIPT

Poorly optimized JavaScript is one of the largest contributors to perceived performance problems. Although major advancements have been made to JavaScript engines, JavaScript issues still plague a number of websites, leading to error messages like the one shown in Figure 12-7.

Figure 12-6: The square on the right is being rendered with hardware acceleration.

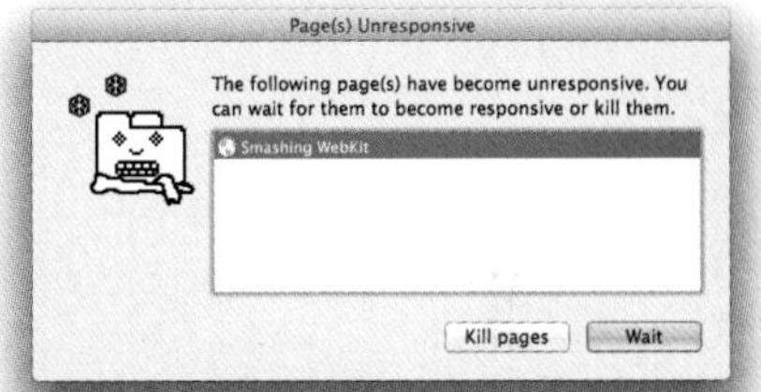

Figure 12-7: This error message displays in Chrome on pages with poorly optimized JavaScript.

317

LOADING JAVASCRIPT

If done improperly, loading JavaScript files can be one of the slowest steps in the page load process. While other assets such as markup, images, and CSS load asynchronously, JavaScript is single-threaded, meaning that the browser has to stop entirely when loading a JavaScript file.

Jake Archibald compares loading JavaScript to the browser sneezing.

For example, if you have a JavaScript file in the middle of a page, the browser parses all markup up until the JavaScript, and then waits to parse any additional markup until after that JavaScript loads completely.

This problem is exacerbated by external JavaScript files because the browser not only has to execute the JavaScript, but also wait for it to download before doing anything else.

Browsers don't load JavaScript asynchronously because JavaScript can affect the markup on the page, and the markup on the page can also affect the JavaScript.

DOM Position

One of the easiest ways to avoid issues related to JavaScript loading is to place it in the right place in the DOM. Although conventional wisdom states that it is best to put JavaScript files in the document head, that's usually the worst place to put them because JavaScript files in the head must be downloaded and executed before anything else on the page.

It's often better to place your JavaScript files at the end of the document, right before the closing </body> tag to ensure that all markup can load before the JavaScript.

However, placing JavaScript at the end of the document is not always optimal because the script loads last on the page. If you have a lot of markup or just want the JavaScript functionality sooner, you have to explore other options.

Defer and Async

You can add two attributes to your script tag to make JavaScript load asynchronously with the other content on the page. These attributes are defer and async:

```
<script type="text/javascript" defer></script>
<script type="text/javascript" async></script>
```

These scripts let the browser know that it can continue loading other content while loading the scripts. In both cases, DOM parsing continues while the script downloads (if it is external).

defer causes the browser to download the script immediately, but not execute it until the DOM is completely parsed. async downloads the script immediately, and then executes it as soon as it is available. async is great for external scripts because it allows the browser to parse the DOM while downloading the script and then execute the script as soon as possible, as shown in Figure 12-8.

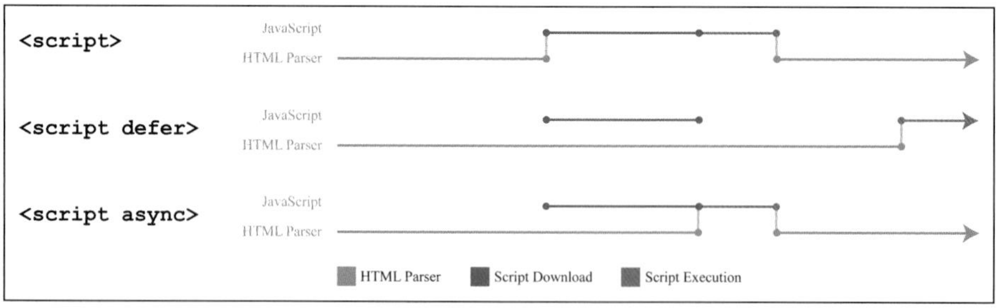

Figure 12-8: A visualization of how normal, deferred, and asynchronous execution work

WebKit-based browsers and Firefox both support defer *and* async. *IE9 and lower only support* defer, *but* async *will be supported in IE10.*

JavaScript Loaders

If you would like more fine-grained control over JavaScript loading, consider using a JavaScript loader. These scripts not only allow you to load JavaScript asynchronously, but also provide capabilities for managing dependent scripts.

Imagine you have two external scripts, such as the jQuery library and a script that uses jQuery. If you load those scripts completely asynchronously, they download at the same time but you can't be certain which will execute first. If the dependent script executes before the jQuery library, you end up with JavaScript errors.

An alternative might be to put both of these scripts at the end of your document, so they do not block any of the page content, but still load synchronously. While this avoids errors, it is not optimal because each script must be downloaded separately.

With a JavaScript loader you get the best of both worlds: the scripts can download simultaneously, and still execute in the proper order.

There are several options when it comes to JavaScript loaders, including LABjs (`http://labjs.com/`) and RequireJS (`http://requirejs.org/`). To explore other options, read this tutorial: `http://net.tutsplus.com/articles/web-roundups/for-your-script-loading-needs/`.

> *A JavaScript loader is an extra script that users must download. Although most loader scripts are small, they should not be used unnecessarily.*

LOOPS

In general, you will see the largest performance gains with the least amount of effort if you focus on code that is executed frequently. Because loops usually run several times, they are a sensible place to start whenever you notice a performance problem.

The core principle for optimizing loops is to avoid doing anything inside the loop that you can just as easily do outside. Following this practice ensures that code isn't executed any more often than it needs to be.

Imagine you have this loop:

```javascript
for ( var i = 0; i < 5; i++ ) {
    var myEl = document.getElementById('my-element');

    // whatever you want to do with myEl
}
```

Assuming that the reference in `getElementById()` doesn't change in each iteration of this loop, there is no need to perform this lookup every time. Instead, cache the DOM reference outside of the loop:

```
var myEl = document.getElementById('my-element');

for ( var i = 0; i < 5; i++ ) {
    // whatever you want to do with myEl
}
```

As Figure 12-9 shows, the cached version is significantly faster.

Testing in Chrome 13.0.782.215 on Mac OS X 10.7.1		
Test		**Ops/sec**

Not Cached	`for ( var i = 0; i < 10; i++ ) {`
	`    var myEl = document.getElementById('my-element');`
	
	`    // whatever you want to do with myEl`
	`}`
		1,160,774
		±0.69%
		90% slower

Cached	`var myEl = document.getElementById('my-element');`
	
	`for ( var i = 0; i < 10; i++ ) {`
	`    // whatever you want to do with myEl`
	`}`
		11,353,816
		±0.73%
		fastest

Figure 12-9: Non-cached versus cached DOM reference. Test URL: `http://jsperf.com/sw-loop-cache`

Faster for() Loops

When using a basic `for()` loop, you can improve performance by being careful with your comparison. For instance, to iterate over the items in an array, you might use:

```
for ( var i = 0; i < myArr.length; i++ )
```

However, each time you iterate through this array, the length value has to be recalculated. Assuming the length will not change in the loop, it's better to cache a variable in the first part of the statement:

```
for ( var i = 0, len = myArr.length; i < len; i++ )
```

This simple change makes a substantial difference in performance, as Figure 12-10 shows.

> *While caching the comparison value improves performance in most browsers, it makes little difference in Chrome.*

Testing in Safari 5.1 on Mac OS X 10.7.1		
	Test	Ops/sec

No caching	`for ( var i = 0; i < myArr.length; i++ ) {`
	`    // blah`
	`}`
		8,091,741
		±1.07%
		42% slower

Caching the length	`for ( var i = 0, len = myArr.length; i < len; i++ ) {`
	`    // blah`
	`}`
		14,023,964
		±0.77%
		fastest

Figure 12-10: Benchmark comparison between these two for loops. Test URL: `http://jsperf.com/sw-for-loop`

Not caching the comparison values can cause further problems if you are dealing with a collection object. For instance, to loop through the `childNodes` of an element, while adding nodes to that element:

```
var myEl = document.getElementById('my-element');

for ( var i = 0; i < myEl.childNodes.length; i++ ) {
    var newChild = document.createElement('div');

    myEl.appendChild(newChild);
}
```

This code results in an endless loop because the array of child nodes gets longer each time you add a child to the element. You can avoid this problem by caching the `length` of the `childNodes`:

```
for ( var i = 0, len = myEl.childNodes.length; i < len; i++ )
```

Avoid For…In Loops

One loop that is particularly important to avoid in JavaScript is `for…in`. As Figure 12-11 shows, the performance of this loop is especially bad.

Testing in Chrome 13.0.782.215 on Mac OS X 10.7.1		
	Test	Ops/sec

For Loop	`for ( var i = 0, len = myArr.length; i < len; i++ ) {`
	`    var item = myArr[i];`
	`}`
		28,466,218
		±1.18%
		fastest

For…in Loop	`for ( var item in myArr ) {`
	`    // blah`
	`}`
		444,878
		±0.30%
		98% slower

Figure 12-11: Iterating through an array with a for…in loop versus a basic for loop. Test URL: `http://jsperf.com/sw-for-in-loop`

If you're using an array, you can simply iterate through the items using a basic `for` loop. Otherwise, consider hard coding the keys of the object you're targeting.

THE SCOPE CHAIN

Every time you look up a variable in JavaScript, the engine must search through the scope chain until it finds the correct reference. Because it checks each member of the scope chain one by one, the order of variables in the chain becomes a performance issue. The earlier the variable is found in the chain, the faster the lookup will be.

That said, scope chain lookups are very fast. Finding a variable one or two places sooner in the chain is a micro-optimization at best. However, considering the huge number of variables saved in an average JavaScript app, these scope chains can get quite long. Thus, understanding the order of the scope chain and ways to improve scope lookups can help you make a substantial difference in performance.

Local Variables

Local variables are always first in the scope chain, so you can get a performance boost by caching any global variables that you use more than once, as Figure 12-12 shows.

Testing in Chrome 13.0.782.215 on Mac OS X 10.7.1		
Test		**Ops/sec**

Not Cached	`function testFunc() {`
	`    // access it 50 times`
	`    for ( var i = 0; i < 50; i++ ) var newVar = myGlobalVar;`
	`}`
	
	`testFunc();`
		3,225,944
		±1.22%
		32% slower

Cached	`function testFunc() {`
	`    var myLocalVar = myGlobalVar;`
	
	`    // access it 50 times`
	`    for ( var i = 0; i < 50; i++ ) var newVar = myLocalVar;`
	`}`
	
	`testFunc();`
		4,776,969
		±0.15%
		fastest

Figure 12-12: Comparing a function that references global variables vs. one that caches them locally. Test URL: `http://jsperf.com/sw-local`

However there is no benefit if you are only using a global variable once because you have to look it up to cache it.

Digging into Objects

Digging into objects is going to be slower than accessing a variable at a higher level because the engine has to step through each level of the object, as you can see in Figure 12-13.

While the higher level variables are faster in most browsers, Chrome uses aggressive caching techniques so there is no significant difference after the first level, as you can see in Figure 12-14.

Testing in Safari 5.1 on Mac OS X 10.7.1		
Test		**Ops/sec**
Variable	`var newVar = myVar;`	323,607,972 ±0.71% fastest
Level 1	`var newVar = myObj.myVar;`	234,848,485 ±0.68% 27% slower
Level 2	`var newVar = myObj.level2.myVar;`	199,627,538 ±0.54% 38% slower
Level 3	`var newVar = myObj.level2.level3.myVar;`	146,778,762 ±0.59% 55% slower

Figure 12-13: Comparing a top level variable with different levels of object lookups. Test URL: `http://jsperf.com/sw-objects`

Testing in Chrome 13.0.782.215 on Mac OS X 10.7.1		
Test		**Ops/sec**
Variable	`var newVar = myVar;`	781,541,684 ±0.18% fastest
Level 1	`var newVar = myObj.myVar;`	323,100,148 ±0.09% 59% slower
Level 2	`var newVar = myObj.level2.myVar;`	782,900,513 ±0.26% fastest
Level 3	`var newVar = myObj.level2.level3.myVar;`	784,606,501 ±0.12% fastest

Figure 12-14: Chrome is the exception when it comes to deep object lookups. Test URL: `http://jsperf.com/sw-objects`

Using Closures Properly

The term closure refers to a JavaScript function that is inside another JavaScript function:

```
function myFunction() {
    function myClosure() {
    }
}
```

> Closures are often compared to the movie Inception (2010) — "A dream within a dream within a dream."

Closures are useful because they are contained within the scope of their parent function. For instance, take these functions:

```
function myFunction() {
    var myLocalVar = 'blah';
```

```
    function myClosure() {
        // can access to myLocalVar
    }
}

function myFunction2() {
    // can not access to myLocalVar
}
```

Because `myClosure()` is contained within `myFunction()`, it can access the parent function's local variables.

Conventional logic states that this can cause performance problems because each closure adds another set of local variables to the top of the scope chain. However, benchmarks in modern browsers do not support this assumption, as Figure 12-15 shows.

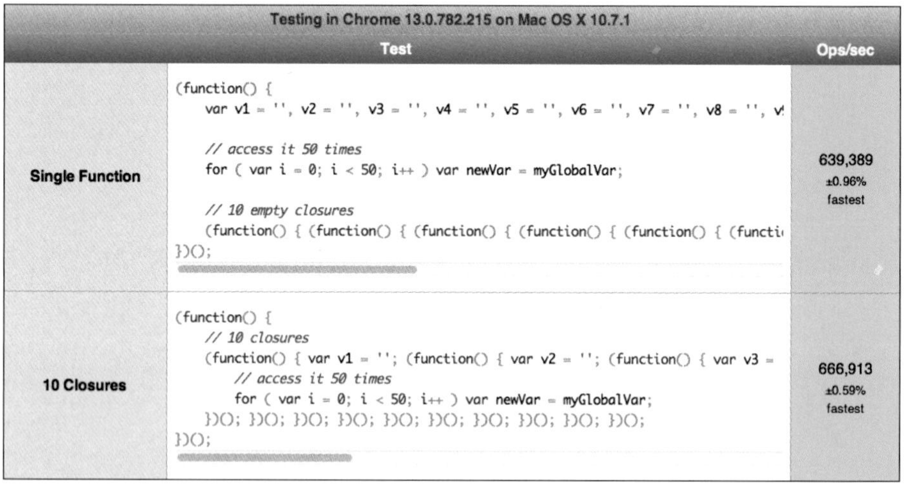

Testing in Chrome 13.0.782.215 on Mac OS X 10.7.1		
Test		**Ops/sec**

Single Function	`(function() {`
	`    var v1 = '', v2 = '', v3 = '', v4 = '', v5 = '', v6 = '', v7 = '', v8 = '', v`
	
	`    // access it 50 times`
	`    for ( var i = 0; i < 50; i++ ) var newVar = myGlobalVar;`
	
	`    // 10 empty closures`
	`    (function() { (function() { (function() { (function() { (function() { (functi`
	`})();`
		639,389
		±0.96%
		fastest

10 Closures	`(function() {`
	`    // 10 closures`
	`    (function() { var v1 = ''; (function() { var v2 = ''; (function() { var v3 =`
	`    // access it 50 times`
	`    for ( var i = 0; i < 50; i++ ) var newVar = myGlobalVar;`
	`})(); })(); })(); })(); })(); })(); })(); })(); })(); })();`
	`})();`
		666,913
		±0.59%
		fastest

Figure 12-15: Closures make little difference in modern browsers. Test URL: `http://jsperf.com/sw-closures`

DOM MANIPULATION

DOM manipulation is one of the most expensive operations in JavaScript, so it should always be handled with care. Although manipulating the DOM is often the primary purpose of JavaScript, there are a couple techniques you can leverage to improve performance.

Batching DOM Manipulation

When manipulating the DOM, try to keep the number of times you actually touch the DOM to a minimum because every time you touch the DOM, the browser must execute a reflow (among other things).

To minimize these reflows, batch DOM changes as much as possible. For instance, you should avoid building a list like this:

```
var myList = document.createElement('ul');

document.body.appendChild( myList );

for ( var i = 0; i < 10; i++ ) {
    var newLi = document.createElement('li');
    myList.appendChild(newLi);
}
```

Here you create a list, append it to the DOM and then append a number of list items. The problem is that each one of these list items affects the DOM.

A better approach, is to build the entire list at once, and then append the whole thing to the DOM:

```
var myList = document.createElement('ul');

for ( var i = 0; i < 10; i++ ) {
    var newLi = document.createElement('li');
    myList.appendChild(newLi);
}

document.body.appendChild( myList );
```

As shown in Figure 12-16, you get a performance boost simply by changing the order so the DOM isn't touched until the end.

Testing in Chrome 13.0.782.215 on Mac OS X 10.7.1		
	Test	**Ops/sec**

Appending Individually	`var myList = document.createElement('ul');`
	
	`document.body.appendChild( myList );`
	
	`for ( var i = 0; i < 10; i++ ) {`
	`    var newLi = document.createElement('li');`
	`    myList.appendChild(newLi);`
	`}`
	
	`// have to remove it at the end for testing purposes`
	`document.body.removeChild( myList );`
		41,061
		±10.14%
		23% slower

Appending At Once	`var myList = document.createElement('ul');`
	
	`for ( var i = 0; i < 10; i++ ) {`
	`    var newLi = document.createElement('li');`
	`    myList.appendChild(newLi);`
	`}`
	
	`document.body.appendChild( myList );`
	
	`// have to remove it at the end for testing purposes`
	`document.body.removeChild( myList );`
		53,431
		±5.66%
		fastest

Figure 12-16: Appending elements to the DOM individually vs. simultaneously. Test URL: http://jsperf.com/sw-dom-manipulation

Faster CSS Alterations

CSS alterations are another DOM manipulation that can cause performance issues in JavaScript.

Whenever possible, it is better to attach a class name from the stylesheet rather than adjust the style attribute of an element directly, as Figure 12-17 shows.

Testing in Chrome 13.0.782.215 on Mac OS X 10.7.1		
	Test	Ops/sec
Class Name	`myEl.className = 'my-class';`	2,152,147 ±0.29% fastest
Style	`myEl.style.color = '#000';` `myEl.style.backgroundColor = '#FFF';`	998,856 ±0.24% 54% slower

Figure 12-17: Adding class names vs. altering styles directly. Test URL: `http://jsperf.com/sw-classes`

In addition to requiring less DOM manipulation, CSS classes allow you to apply a number of styles at once and therefore avoid extra reflows. Reflows are one of the main issues with CSS alterations, and although they are often unavoidable, there are certain measures you can take to keep reflows to a minimum.

First, try to batch these changes as much as possible in your script. For instance, to adjust the height and width of an object, you might write:

```
var newHeight = myEl.offsetHeight + 10;
myEl.style.height = newHeight + 'px';

var newWidth = myEl.offsetWidth + 10;
myEl.style.width = newWidth + 'px';
```

However, this requires an extra reflow because the new height is calculated before reading the old `offsetWidth`. It is much faster to batch the two reads and then execute the two style changes:

```
var newHeight = myEl.offsetHeight + 10;
var newWidth = myEl.offsetWidth + 10;

myEl.style.height = newHeight + 'px';
myEl.style.width = newWidth + 'px';
```

This small change produces a significant performance increase, as shown in Figure 12-18.

If you are making a number of style changes that trigger reflow, it is possible to further batch the changes so they only trigger two reflows. The trick is to apply `display: none` to the element, apply all the changes, and then set the display back to `block` (or `inline`, `inline-block`, and so on).

Testing in Chrome 13.0.782.215 on Mac OS X 10.7.1		
	Test	Ops/sec

Separated Reflows	`var newHeight = blah.offsetHeight + 10;`
	`blah.style.height = newHeight + 'px';`
	
	`var newWidth = blah.offsetWidth + 10;`
	`blah.style.width = newWidth + 'px';`
		3,988
		±0.21%
		47% slower

Batched Reflows	`var newHeight = blah.offsetHeight + 10;`
	`var newWidth = blah.offsetWidth + 10;`
	
	`blah.style.height = newHeight + 'px';`
	`blah.style.width = newWidth + 'px';`
		7,574
		±0.46%
		fastest

Figure 12-18: Comparing separate and batched reflows. Test URL: `http://jsperf.com/sw-batching-reflows`

In most cases this alteration occurs so quickly that the user cannot see the element disappear and reappear.

OPTIMIZING CSS

The main task of browsers is rendering web pages, which means that rendering CSS is generally very fast. However, there are a number of steps you can take to make it even faster, from using better selectors to avoiding slower properties. These techniques not only speed up the initial page load, but also improve JavaScript performance wherever it alters rendering.

FASTER SELECTORS

Including faster selectors reduces the amount of the time the browser spends rendering your web page. This affects both the initial page load and any JavaScript manipulation that triggers a reflow or repaint.

How Selectors Work in WebKit

The WebKit rendering engine and other modern rendering engines such as Gecko (Firefox) parse CSS selectors from right to left. Given a selector like `div p.my-class`, the renderer first checks to make sure the element matches the right side (`p.my-class`), and then checks to see if it has an ancestor that matches the left (`div`).

The reason renderers analyze selectors from right to left has to do with how they parse the DOM and apply styles.

When conceptualizing selectors, you may think that the renderer finds any element that matches the left side of a selector, and then checks descendants to match the rest. However, renderers do not apply styling all at once.

Rather, DOM parsing goes from top to bottom, with style rules being applied as each node is parsed. Because styling is applied to each node individually, it makes more sense to match the right side of the selector, and then check the ancestors.

327

Selector Best Practices

Because the renderer moves from right to left, it is best to be very specific on the right, and very general on the left.

Being specific on the right means that the renderer won't have to perform ancestor checks for as many elements because most elements fail the first test (the right-most selector).

Being general on the left means that any necessary ancestor checks execute more quickly because they do not have to match as much.

Thus, the age-old wisdom of "descending from an ID" is actually bad practice. Given the selector `#my-list li`, the browser takes every `li` in the DOM, and checks every single one of its ancestors to see if it has the ID `my-list`.

It's wise to be specific on the right. Although this doesn't necessarily mean including an ID, you should try to include both a class name and element tag in your right-most selector. (However, don't add classes in your markup just to speed up selectors.)

Additionally, avoid chaining together too many selectors. As a rule, you should try to avoid chaining more than two selectors unless it is absolutely necessary.

It's also best to avoid selectors such as `div *`. With this selector, the renderer has to check every element on the page to see if it has a `div` ancestor.

> Page Speed (`http://code.google.com/speed/page-speed/`) provides a tool you can use to analyze selectors. Page Speed is offered as an extension for both Chrome and Firefox.

Sharing Rules

It is better for performance to share CSS rules as much as possible across elements. Thus, you should adopt some object-oriented CSS principles: general class names to style multiple elements, with additional classes to alter specific styles.

For instance, avoid rules like this:

```css
.button-1 {
    color: white;
    font-size: 1.4em;
    background-color: blue;
}

.button-2 {
    color: white;
    font-size: 1.4em;
    background-color: gray;
}
```

And instead use rules like this:

```
.button {
    color: white;
    font-size: 1.4em;
}

.button-1 {
    background-color: blue;
}

.button-2 {
    background-color: gray;
}
```

PROPERTIES TO AVOID

You can also improve CSS performance by staying away from expensive properties. Although most properties render quickly, a few CSS3 properties, and even some older CSS2 properties, can create problems.

These properties are often necessary for styling the page. However, it is important to be aware of which CSS properties may be causing performance issues.

Gradients

CSS3 gradients are one of the slowest CSS properties to render, but this does not mean you should avoid them entirely. When compared to loading an external image with an HTTP request, a CSS3 gradient is almost always faster.

Gradients can cause problems if you start animating them. Because they stretch to fill the element, gradients must be re-rendered every time the dimensions of that element change. The re-rendering can cause noticeable performance issues during certain animations, even to the point of flickering and flashing during reflows.

> *Repeating gradients do not stretch to fill the element, but still must be re-rendered when dimensions change.*

Opacity

Opacity does not cause noticeable performance issues by itself, but it can cause problems when a lot of translucent elements are layered on top of one another. That's because the renderer must generate a composite color for these elements, as shown in Figure 12-19.

329

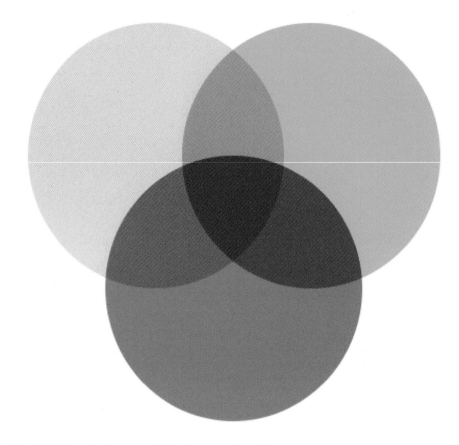

Figure 12-19: Composite colors are created when layering translucent elements.

This issue occurs both when using `opacity` and alpha transparency in RGBa (which is covered in Chapter 3).

Composite opacity issues are more pronounced during animation.

Font Face

`@font-face` is a very slow property for a variety of reasons. First, the embedded font is typically included with an external HTTP request.

> It is difficult to avoid the HTTP request for `@font-face`. Although you could use data URIs, there are a number of different formats you need to include for different browsers, which means that you would have to include the raw data for several files in your stylesheet (or serve separate CSS across browsers).

Another problem with web fonts is flash of unstyled text (FOUT). With FOUT, the fallback font shows until the custom font loads and triggers a reflow. This issue has been resolved in WebKit, but it can still present problems in IE and older browsers.

Font files can be large, but there are a couple ways to reduce their size and remove unnecessary bytes. If you need only basic characters, you can remove other subsets to reduce the number of characters in the font file. There is an option for this in the Font Squirrel generator (which you learned about in Chapter 5), and you can also set this in Google Web Fonts (`http://code.google.com/apis/webfonts/docs/getting_started.html#Subsets`).

Another component that increases the size of font files is hinting data. Although hinting is essential for improving font rendering in Windows, it is completely ignored in Mac. Font Squirrel's generator allows you to remove this data, but that's helpful only if you are serving separate CSS to Windows and Mac. Google Web Fonts handles this automatically.

Box Shadow

In Chapter 3 you learned how to render drop shadows using `box-shadow`. Although rendering times for this property have improved, there are still times that `box-shadow` can lead to performance issues.

`box-shadow` allows you to stack any number of drop shadows in an element. If you are adding a great deal of shadows to an element, you may experience performance issues. Even in single shadows the renderer may have problems with a really large blur radius.

OPTIMIZING IMAGES

Image data makes up a lot of the file size on the Internet, so you can see substantial performance improvements by properly optimizing your images. That saves download time for the user and also reduces demand for network resources.

SAVE FOR WEB

Photoshop includes an excellent Save For Web feature that compresses images for the web. This easy-to-use interface allows you to dramatically reduce the size of your images, as shown in Figure 12-20.

The Save For Web dialog allows you to control a variety of features, such as the quality level for JPEGs and palette for indexed formats like PNG8 and GIF. Files saved using this method are substantially smaller than those saved normally (even using the same file types and quality settings).

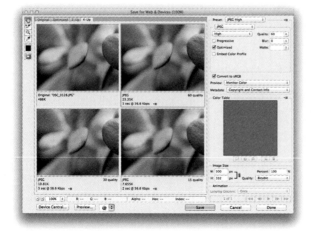

Figure 12-20: Photoshop's Save For Web dialog

WEBP

WebP, an open-source image format released by Google, provides significant file size savings for photographic images. When compared to JPEG, WebP images are on average 39.8% smaller.

Best of all these file size savings do not come at the expense of image quality, as Figure 12-21 shows.

JPEG (24.9 KB)   WebP (9.9 KB)

Figure 12-21: There is little difference in quality between JPEG and WebP.

Unfortunately, at the time of this writing WebP is available only in Chrome (and Chrome Frame). That means you should avoid using it for the time being, unless you want to serve a special WebP version to Chrome users.

To learn more about WebP, visit http://code.google.com/speed/webp/.

USE A COOKIELESS DOMAIN

Part of the reason HTTP requests are so slow is that each request includes a request header in addition to the data that is being requested. When used on a site with cookies, these headers can get very bloated because all of the cookie data is relayed with every request.

Every image, stylesheet, and JavaScript file gets served with all the cookies you have saved on your domain, even though these assets rarely need any cookie information.

Thus it is a good idea to set up a content domain, either a subdomain of your main domain, or using a CDN like Amazon Simple Storage Service (Amazon S3) (`http://aws.amazon.com/s3/`). As long as you make sure not to save any cookies on the content domain, there will be a noticeable size reduction in any images it serves.

WEB SOCKETS

HTML5 introduces web sockets, a revolutionary new concept for passing information back and forth from the server. This API dramatically reduces overhead associated with two-way communication with a remote host because it builds a direct tunnel to the backend that does not rely on HTTP requests. This capability to stream data directly is particularly useful for applications that rely on real-time information.

ADVANTAGES OF WEB SOCKETS

Web sockets provide an enormous reduction in network traffic and latency, leading to substantial performance gains for apps that require a large amount of communication with the backend.

No HTTP Requests

The main benefit of web sockets is that they avoid HTTP requests and the associated overhead. HTTP requests are extremely slow for a variety of reasons, including the following:

- Communication must be established between the front and back ends, meaning latency time from the file lookup and acknowledgement for every single request.
- HTTP requests can be very bloated, containing the actual data you are requesting and unnecessary header data, such as the cookie data you learned about earlier.

Real Time Data

Streaming directly to the server is ideal for any application that depends on real-time data because the data can be returned whenever it is available.

HTTP requests must be sent from the front end, and then wait for the request to be processed and a confirmation to be returned from the backend. In this span of time the data you are requesting may have changed.

Web sockets relay information in a steady stream, whenever it is changed. Conversely, with XMLHttpRequest (XHR), you have to send new HTTP requests every time you want to update the data. It is difficult to know how often to send these requests: too many overload your server and too few cause stale data.

JavaScript API

The web socket API is simpler than AJAX scripts. That's because the API processes the requests directly through JavaScript, instead of relying on a bootstrapped AJAX script to send XHRs and execute a callback when a response is received.

BROWSER SUPPORT

Web sockets are available in a variety of mobile and desktop browsers. They are currently supported by iOS Safari, Desktop Safari, Chrome, and Firefox.

Opera 11+ supports web sockets, but only if they are enabled manually by the user (due to an as-yet unresolved security concern: `www.ietf.org/mail-archive/web/hybi/current/msg04744.html`).

IE9 does not support web sockets, but it is rumored that they will be supported in IE10.

At the time of this writing Android browser does not support web sockets, although there is a PhoneGap plugin that enables them for Android: `https://github.com/FreakDev/PhoneGap-Android-HTML5-WebSocket`.

HOW TO USE WEB SOCKETS

Using web sockets is very straightforward due to the easily accessible JavaScript API.

Web Socket Servers

There are a variety of implementations you can leverage to set up a web socket server on the backend:

- PHP and Web Sockets (`http://code.google.com/p/phpwebsocket/`)
- Socket IO (Node) (`http://socket.io/`)
- jWebSocket (Java) (`http://jwebsocket.org/`)
- Web Socket Ruby (`https://github.com/gimite/web-socket-ruby`)

Follow the instructions for your particular implementation.

Socket IO and jWebSocket provide fallbacks for non-supportive browsers.

Connecting to a Web Socket

After setting up a web socket server, you can establish connection to the socket in JavaScript:

```
var myWS = new WebSocket('ws://www.smashingwebkit.com');
```

Then, you can set up a callback to execute when the web socket connection is established:

```
myWS.onopen = function() {
    // what to do when the connection opens
};
```

Communicating with the Web Socket

To communicate with your web socket, simply send data using the `send()` API:

```
myWS.send('My data');
```

Make sure not to send this before the connection is opened, by taking advantage of the onopen callback.

Set up a callback function to process any returned data:

```
myWS.onmessage = function(e) {
    alert('Received Message: ' + e.data);
};
```

This callback fires whenever the server sends new data.

Closing the Connection

To close the connection, use the `close()` method:

```
myWS.close();
```

You can also set up a callback to fire when the connection closes:

```
myWS.onclose = function() {
    // what to do when the connection closes
};
```

SUMMARY

Improving performance is tantamount to improving user experience. Although users may not notice when a site is running fast, they certainly notice when it is running slow. For most users, the speed of a website or app is just as important as its content or features.

When optimizing your site, it is important to first determine where the problems exist. Optimizing the wrong parts not only wastes time but can reduce the integrity of the code and make your site less maintainable.

If you have a performance problem, there are a number of measures you can take to make things run faster, such as optimizing animation, JavaScript, and even CSS. There also are proactive techniques you should always use to reduce file size and HTTP requests. When building a page it is best to consider final render size and speed, rather than only optimizing once you notice a problem.

13

THE FUTURE OF WEBKIT

SINCE THE EARLY days of Safari, WebKit has been considered on the cutting edge of rendering engines. In fact, many of the standards used in today's browsers originated as innovative features in WebKit. Now the engine retains its position as a market leader by developing new features to push web and application rendering into the future.

The WebKit team is continuously improving the WebKit core by building new components as well as patching existing features with bug fixes, enhancements, and performance optimizations. But the core team can't do it alone. As an open source project, WebKit depends on a lot of this support from the community.

This chapter explains how to keep on top of the latest features in WebKit using the WebKit nightlies and how to file bug reports for any issues that occur in the latest build. If you are comfortable with desktop app development, you learn how to contribute to the WebKit core and submit patches for review. You also learn how to assist with writing WebKit documentation.

You look at features currently in development and read about new components such as Mathematical Markup Language (MathML) as well as improvements to existing features such as CSS, SVG, and DOM.

WEBKIT NIGHTLIES

Typically, each Chrome and Safari update includes a newer version of WebKit. These updates are relatively infrequent and only include stable components. However, you can keep up with all the latest changes to WebKit by downloading nightly builds.

The WebKit nightlies compile all the latest patches to the WebKit core, with a new version released every night here: `http://nightly.webkit.org/`.

You can download nightly builds for Mac and Windows, and even download older versions from the archive. Additionally, you can download the latest source code if you would like to contribute to the WebKit core.

GETTING INVOLVED WITH WEBKIT

WebKit is an open-source project that depends greatly on support from the community. Getting involved with the WebKit project not only improves the browser, but also provides you with a deeper understanding of how WebKit applications work.

When you first open a WebKit nightly, you are presented with a screen detailing how you can contribute to the project, as shown in Figure 13-1.

There are a number of ways to contribute to WebKit: you can report bugs, fix known issues, develop new features, and even write documentation.

FILING BUG REPORTS

One of the best ways to contribute to WebKit is by filing bug reports for any issues you notice.

Reporting bugs requires no knowledge of the WebKit core, and is a great way for web app developers to assist the WebKit team. Best of all, it helps ensure that WebKit browsers remain error-free in the specific components you use in your websites.

How To File a Bug Report

The first step to filing a bug report is to check WebKit's Bugzilla repo (`https://bugs.webkit.org/query.cgi`) to determine if the bug has already been submitted by another user.

If it hasn't been reported, you can create a Bugzilla account and file the bug. And even if it has been reported, it's still a good idea to comment on the report with your individual usage information. Additional usage information not only helps clarify the cause of a bug but also keeps the bug fresh, signaling that users are still experiencing the problem.

Thank you for testing WebKit!

Quick Links:

- WebKit.org
- WebKit Blog
- Nightly Builds
- Contact Us
- Mailing List

Individuals like yourself who download and test the latest nightly builds of WebKit help us to create the highest quality product. For that, we thank you.

How can I help?

The number one way you can help is to report issues you encounter while using WebKit.

👤 Tester Center	⚒ Developer Center
Bug Reporting Tips A guide to writing a good bugreport for the developers.	**Bugs With Reductions** Bugs that have reduced testcases attached.
Bugs Needing Reduction Bugs that need a reduced testcase made.	**High Priority Bugs** The most important bugs to fix.
Unconfirmed Bugs Bugs that need a clear list of steps for reproduction.	**Forgotten Patches** These bugs are good starting points.
How to Reduce a Bug A guide to making a good testcase that will help us.	**Patches awaiting Review** Patches that are awaiting review.
Bug Life Cycle Describes the life cycle of a bug in the WebKit project.	**Approved Patches** Patches with positive reviews that need to be landed.

Where did my home page go?

Figure 13-1: The WebKit nightlies are geared toward testing and debugging the framework.

Making Bug Reports More Useful

There are a few quick steps you can take to help the WebKit team track down and fix the issue you're submitting.

Most important is accurate information about the specific version of WebKit. So make sure your bug report includes the WebKit revision number as well as the platform and OS version you are using.

If you know the precise cause of the bug, you can assign it to the appropriate component—CSS or HTML editing, for instance. You also can add useful features such as a URL containing the issue or a screenshot for any visual bug to your bug report.

Try to determine the problem as specifically as possible. One technique for honing in on a given issue is test case reduction. With this approach, you remove components from the page one at a time until the actual cause of the bug is apparent.

> *Test case reduction can be time-consuming and is not necessary to include in every bug report.*

For more information on writing good bug reports, go here: `www.webkit.org/quality/bugwriting.html`.

CONTRIBUTING TO THE WEBKIT CORE

The WebKit core is written primarily in C++ and Objective C, so web developers may have trouble contributing code unless they have desktop programming experience.

Developers with experience in these technologies can help improve the codebase.

Ways to Contribute

There are a number of ways to contribute code to the WebKit core. First and foremost, you can fix bugs that are reported on Bugzilla. When working on a bug, it is important to follow the guidelines in the Bug Life Cycle (`www.webkit.org/quality/lifecycle.html`). For instance, it is a good idea to comment in the bug report whenever you start working on a given issue.

Working bugs is a great way to get your feet wet with the codebase before digging into other contributions. Once you are comfortable with the WebKit core, you can move on to improving performance in any number of components, or cleaning up code to make the core more maintainable. You also can work on any of the new features currently being developed.

> *When contributing to the WebKit core, make sure to follow the code style guidelines, which you can find at `www.webkit.org/coding/coding-style.html`.*

Submitting Patches

After you've finished creating your patch, you can submit it to Bugzilla. Use the `svn-create-patch` script, and then add it as an attachment in the appropriate bug report. When adding the patch, check the Patch check box and choose the question mark (?) option from the Review drop-down list. This tells the WebKit team your patch is ready for review.

WRITING DOCUMENTATION

Open source projects like WebKit are only as good as their documentation, so contributing to this effort is another excellent way to help fellow developers.

There are a variety of documentation efforts to which you can contribute:

- Web developers can help write the developer documentation, outlining DOM methods and CSS properties that are supported by WebKit.
- Desktop developers can help write the core documentation.
- Anyone who uses WebKit can help with the overall documentation for the project.

For more information on writing WebKit documentation, go here: `www.webkit.org/projects/documentation/`.

WHERE IS WEBKIT HEADED?

With frequent updates to the core, the WebKit team ensures that the project remains at the forefront of web and application rendering. This includes a variety of new features as well as ongoing improvements to the codebase.

FEATURES IN DEVELOPMENT

There are a number of features currently being developed by the WebKit team. They are working on everything from building completely new features such as MathML, to fleshing out and debugging already developed features such as CSS3 and SVG.

MathML

MathML is a system for describing mathematical equations and expressions through HTML markup. This special markup not only defines a system for rendering equations visually in the browser, but also relays information regarding the content of these equations.

Without MathML, mathematical equations are typically included in websites as static images. Although there are backend scripts that can generate images from mathematical markup, this extra step is arduous which has prevented a lot of educational and scientific work from being presented online. Additionally, the images created by these scripts are completely static, and can't be interpreted or interfaced with JavaScript.

> *One backend equation renderer is Mathematical Formulae (`http://developer.mindtouch.com/App_Catalog/Math`), an open source ImageMagick extension.*

MathML uses a number of special elements to denote different mathematical operators and components. These elements are wrapped in a `<math>` element.

For instance, you can use MathML to write the quadratic equation:

```
<math xmlns="http://www.w3.org/1998/Math/MathML">
  <mrow>
    <mi>x</mi>
    <mo>=</mo>
    <mfrac>
      <mrow>
        <mo form="prefix">&#x2212;<!-- &minus; --></mo>
        <mi>b</mi>
        <mo>&#x00B1;<!-- &PlusMinus; --></mo>
        <msqrt>
          <msup>
            <mi>b</mi>
            <mn>2</mn>
          </msup>
          <mo>&#x2212;<!-- &minus; --></mo>
          <mn>4</mn>
          <mo>&#x2062;<!-- &InvisibleTimes; --></mo>
          <mi>a</mi>
          <mo>&#x2062;<!-- &InvisibleTimes; --></mo>
          <mi>c</mi>
        </msqrt>
      </mrow>
      <mrow>
        <mn>2</mn>
        <mo>&#x2062;<!-- &InvisibleTimes; --></mo>
        <mi>a</mi>
      </mrow>
    </mfrac>
  </mrow>
</math>
```

In browsers that support MathML, this markup renders as an equation as shown in Figure 13-2.

WebKit includes a development version of MathML, which is already implemented in the WebKit nightlies as well as Safari 5.1. At the time of this writing, MathML is not available in Chrome.

Although WebKit's rendering of MathML is far from perfect, various issues are being addressed, and support for this standard will improve over time.

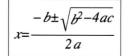

$$x = \frac{-b \pm \sqrt{b^2 - 4ac}}{2a}$$

Figure 13-2: The quadratic equation rendered with MathML

CSS

While the majority of CSS improvements in the WebKit core are related to CSS3 properties, you may be surprised to discover that the core team is still working on certain aspects of CSS2.1 (and even debugging some minor issues in CSS1).

At the time of this writing, a number of bugs exist in CSS1 surrounding the `text-transform` attribute. CSS2.1 has been mostly implemented, although WebKit still does not support the `white-space` values `pre-wrap` and `pre-line`.

A few CSS3 selectors still need to be implemented, and experimental CSS3 attributes are continuously being refined. You can expect WebKit to continue innovating new CSS3 attributes.

SVG

The new SVG element is supported by WebKit, but it is in the experimental phase. Basic rendering is complete, although certain advanced features such as animation and SVG fonts need to be finalized. There are also a number of bugs that need to be fixed.

DOM

While WebKit's DOM model is basically finished, there are a variety of bugs and compliance issues that still need to be resolved. You learned about some of these, such as the bugs in the canvas composite blend modes, earlier in this book.

GENERAL IMPROVEMENTS

In addition to the specific items in development, there are a number of ongoing improvements to the WebKit core:

- Various components are always being optimized for better performance.
- The codebase is constantly being refined and cleaned up for easier maintenance.
- Compatibility across different implementations as well as backward compatibility for older applications are consistently being improved.

THE FUTURE OF WEBKIT

WebKit's feature-rich and fast engine is ideal for desktop applications and its lightweight yet powerful engine has become the new standard for mobile devices.

In the early days of Safari, WebKit stood apart as the only engine that could render a variety of complex CSS3 properties such as rounded corners and gradients. Today, WebKit stays ahead of other renderers by creating innovative CSS3 properties, supporting the newest standards, and fleshing out previously developed features.

In the future, you can expect WebKit to continue its trend of pushing document rendering to the next level. WebKit remains the rendering engine to follow, as it continuously develops the newest features on the Web, and in turn creates new standards in web development.

Happy coding!

Index

346

349